**Environmental Management
and Business Strategy**

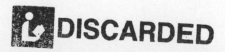

Environmental Management and Business Strategy

**Richard Welford and
Andrew Gouldson**

Pitman Publishing
128 Long Acre, London WC2E 9AN

A Division of Longman Group UK Limited

First published in 1993
Reprinted 1993

© 1993 Richard Welford and Andrew Gouldson

British Library Cataloguing in Publication Data
A CIP catalogue record for this book can be obtained from
the British Library

ISBN 0 273 60097 4

Typeset by Mathematical Composition Setters Ltd, Salisbury, Wiltshire
Printed by Bell and Bain Ltd, Glasgow

For Chris and Hayley

CONTENTS

CONTENTS

PREFACE

In the last five years we have seen a fundamental change in the way that industry views the protection of the environment. This is not suggesting that industry has done nothing in this respect in the past; it has, but recently we have seen the dominant ideology among senior management in industry shifting towards a less ruthless view of the planet in which we live. Huge steps forward have been made in the field of environmental management and much bigger steps are yet to be made. Indeed, unless they are made the planet could become uninhabitable within a very short space of time.

The other shift that we have seen has been on the part of pressure groups who now see the environmental situation as so serious that, rather than expend time and money abusing the activities of industry, they are now cooperating in an attempt to encourage change. Even Greenpeace with their reputation for aggressive campaigning now publish a newsletter with the title 'Greenpeace Business'. Politicians have also been eager to jump on the green bandwagon in an attempt to gain valuable votes. But that reflects not cynicism but growing pressure on the part of the public to see action on the environment.

Our focus is nevertheless on industry. Industry has a very important part to play in protecting and improving the environment in which we live. By using the management tools and techniques developed in this book it can begin to respond to the global environmental challenge. While industry has to change and develop in a sustainable way, we cannot afford wholesale closure of industry in order to bring about environmental improvement because that simply brings with it different problems. There is a need to develop strategies which provide for a new, often radical and committed approach to the environment.

It is for these reasons and a personal commitment to see environmental improvement that we have written this book. It focuses on how industry can improve its own environmental performance and aims to equip the reader with a knowledge of the issues surrounding environmental management and an understanding of the techniques used to achieve environmental improvement. The book is relevant to a wide range of readers including students taking courses in environmental management and business studies. It will also be of direct use to managers in industry who are concerned with the environmental impact of their own organisation.

The book is structured in order to provide readers with an understanding of the background to environmental management. It discusses the legislative framework before moving on to consider the strategies for environmental improvement. These strategies deal with the design of a plant, through to the operation of plants and processes, on to specific product and marketing issues and ending with an examination of opportunities for regional cooperation. Throughout the book we emphasise the need for an integrated and systematic approach to the issue of environmental management. We also stress the need for management at the highest levels to be involved in environmental management strategies and along with this, the need for commitment and participation throughout the organisation. In addition, companies have to be honest about their approach to environmental management and we stress the need for credible strategies which go beyond traditional approaches to business.

The structure of the book is as follows: Chapter 1 looks at the environmental challenge facing industry and at some common principles that can be applied to environmental management. Chapter 2 extends this by looking at the legislative framework in the EC and the UK and establishes the need for a proactive approach in this area. Chapter 3 begins to look directly at corporate strategy in examining the process of environmental impact assessment (EIA). This technique, increasingly being adopted by firms on a voluntary basis, puts consideration of environmental impacts onto the business agenda at the planning stage of a plant or new development.

Chapters 4, 5 and 6 are best read together and establish what is the central focus of the book, namely the need for an integrated and ongoing strategy aiming at a continuous cycle of environmental improvement. Specifically, Chapter 4 examines the design of an environmental policy within the business, focusing on the requirements of an environmental review and on the important concept of the measurement of environmental impacts. These issues are closely related to each other. Chapter 5 looks in detail at the design of the environmental management system which will drive the process of environmental improvement and Chapter 6 examines the process of environmental auditing in relation to that management system.

Chapter 7 examines the important issue of product and process design with a particular emphasis on waste management. This begins the analysis of product management as opposed to organisational management and Chapter 8 continues this by examining green marketing. However, as we stress throughout these chapters, product strategy and the internal environmental management strategy cannot be seen as completely separate issues.

The last two chapters examine the tools developed throughout the book in the context of two specific cases. The first, in Chapter 9, is that of small and medium-sized enterprises where it is our assertion that much can be achieved by combining environmental management strategies with the best practice observed in small businesses. The final chapter looks at how environmental management strategies can be developed at a regional level where much can be gained from cooperative rather than competitive strategies.

This book would not have been possible without the help, advice, support and contributions of a number of people. These include Jonathan Wilson,

Donal O'Loaire, Edwin Kok, Nigel Roome, Denis Smith, Elaine Fazakerley, Elaine White, Carol Charlton, David Fleming, John Oakland, Peter Roberts, Geoff Taylor and Stefanos Tsipas. We would also like to acknowledge the help and support of Jennifer Mair and Penelope Woolf of Pitman Publishing. Any errors in the text are, of course, our own responsibility.

CHAPTER I

Introduction: the environmental challenge and business strategy

Environmental issues have been a matter of public concern for over a quarter of a century. As knowledge relating to the cause and effect of environmental damage has become more complete, the pressure to change the ways in which we behave has increased. Much of this pressure has been targeted towards industry which is often identified as the major source of pollution. Individuals are also changing their patterns of behaviour and industry is having to respond to the seemingly endless demands of the modern, environmentally aware consumer.

Until recently, the environmental debate in industry has largely been one of rhetoric rather than action. While it is difficult for industry to refute the general need for environmental protection, to date there has been little practical guidance as to how real progress might be made. The need now is to develop practical solutions to meet the environmental challenge. Businesses are at the core of the environmental debate and are central both to the problem and to the solution.

By providing the goods and services demanded by the public, businesses fulfil many vital social needs and many not-so-vital social wants. The investments and innovations of industry drive economic growth and satisfy the demands of the consumer. However, in doing so, be it because of the resources that they consume, the processes that they apply or the products that they manufacture, business activity is a major contributor to environmental destruction. To protect the environment, we must find ways to meet the needs of both current and future generations. In part we need to find new technologies and to develop more efficient methods of production. However, this technological solution is insufficient in itself. There is a need for a change in attitudes towards both consumption and production. There is no doubt that industry has been innovating and improving efficiency for many years and many firms have made major advances in their environmental performance. Other firms have done little, however, and unless change occurs rapidly environmental degradation may become irreversible.

If harnessed correctly, the market mechanism can be utilised to develop the solutions which are so vital if the environment is to be protected. This depends on cooperation between government, which must provide fiscal incentives for environmental improvement, industry and consumers. Industry to date has been driven by profitability and while that profitability might be seen as vital to economic growth we should begin to demand that industry puts other objectives, such as environmental improvement, into its strategic plan. Much of this implies a change in corporate culture based on a commitment to see environmental improvements. There is no doubt that we are seeing the beginnings of a change in societies' attitudes to the environment and industry needs to respond to this.

Within the pluralist society in which we live a whole range of pressures are beginning to create the preconditions which are necessary to encourage businesses to respond to the environmental challenge. Industry is beginning to develop the new technologies and techniques that will move the global economy toward sustainability and must continue to do so. The rapid growth of public environmental awareness in recent years has placed new pressures on industry. These pressures can take many forms as individuals collectively exercise their environmental conscience as customers, employees, investors, voters, neighbours and fellow citizens. However, whether it is due to intellectual fatigue with environmental issues, a lack of conviction that an individual's own actions will have an impact on environmental improvement or a reluctance to reduce private consumption for public welfare, many individuals seem to ignore their own responsibilities. Consumers have a major part to play in environmental improvement and it is wholly wrong to expect industry to respond without a parallel effort made by those who consume the goods produced. However, given the inherent public reluctance to reduce their own levels of consumption which we have seen to date, it is apparent that government and industry must respond in order to effectively protect the environment.

Throughout the developed world the approach of governments has been to respond to increasing public concern for the environment by developing policy frameworks for environmental protection. Environmental policies and their associated legislation impose new costs and generate new opportunities for industry and change the competitive climate that faces industry. In the marketplace, survival and success is linked to the ability of companies to be flexible and to respond to the new pressures put before them. Rather than being seen as the cause of the environmental problem, industry must respond and show itself to be the solution to the problem. Once again, though, that requires commitment to the idea of environmental improvement and access to the management tools, developed throughout this book, to achieve change.

Individual businesses have always been faced with a range of competitive market conditions which threaten their survival. In many cases, requirements for improved environmental performance are perceived to add to this threat. It is now clear, however, that the demands placed upon industry to improve its environmental performance will continue to grow. Companies which respond to this challenge will see themselves at the forefront of industry, developing new products in new markets and gaining a competitive edge over their competitors. Not only is it ethical for a company to improve its environmental performance, but it is sound business practice. What we cannot expect, however, is for industry to change overnight. We can nevertheless expect a gradual and continuous effort to improve environmental performance and in time this will move the global economy towards a more sustainable pattern of production.

INCREASING ENVIRONMENTAL PRESSURES

While it may not have impacted directly on the day-to-day lives of most western citizens, all the available indicators suggest that the quality of the environment upon which human life and economic activity depend is deteriorating rapidly. Environmentalism is no longer associated with the alternative movements of the 1960s and the scientific evidence surrounding environmental degradation is too strong to ignore. At the global level, the greenhouse effect and the depletion of the ozone layer represent a serious threat to the continued viability of ecosystems. At a more local level, the decline in urban air quality, the pollution of oceans and water courses, the degradation of soil quality, the loss of habitat and species and the consumption and contamination of natural resources are ubiquitous. Collectively, these local pressures combine to add to the threats facing the global environment. While there may be some disagreement relating to the scale of the problem or the ways in which it should be addressed, there is a general consensus that the problems are extremely serious.

Since 1950, industrial output has increased by a factor of seven. Between 1950 and 1987 the global population doubled and is expected to double again by 2030 (World Commission on Environment and Development, 1987). Due to the distribution of economic wealth, few would argue that for the vast majority of the global population living standards are sufficient. Therefore, to maintain as an absolute minimum the current levels of strain placed upon the environment, industry must meet the demands of a rising population by supplying more with less, both in terms of the materials that it consumes and the pollution which it generates.

The magnitude of the environmental challenge facing industry is enormous. In assessing this we might use the approach of Ehrlich and Ehrlich (1991) and Stikker (1992) in defining the global environmental burden in a simple equation:

$$\text{Global environmental burden} = \text{Global population} \times \frac{\text{GNP}}{\text{per capita}} \times \frac{\text{Environmental impact}}{\text{per unit of GNP}}$$

Let us then make some assumptions relating to the independent components as follows:

- The 1987 global population of 5 billion generates the maximum acceptable environmental burden.
- World population will double its 1987 level to reach 10 billion within 40 years.

● GNP per capita should increase by 5 per cent per year, and will therefore rise by a factor of 5 within 40 years.

The conclusion of commentators such as Stikker (1992) is therefore that to maintain the current global environmental burden, the environmental impact per unit of GNP must fall by 90 per cent within 40 years.

Of course the assumptions made here simplify some extremely complex issues. Nevertheless, the conclusion generated gives an indication of the scale of the environmental challenge facing industry. It suggests that if industry is to operate within a level of global environmental quality that is not deteriorating, it must reduce its global environmental impact by 90 per cent within the next 40 years. Moreover, that position maintains current levels of degradation which many see as already unacceptable and even bigger advances would clearly be desirable. It is therefore apparent that individual companies must commit themselves to a plan of action to make their own contribution to this global environmental challenge.

The problem is even more serious if we accept that we have already crossed the threshold of an acceptable or sustainable level of environmental quality. The deterioration of the environment in recent years has been alarming. Furthermore, many environmental phenomena have a lag between cause and effect so that regardless of any actions taken now, environmental quality will continue to deteriorate well into the next century. This is certainly the case in relation to global warming and ozone depletion. Additionally, it may be argued that industry in the developed world should achieve greater reductions in environmental impact than the less advanced industries in the Third World. If these views are accepted, then industry must aim to exceed by significant amounts the target of a 90 per cent reduction in resource depletion and environmental pollution by 2035.

SUSTAINABLE DEVELOPMENT

The continuing ability of the environment to supply raw materials and assimilate waste while maintaining bio-diversity and a quality of life is being increasingly undermined. If development is to continue we have to find a way of doing it that will not further degrade the environment in which we live. In its simplest form, sustainable development is defined as development that meets the needs of the present generation without compromising the ability of future generations to meet their own needs (World Commission on Environment and Development, 1987). Such a simple statement has profound implications. It implies that all human activity must refrain from causing any degree of permanent damage through its consumption of environmental resources. These resources may be the material and energy inputs used in production or the services that the natural environment provides as it assimilates waste. As an ultimate objective, the concept of sustainability is immensely valuable.

However, strategies are needed to translate conceptual theories into practical reality.

The challenge that faces the economic system is how to continue to fulfil its vital role within modern society while working towards sustainability. There is a need to carefully assess how development can be made sustainable and this implies acceptance of the view that not all development will be good. Sustainability is not something that will be achieved overnight but in the longer term. Entire economies and individual businesses need to look towards a new type of development and growth.

One major obstacle preventing sustainability from being achieved is the overall level of consumption experienced in the Western world. Consumers who are relatively wealthy seem reluctant to significantly reduce their own levels of consumption. While increasingly governments are adopting economic instruments such as taxes, subsidies and product labelling schemes to reduce and channel consumption towards more environmentally friendly alternatives, there is also a need for education among consumers. In addition, industry itself must be encouraged to further increase environmental efficiency.

At the centre of sustainable development, industry must seek to provide the services demanded by consumers with the minimum environmental impact at all stages. This is a far reaching challenge as it involves a reformulation not only of production processes but also of the products themselves. Conceptually, consumers rarely buy a physical product, but the set of services and utilities, however intangible, that the product provides. For instance, consumers do not necessarily buy an aerosol can, but a container which propels liquids as a spray. If manufacturers can provide the same services with a reduced environmental impact then, perhaps with some persuasion, consumers will alter their consumption patterns and purchase manual rather than aerosol sprays, for example.

While many consumers may be unwilling to reduce the overall levels of consumption to which they have become accustomed, they have proved willing to select the good which produces a reduced environmental impact. Companies which can supply goods with a sustainable differential advantage will be well placed to satisfy these new consumer demands at a profit. In so doing the producer has to accept the responsibility for the environmental impact of the materials and processes used at the production stage and for the final product and its disposal. In many ways therefore, industry has to take on a whole range of new responsibilities towards the environment.

Sustainability challenges industry to produce higher levels of output while using lower levels of inputs and generating less waste. To some extent, consistent structural change during the post-war period has led to continued increases in environmental efficiency and environmental impact per unit of GNP generated has been reduced. This is particularly evident in relation to energy-intensive industry. The problem that remains is that while relative environmental impact per unit of output has fallen in some sectors, increases in levels of output and hence environmental impact have more than offset any gains in relative environmental efficiency. Higher levels of output have been a direct response to higher levels of consumption and we can see that sustainability requires action from both industry and consumers.

Sustainable development is not only about direct impact on the environment, however. A key part of the concept is about equity. The massive inequality in wealth and standards of living displayed across the world make sustainable development harder to achieve. Those living in the Third World often aspire to the standards of living of the First World and we know from an environmental stance such aspirations are presently not achievable. But what right does the First World have to deny other human beings development in the same unsustainable way in which they themselves have developed? Therefore we can see that environmental improvement is inextricably linked to wider issues of global concern which do need to be addressed.

THE CHALLENGE OF ENVIRONMENTAL MANAGEMENT

Before moving on to introduce the elements of management practice and strategy which will facilitate improved environmental performance in industry, it is important to relay some of the factors which together serve to encourage industry to respond to the environmental challenge.

Environmental efficiency

Companies often strive to minimise the costs of their operations. This is especially relevant in relation to the efficiency with which they use their material inputs. As the ability of the environment to supply raw materials and accept waste is diminished, the costs of these services to industry will increase. As a result, more efficient raw material utilisation and a decrease in the amount of waste generated are key factors which will encourage industry to minimise its environmental impact. Particularly in relation to waste products, companies are experiencing increasingly stringent legislation which increases the costs of waste management. Waste should be viewed both in terms of physical waste generated and the less tangible losses experienced through an inefficient use of resources. Avoiding these losses improves both the business and environmental performance of a company. As a result, many companies have pursued a strategy of waste minimisation for a number of years and have experienced short payback periods on investment in waste management.

In efforts to increase the efficiency of their operations, many companies have developed integrated management systems to reduce inefficiencies and the likelihood of errors. Most commonly to date, these have centred around the promotion of quality. There are clear parallels between quality management and environmental management which are further explored in Chapter 6.

The influence of government

The main impact of government on the environmental performance of industry has been through the development of environmental legislation. Environmental considerations have been built into the legislative framework for many years. Initially, establishing rights of ownership over natural resources led to the development of a legal system to protect those rights. Subsequently, the impact of industrial activity on the health of employees and the surrounding community led to the creation of public health and safety legislation. Measures have also been introduced to control the use of products, processes and wastes which may harm the environment. The impact of environmental legislation on the operation of industry has been profound and is set to become ever more tough.

As the strain placed upon the environment mounts and knowledge of the causes and effects of environmental degradation becomes more complete, the extent and impact of environmental legislation will continue to develop. Thus, industry must satisfy an increasing number of legal obligations in relation to the effect that its activities have upon the environment. As a result, in all of its operations, industry must plan ahead to meet the demands of current and forthcoming environmental legislation. By developing proactive responses to legislative pressure, industry will reduce its costs and exposure to risk. While in the short term, legal obligations undoubtedly increase the costs of production that fall upon the firm, it is up to each firm to comply with legislation in the most cost-effective way. The development of proactive strategic responses to the demands of legislation will reduce these costs.

In parallel with the development of environmental legislation, governments are increasingly applying market instruments to achieve environmental objectives. Actions of this nature may include the imposition of taxes on environmentally damaging goods, subsidies on environmentally friendly goods or the provision of information relating to the environmental performance of companies or products. Market instruments are intended to channel the choice of consumers or other stakeholders towards the better environmental option. Thus through a combination of legislative and market instruments, by encouraging certain activities and discouraging others, governments seek to accelerate the structural change which encourages improved environmental efficiency in the economy as a whole.

The development of stakeholder influence

Individual businesses interact with a number of stakeholders, all of whom have an interest in the performance of that company. Traditionally the main focus of stakeholder interest has been upon the financial performance of the company. Increasingly, however, stakeholder pressure is concentrating on the environmental performance of the company. The range of stakeholders which demand high environmental standards is displayed in Figure 1.1 and it would be useful to deal with each one in turn.

1. Customers

The relationship between a company and its customers is obviously of paramount importance. In relation to environmental considerations, the potential importance of green consumerism cannot be overstated. The range of characteristics that underlay the purchasing decision are a fundamental consideration for all businesses. Increasingly, the environment is being accepted as one such characteristic by consumers. At present, however, the influence of green consumerism on most businesses is marginal. Of the myriad of products that each consumer buys, very few are chosen on the basis of their environmental credentials alone. Nevertheless, it is certain that credible claims relating to environmental performance constitute one positive element among the many characteristics upon which consumers base their purchasing decision. Companies which can validate and communicate the environmental performance of their products will enhance their competitive position.

Governments are also seeking to increase the potency of green consumerism by providing the consumer with the information necessary to make an informed choice in relation to the environmental performance of each product within the product range. For this reason for example, we saw the introduction of the EC's eco-labelling scheme in 1993 (see Chapter 8).

2. Trading partners

Many businesses do not sell into 'end-consumer' markets and may therefore perceive themselves to be remote from any consumer pressures to improve their environmental performance. Increasingly, the pressure to improve environmental performance is emanating from trading partners rather than the

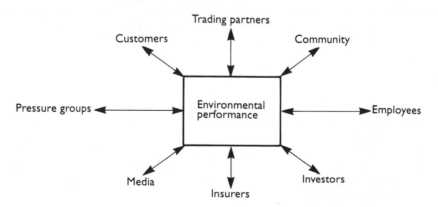

Figure 1.1 Stakeholder pressure and environmental performance

ultimate consumer. In efforts to improve overall environmental performance, many companies are exercising their own rights both as purchasers and as vendors and are demanding that all of the companies within their supply chain seek to minimise their own environmental impacts. Hence, demands to improve environmental performance at all stages in the supply chain are being diffused beyond those companies that are directly exposed to the pressures of green consumerism. An increasing number of companies are preferring to buy their resources from or sell their products to companies which meet certain standards of environmental performance.

The provision of information on company environmental performance through standards such as BS7750, the British Standard on Environmental Management Systems, and the EC's eco-management and audit scheme (see Chapters 5 and 6 respectively) will increasingly be written into contracts in the future. Increasing environmental concern and the improved provision of information relating to environmental performance will reward those companies which achieve and communicate high environmental standards with a competitive advantage.

3. The community

Industry shares its surrounding environment with the local population. Increasingly this population is demanding a high level of environmental performance from its industrial neighbours, and seeks some degree of reassurance that they are not exposed to significant environmental risk due to a company's operations. This concern has been recognised for many years and was initially recognised in public health legislation. Trends towards freedom of access to environmental information will give greater power to local communities when they question the activities of local industrial co-habitants. In order to foster a positive working relationship, companies must improve their environmental performance and communicate their efforts to the surrounding communities. This is true both for future developments and existing operations.

4. Employees

The population in the community surrounding a company also includes the workforce of that company. The pressure to provide a healthy living environment is magnified within the workplace. Employees seek healthy and secure working conditions, and can draw on an established framework of health and safety legislation in this respect. However, employees' concerns relating to the environmental performance of their employers goes beyond the impact of operations on the working and living environment. Increasingly people wish to work for ethical and responsible companies. Companies that reflect the environmental concerns of the public will find it easier to attract, retain and motivate a quality workforce.

5. Investors and insurers

The pressures to improve environmental performance also emanate from the investors and shareholders of a company. The rapid growth of ethical investment schemes in recent years reflects the desire of many investors only to lend their financial support to companies which behave in a responsible manner. There are also a number of very good business reasons why investors prefer to work with companies that have a proven track record of environmental integrity. The structure of legal liability for environmental damage dictates that any party that causes environmental damage may be fined and required to bear the costs of remediating that damage and to compensate the affected parties for any associated losses. It is increasingly difficult and expensive to obtain insurance to cover such issues. Consequently, companies associated with a significant environmental incident may suffer significant financial losses. These losses are then translated into reductions in the share price and the associated dividends.

Banks that lend to companies secure the loans on the basis of the physical assets of the company and often on the land upon which any investment takes place. Should the company cease to be viable, the bank assumes ownership of those assets which are then sold to cover any outstanding debts. However, should the physical assets of the company be contaminated, then the value of the assets is significantly reduced. Indeed, the banks may inherit any environmental liabilities that the liquidated company generated. Commercial lenders are therefore reluctant to lend money to any company which may develop any environmental liabilities or to secure loans on the value of an asset which may be eroded through contamination. As a result, companies which cannot demonstrate a high level of environmental performance associated with low environmental risks will find it increasingly difficult and expensive to attract and retain investment and insurance for their operations.

6. Media and pressure groups

A combination of increased public awareness of environmental issues and freedom of access to information on the environmental performance of companies will serve to magnify media and pressure group interest in the environmental performance of industry. In order to manage media and pressure group attention, companies must be able to state that they have made efforts to reduce their environmental impact. However, while it may be tempting to allow the PR or marketing departments to lead the way in convincing all stakeholders of this commitment, any shallow or spurious claims will soon be uncovered. Claims which cannot be substantiated are likely to be seized upon and will be very detrimental to a company's public image. Companies which seek to communicate responsible environmental performance must base any claims that they make to this effect on hard facts which they are willing to communicate (see Chapter 8).

STRATEGIC RESPONSES TO THE ENVIRONMENTAL CHALLENGE

Given the internal and external demands to improve the environmental performance of a company, those companies that achieve high standards of environmental performance will benefit in a number of ways. These are summarised in Figure 1.2. Many of these benefits are directly related to cost reduction and as such are not inconsistent with principles of profit maximisation. But those benefits also reflect a more ethical approach to business where profits will not be the sole motivation and where due care and responsibility towards the environment are integral parts of doing business.

In order to realise a competitive advantage based on environmental management, companies must seek to develop strategies which translate actions into benefits, improving their environmental performance and addressing the environmental demands placed upon them by government and stakeholders. By incorporating the increasingly important environmental dimension into the decision-making processes and strategies of the firm, managers can seek to reduce costs and exploit the opportunities offered by increased public environmental concern within a dynamic market-place. Such a strategy must be proactive and honest. It may also be evangelical, educating and campaigning. But more than anything it must be ethical. The environment is too important an issue to be treated as a gimmick for short-term advantage.

The general principles of such a strategy are embodied within the International Chamber of Commerce's *Business Charter for Sustainable*

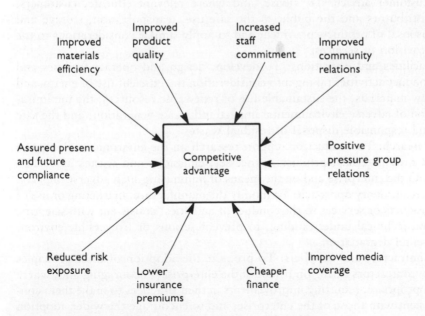

Figure 1.2 The constituents of competitive advantage

Development. The key elements to this strategy are embodied in sixteen 'Principles for Environmental Management'. Companies are therefore encouraged to endorse the following aims:

1. **Corporate priority**: To recognise environmental management as among the highest corporate priorities and as a key determinant to sustainable development; to establish policies, programmes and practices for conducting operations in an environmentally sound manner.

2. **Integrated management**: To integrate these policies, programmes and practices fully into each business as an essential element of management in all its functions.

3. **Process of improvement**: To continue to improve corporate policies, programmes and environmental performance, taking into account technical developments, scientific understanding, consumer needs and community expectations, with legal regulations as a starting point; and to apply the same environmental criteria internationally.

4. **Employee education**: To educate, train and motivate employees to conduct their activities in an environmentally responsible manner.

5. **Prior assessment**: To assess environmental impacts before starting a new activity or project and before decommissioning a facility or leaving a site.

6. **Products and services**: To develop and provide products and services that have no undue environmental impact and are safe in their intended use, that are efficient in their consumption of energy and natural resources, and that can be recycled, reused, or disposed of safely.

7. **Customer advice**: To advise, and where relevant educate, customers, distributors and the public in the safe use, transportation, storage and disposal of products provided; and to apply similar considerations to the provision of services.

8. **Facilities and operations**: To develop, design and operate facilities and conduct activities taking into consideration the efficient use of energy and raw materials, the sustainable use of renewable resources, the minimisation of adverse environmental impact and waste generation, and the safe and responsible disposal of residual wastes.

9. **Research**: To conduct or support research on the environmental impacts of raw materials, products, processes, emissions and wastes associated with the enterprise and on the means of minimising such adverse impacts.

10. **Precautionary approach**: To modify the manufacture, marketing or use of products or services to the conduct of activities, consistent with scientific and technical understanding, to prevent serious or irreversible environmental degradation.

11. **Contractors and suppliers**: To promote the adoption of these principles by contractors acting on behalf of the enterprise, encouraging and, where appropriate, requiring improvements in their practices to make them consistent with those of the enterprise; and to encourage the wider adoption of these principles by suppliers.

12. **Emergency preparedness**: To develop and maintain, where appropriate hazards exist, emergency preparedness plans in conjunction with the emergency services, relevant authorities and the local community, recognising potential cross-boundary impacts.
13. **Transfer of technology**: To contribute to the transfer of environmentally sound technology and management methods throughout the industrial and public sectors.
14. **Contributing to the common effort**: To contribute to the development of public policy and to business, governmental and intergovernmental programmes and educational initiatives that will enhance environmental awareness and protection.
15. **Openness to concerns**: To foster openness and dialogue with employees and the public, anticipating and responding to their concerns about the potential hazards and impacts of operations, products, wastes or services, including those of transboundary or global significance.
16. **Compliance and reporting**: To measure environmental performance; to conduct regular environmental audits and assessments of compliance with company requirements and these principles; and periodically to provide appropriate information to the Board of Directors, shareholders, employees, the authorities and the public.

The key to environmental strategy must be integration. This is not only reflected in the ICC Charter but is also implicit in the Environmental Protection Act (1990) in the UK and within the EC's Fifth Environmental Action Programme (see Chapter 2). This common element of integration implies that a firm must examine every aspect of its environmental performance. That is not to suggest that priorities should not be set, indeed they should, but that every aspect of an organisation's environmental impact must be recognised. In so doing it then becomes possible to design strategies that are holistic rather than piecemeal. It would be no good improving the environmental impact of one part of a firm's activities if this simply meant shifting it to another division. Real environmental improvement should be a Pareto improvement, that is, an improvement with no offsetting deterioration elsewhere.

Environmental strategy must therefore begin with real commitment on the part of the whole organisation. This may mean a change in corporate culture and management has an important role to play in leading that commitment and laying out the organisation's corporate objectives with respect to the environment; management has to be the catalyst for change. Moreover, that change has to be ongoing and management must be ever mindful of the full range of objectives to which it is subject. Management has to find compromise between these objectives if they conflict and design corporate strategies which are operational, consistent and achievable. To help in this process there are a number of questions which need to be considered:

1. What are the key aspects of the business?

2. Which areas of the business make the biggest contribution to achieving corporate objectives?
3. What are the strengths, weaknesses, opportunities and threats most apparent in the business?
4. What future scenarios are achievable and consistent with corporate objectives?
5. What future scenarios would be deemed undesirable?
6. Of the positive scenarios, what efforts are required to achieve them?
7. What activities should be ceased which would otherwise hamper the achievement of the desirable scenarios?
8. Which corporate strengths should the organisation build on to achieve its goals?
9. Which corporate weaknesses need to be remedied in the short run?
10. What sorts of investments are required to achieve the desirable scenarios?

These questions have to be addressed in a systematic way, dealing with the company as a whole rather than in a compartmentalised way. There is a need to look towards the 'larger picture' rather than being driven by product-specific considerations. Moreover, corporate structures should not be seen as rigid and the identification and development of corporate strengths seen as more important than the continuation of 'business as usual'. When it comes to the integration of environmental considerations, cooperative strategies need also to be considered. All too often competition has been the dominant ideology in business, but increasingly cooperative strategies between businesses and involving the public and regulatory agencies can bring about benefits which are environmentally sustainable. Single-minded competitive strategies run the risk of isolating businesses from new developments, expertise and public opinion which are invaluable to the environmentally aware company.

ENVIRONMENTAL MANAGEMENT TOOLS

The ICC Charter begins to offer some of the detail that is necessary to translate the philosophies of environmental concern into practical strategies to improve environmental performance. Statements of principle and environmental policies are important in gaining the commitment needed to implement environmental improvement and in telling stakeholders about this commitment. But in order to introduce effective environmental management environmental information and analysis are required. Industry is in the process of developing ever more sophisticated tools to achieve this. These are dealt with in detail throughout this book but it is worth summarising their contribution to the overall company approach.

Environmental impact assessment (EIA) provides companies and the public with information and analysis on the development of a new plant or facility.

Environmental reviews offer a snapshot of an existing plant's environmental performance at one point in time and environmental audits provide an ongoing check on a company's environmental improvement. Techniques associated with waste management help us to consider and reconsider aspects of product and process design. These tools should be part of a company's overall environmental management system which should represent a systematic and integrated approach to a company's environmental improvement strategy.

The company will also have open to it a range of tools associated with green marketing. Environmental considerations need to be firmly encapsulated within a company's traditional marketing mix. Green products, for example, must be assessed from cradle to grave, that is, their environmental impact must be assessed on the basis of raw material inputs, production processes, use and disposal. For many, accepting responsibility for a product once it has left the factory gates represents a fundamentally different mind set but the introduction of life cycle assessment (LCA) means that we can seek to identify the widest aspects of a product's environmental impact.

THE MARKET ASSOCIATED WITH ENVIRONMENTAL IMPROVEMENT

The environmental strategies discussed above and the need for new environmental technology themselves produce new opportunities and demands for new products, thereby expanding the market for these goods and services. The significance of the environmental protection industry as a quickly expanding industrial market can no longer be denied. Even if we do not account for the considerable expenditures made for the improvement of the environment in the general context of improved production methods or products, a number of studies have estimated the size of the market for environmental improvement in 1990 at $200 billion of which 85 per cent is accounted for by developed economies. An EC document on 'The Industrial Competitiveness and Protection of the Environment' (1992) estimates the Community market at $50 billion.

According to Environmental Data Services (1992) the UK market for environmental consultancy services alone was worth £400 million in 1992 with annual sales of £1 billion expected by the year 2000. The sector's continuing expansion underlines the importance of legislation in creating new opportunities for business but also reflects voluntary initiatives by industry and commerce. This sector is dominated by 70 firms which take 80 per cent of the available work.

The world market for environmental goods and services is likely to expand at a rate of around 5.5 per cent per year to the year 2000. Within the equipment sector, demand for products for waste management and land remediation is expected to show even stronger growth. Not surprisingly, the largest exporters of environmental products are those countries with the most advanced environmental policies and frameworks. Germany is the world's leading exporter of pollution abatement equipment, for example.

Increasingly we may also expect much more significant research funding from governments in this area. Presently such expenditure is increasing although it remains low compared with other research domains. But we are seeing a major growth in international cooperation in this area reflecting the global dimension of the environmental challenge. In time this international cooperation will lead to a greater harmonisation of environmental standards and improved cross-boundary data collection.

A major spin-off for firms who take the environment seriously therefore could be a share in a new environmental market. The market for environmental products and services may well be an area into which firms can diversify and there is clear synergy between a firm's own strategies for environmental improvement and its ability to sell-on its expertise and technology. Once again we see great scope for cooperative efforts in this new and developing area. Although such new product and service developments are beyond the scope of this book, they nevertheless provide an additional focus which many firms will wish to consider.

CONCLUSION

The main focus of this book is on the strategies which firms can adopt to improve their environmental performance. We have established that there is a need and indeed a desire on the part of industry to change the way it views the environment and there is a need to look in detail at the tools available to achieve this. Before we proceed however, it is useful to review some key issues which will come up over and over again. The following ten propositions underlie the general approach to environmental management and business strategy which will be developed more fully in subsequent chapters:

1. Industry needs to take a systematic approach to environmental improvement and management has a key role to play in implementing environmental management systems.
2. The approach also has to be an integrated one which identifies all sources of pollution and environmental damage and takes a holistic approach to its remediation.
3. It may be necessary to decide on priorities for action but the long-term target must be the elimination of all negative impacts on the environment and this can be achieved via a continuous cycle of improvement.
4. Environmental information is at the heart of any business strategy to improve environmental performance and this needs to be collected and assessed at regular intervals.

5. Legislative frameworks are becoming more sophisticated and more stringent and to stay ahead of the growing legislative demands, industry needs to take a proactive response.
6. Industry needs to take an honest, credible and ethical approach to environmental improvement and carefully consider changes to its corporate culture.
7. When it comes to the assessment of individual products, environmental impact has to be measured from cradle to grave.
8. Cooperative strategies to environmental improvement may sometimes be superior to competitive ones.
9. Industrial development needs to be sustainable development.
10. Environmental management represents a new partnership between an industry and its stakeholders and its successful implementation depends on every party playing its role.

References

Commission of the European Communities (1992) 'Industrial Competitiveness and the Protection of the Environment', communication of the Commission to the Council and to the European Parliament, (SEC (92) 1986 final), November.

Ehrlich, P. and Ehrlich, A. (1991) *The Population Explosion*, Arrow Ltd, London.

Environmental Data Services (1992) 'Environmental Consultancies Ride the Recession', News Release, 14 December.

International Chamber of Commerce (1990) *The Business Charter for Sustainable Development*, ICC, Paris.

Stikker, A. (1992) 'Sustainability and Business Management', *Business Strategy and the Environment*, Volume 1, Part 3, Autumn.

World Commission on Environment and Development (1987) *Our Common Future*, Oxford University Press, Oxford.

CHAPTER 2

The legislative framework

The development of environmental legislation is singularly the most important factor influencing the behaviour of industry in the field of the environment. While issues of business efficiency or the drive for competitive advantage are vital components in the development of environmental management in industry, proactive strategic responses to environmental issues are the exception rather than the rule. Indeed, many proactive responses are themselves driven by environmental legislation, seeking to minimise the costs of future legislation or to exploit the new opportunities offered by the advance of environmental policy. For the vast majority of firms, particularly in the small and medium-sized enterprise sector, issues of environmental management are usually manifested through reactive responses to tightening legislation.

There has been a rapid advance of environmental legislation in recent years both from the European Community and from the Member States. The environmental policies of the EC are increasingly driving the environmental policies of the Member States. It is in developing their responses to the progress of environmental law that many companies realise the fundamental strategic implications of the environmental issue, also realising that the protection of the environment is not a passing irrelevance, but a potentially costly threat to the continuing survival and success of the company. However, while advancing environmental legislation will represent higher costs for some companies, increased costs in one company are reflected by increased revenues in another. The advance of environmental pressure, led by the development of environmental policy, therefore offers both a threat and an opportunity.

It is therefore vital that companies understand the framework of environmental policy so that they can positively respond to the challenges that confront them. This chapter discusses the development of environmental policies in Europe. It will explain the organisational structure of the EC, the aims and objectives of the EC relating to environmental policy in the coming years, the areas that will be addressed and the instruments that will be applied. However, under the terms of subsidiarity, the objectives of the EC are applied within the legislative frameworks which exist in each Member State. Therefore, this chapter will also discuss the background and development of environmental law in the UK, suggesting that positive and proactive strategic responses to environmental legislation generate new opportunities while reactive, *ad hoc* solutions generate extra costs.

THE DEVELOPMENT OF EUROPEAN COMMUNITY ENVIRONMENTAL POLICY

Within the Treaty of Rome which founded the original European Community in 1957 there was no mention of environmental policy. Indeed, until 1987 and the Single European Act, the European Community had no explicit legal basis in relation to environmental policy. Despite the absence of a clear legal founding for EC environmental actions, the EC had embarked on its Fourth Environmental Action Programme before being given a clear mandate for environmental action under the Single European Act in 1987. Prior to 1987, action was taken under the auspices of the EC's mandate for action in relation to the creation of a 'level playing field' within a common market and the protection of the welfare of its citizens.

The first environmental action plan in 1973 set out a number of principles which have formed the basis of environmental action in the EC ever since. The aims are clearly set out, stating that:

1. Prevention is better than cure.
2. Environmental effects should be taken into account at the earliest possible stage in decision making.
3. Exploitation of nature and natural resources which causes significant damage to the ecological balance must be avoided. The natural environment can only absorb pollution to a limited extent. Nature is an asset which may be used but not abused.
4. Scientific knowledge should be improved to enable action to be taken.
5. The 'polluter pays' principle; the polluter should pay for preventing and eliminating environmental nuisance.
6. Activities in one Member State should not cause environmental deterioration in another.
7. Environmental policies of Member States must take account of the interests of developing countries.
8. The EC and Member States should act together in international organisations and also in promoting international environmental policy.
9. Education of citizens is necessary as the protection of the environment is a matter for everyone.
10. The principle of action at the appropriate level; for each type of pollution it is necessary to establish the level of action which is best suited for achieving the protection required, be it local, regional, national, EC-wide or international.
11. National environmental policies must be coordinated within the EC without impinging on progress at the national level.

(*Source*: Haigh, N. (1992) and *Official Journal of the European Communities*: C112 20 December 1973)

The main activities of the EC in the environmental policy arena until 1987 were centred on the application of nearly 200 command and control directives in areas as diverse as lead in petrol and aircraft noise. The objectives and nature of EC environmental policy have since been expanded within the Single European Act and most recently within the Fifth Environmental Action Programme. Realising that environmental policy is of little use unless enforced, EC environmental policy has given increased emphasis to the improved enforcement of existing legislation rather than the rapid adoption of new legislation. Emphasis has also shifted from the use of command and control instruments in environmental policy to the application of economic market-based instruments such as the proposed carbon tax and voluntary agreements such as the eco-labelling and eco-management and audit schemes. The aim of such measures is to encourage change in all sectors of industry and society in a more general way than can be achieved through the use of tightly defined legislative instruments. The use of economic instruments and voluntary measures is seen as a complement rather than a substitute to the more traditional application of command and control measures.

Before discussing the relationships between environmental policy, the Single European Act and the Fifth Environmental Action Programme which sets out the aims of the EC for environmental policy between 1993 and 2000, it is important to understand the organisational structures of the European Community and the instruments available to it in relation to environmental policy. Increasingly there are opportunities for industry and other interested parties to become more closely involved with the development of EC legislation. While becoming involved in the design of new legislation and policy may be the most proactive stance of all, understanding the processes and monitoring the development of EC legislation allows scope to exploit first-mover advantage and enables better-formulated strategic planning. These are essential elements of business success in such a rapidly developing market-place.

The EC decision-making structure

The organisational structure of the European Community has traditionally centred on the three institutions: the Council of Ministers, the European Commission and the European Parliament. The structure and role of each institution is as follows:

The Council of Ministers

The Council, composed of one relevant minister from each Member State, is the body responsible for adopting and approving legislation. Within the Council, each country has a number of votes weighted in relation to its population: Britain, France, Germany and Italy have 10 votes each; Spain has 8; Belgium, Greece, Netherlands and Portugal have 5 each; Denmark and Ireland have 3 and Luxembourg has 2. Under the Maastricht Treaty, legislation can be adopted in most areas through a system of 'Qualified Majority Voting'

(QMV) which is aimed to encourage more efficient decision making by reducing the ability of any one country to veto proposed legislation, apart from some specific exceptions where unanimity is required. Exceptions include areas such as fiscal policy, aspects of energy, water and land management or in rejecting amendments made by the European Parliament to proposed legislation.

The European Commission

The Commission is made up of 17 Commissioners who are civil servants elected by, but independent from, the national governments. Larger Member States such as the UK elect two Commissioners, smaller States only one. The Commission is divided into 23 Directorates General (DGs), including DGXI for the Environment, Nuclear Safety and Civil Protection. The Commission, through the DGs and the associated working groups, is responsible for drawing up proposals for legislation, putting them into effect and their subsequent management.

The European Parliament

The Parliament is made up of 518 MEPs elected every five years from throughout the Member States. It operates through a structure of committees in relevant areas which must offer opinions on legislation proposed by the European Commission before that legislation can be passed. The relevant committee considers the proposals of the Commission and reports to the Parliament which then offers an opinion. This opinion is then taken into account as the development of the legislation progresses.

The interpretation and adjudication of EC legislation in Member States is undertaken through the Court of Justice where relevant competencies apply. The development of EC policy also draws on the Economic and Social Committee (ECOSOC), an advisory body made up of employers, employees and other interest groups.

There are three main legislative instruments available to the EC. The most commonly used instrument up to now has been the Directive. Directives set legal obligations that each Member State must reach within a set period of time while accommodating different conditions within each nation by leaving open the means through which the ends are to be met. Regulations do not offer such administrative flexibility, but set out applicable law in each Member State. They have been rarely used in the development of environmental policy, although the eco-labelling scheme, eco-management and audit scheme and the European Environment Agency are all being established through the use of EC Regulations. The Community may also release Decisions which are tightly focused demands for action addressed to specific parties. As they do not address general concerns, they are not commonly issued in relation to environmental policy.

THE FIFTH EUROPEAN COMMUNITY ENVIRONMENTAL ACTION PROGRAMME

The EC view of the future of environmental policy and its interface with industrial development is clear. With some 340 million inhabitants, the Community is the largest trading bloc in the world, and is therefore in a critical position to take the lead in moving towards sustainability. The Commission accepts that tighter environmental policy will impact on the costs of industry, however, it states that:

> A high level of environmental protection has become not only a policy objective of its own but also a precondition of industrial expansion. In this respect, a new impetus towards a better integration of policies aiming at consolidating industrial competitiveness and at achieving a high level of protection of the environment is necessary in order to make the two objectives fully mutually supportive. (SEC(92) 1986 final).

These views are given more substance within the EC's Fifth Environmental Action Programme. While this programme sets out the likely developments of EC environmental policy in a general sense, a number of specific measures relating to industry are included. Perhaps most importantly the commitment of the EC to strengthen environmental policy is underlined. The EC shares the view that urgent action is needed for environmental protection, and that many of the great environmental struggles will be won or lost during this decade. Further, it states that achieving sustainability will demand practical and political commitment over an extended period and that the EC as the largest trading bloc in the world must exercise its responsibility and commit itself to that goal.

However, as set out within the Fifth Environmental Action Programme, there have been a range of problems in the development and implementation of EC environmental policy:

- Firstly, and somewhat unavoidably, there has been a lack of coherence in the development of environmental policy as the scope and nature of the agenda has changed over the last twenty years.
- Secondly, the choice of instruments to date has been too narrowly focused on the use of command and control legislative instruments. Environmental concerns have also been insufficiently integrated with wider Community activities.
- Thirdly, prior to the Single European Act in 1987 and the adoption of qualified majority voting, the need for unanimity led to compromise of legislation to such an extent that the practical operation of EC environmental law was unclear.
- Fourthly, the reliance placed on the use of Directives which set Community-wide objectives but rely on the alteration of national legislation to achieve these ends has led to some difficulties (particularly in federal countries such as Germany, Belgium and Italy) and inconsistencies in interpretation and achievement.
- Finally, there have been deficiencies in management at all levels.

Reforms will therefore include better preparation of measures, improved consultation, more effective integration of environmental policy into the wider policy agenda, better practical follow-up to legislative measures and stricter compliance checking and enforcement. These areas are all addressed within the Fifth Environmental Action Programme of the EC which sets out the aims of the Community for environmental policy from 1993 to 2000.

A number of more specific developments are planned in relation to the problems that have been experienced in the past. Until recently, the Community's environmental policy has been aimed at controlling or reducing the environmental impact of industry. However, the EC now suggests that the promotion of industrial competitiveness requires a change in emphasis from this reactive stance to a proactive stance based around the adoption of clean technologies and the development of markets for environmentally sound products. Two key instruments available to the EC in this field are the eco-management and audit scheme (see Chapter 6) and the eco-labelling scheme (see Chapters 7 and 8). However, these will be complemented by a range of other market measures including greater public access to environmental information at all levels (including on the environmental performance of individual companies) and the application of levies, incentives and civil liabilities for environmental damage to channel decisions and behaviour toward sustainability.

The increased adoption of market-based instruments is seen as a complement rather than a substitute to the use of command and control legislation. Thus, there are a range of Directives which Member States will have to implement including those relating to packaging wastes, landfill control, priority waste streams, integrated pollution prevention and control, incinerators and toxic releases. Indeed, the EC expects the pace of environmental policy development to accelerate during the decade. It suggests 1992 to 1995 is a priming period focusing on the enforcement of existing legislation and setting direction for the future. The period from 1996 to 2000 will be where the objective of moving the European Community towards sustainability will become fully operational.

As part of the advance of environmental policy, the Fifth Environmental Action Programme proposes the development of a number of dialogue groups to assist in the design, application and enforcement of future environmental policy. Firstly, the use of a consultative forum for debate and the exchange of information between industrial sectors, business, regional and local authorities, professional associations, trade unions, environmental and consumer organisations and the relevant Directorate Generals within the Commission. Secondly, the use of an implementation network to aid the practical application of EC legislative measures. This will include the relevant national authorities and EC departments with expertise that can be called upon by local and national authorities to assist in application and compliance. Finally, an environmental policy review group will be utilised to develop mutual understanding and the exchange of views on environmental policy measures between the Community and Member States.

It is therefore likely that there will be greater transparency and accessibility surrounding the policy development framework. This will better enable industry and its associations (among others) to influence and track the development of European environmental policy and to incorporate its demands into the strategic framework. Given the increased access to the decision-making process within the EC, the first reaction of industry and associations when facing tighter and apparently more costly environmental legislation would be to lobby for a more lenient approach. While this is an understandable reaction, two points should be borne in mind.

Firstly, the EC views the development of environmental legislation as a prerequisite of industrial expansion and competitiveness. At the business level, it is the view of the EC that environmental efficiency drives long-term competitiveness. At the national or Community level, countries which demand high environmental standards encourage their industries to develop technologies and techniques which can be marketed to other less advanced countries when they are forced to adopt similarly strict standards. As stated in Chapter 1, the scale and growth rate of the environmental market suggests that it is a market that cannot be ignored. Accepting such competitive advantage, the EC will continue to develop strict environmental standards and will channel the macro-economic development of the EC economy towards more environmentally benign forms of industry. The dynamics of structural change suggest that while some sectors will grow, others will shrink. This is an inevitable consequence of a changing legislative climate. Lobbying for less stringent environmental legislation is therefore unlikely to prove successful as the EC adopts the view that the Community can have both a competitive and a sustainable economy.

Secondly, while strict environmental legislation imposes significant extra costs on some companies, these extra costs will be reflected by increased revenues for other companies. Companies that have developed the best available technologies and techniques in environmental management will benefit from stringent legislation which will channel demand towards their products and services. Advanced countries, industries and business are therefore pressing the EC to adopt tighter legislation. Once again therefore, it is probable that lobbying for a more lenient approach in the development of EC environmental legislation will be unsuccessful.

For industries and companies that are facing a rising tide of environmental legislation, it is essential that attempts are made to find out about and then positively address the legislative pressures which they are under. However, the Fifth Environmental Action Programme focuses on the improved enforcement of existing legislation rather than the adoption of new legislation. To some extent this should allow industry to take stock of the rapid increase in environmental legislation that has taken place in recent years and to focus on achieving compliance with existing legislation. Despite the stated objective to concentrate on the effective implementation of existing policy, there are many pieces of environmental legislation in the EC policy-pipeline which are awaiting final adoption. Many of these measures have fundamental implications for business and the need to track forthcoming legislation will remain essential.

Furthermore, the Maastricht Treaty and the Fifth Environmental Action Programme require that environmental policy should be fully incorporated into all other Community policies. Therefore, while it may become easier to track the development of policies which are explicitly environmental, it will become more difficult to monitor the development of environmental policy throughout the activities of the Commission as a whole. The establishment of the European Environment Agency which will collect data and monitor compliance throughout the Community could help to disseminate information to all interested parties. In the meantime, the delay between the release of EC legislation and its subsequent implementation in Member States offers vital planning time for those companies who monitor the development of European environmental policy in order to avoid the costs and exploit the opportunities which are undoubtedly generated.

The strategic significance of the EC's views cannot be overstated. By taking a long-term, Community-wide perspective and accepting that industrial competitiveness is enhanced by tight environmental legislation, the policy framework within which all European companies must participate will reflect these views. Some companies, some regions and some nations will benefit. If the views of the EC are correct, the economic prospects of the Community as a whole will benefit and the environment will certainly benefit. However, at the company level realising these benefits will not be automatic. Strategic planning and proactive responses to the changing policy climate are imperative if success is to be secured. Information must be gathered, its implications assessed and the necessary action taken in a systematic and integrated way.

SUBSIDIARITY AND ENVIRONMENTAL POLICY

Under the terms of subsidiarity, the development of European Community environmental policy is implemented within the legal and institutional frameworks of each Member State. Subsidiarity therefore offers each Member State the flexibility and freedom to work within existing or established procedures for environmental regulation and protection. Hence, in each Member State the objectives of environmental legislation are increasingly determined by the EC while the mechanisms through which these objectives are to be reached are determined nationally.

As each country has a separate regulatory infrastructure for pollution control, it is impossible to discuss specifically the environmental policies of each Member State. However, as the objectives of EC policy take precedence over any national objectives, it can be expected that the end results of environmental policy will be harmonised throughout the EC. This is particularly evident in relation to integrated pollution control (IPC), which simultaneously controls emissions to air, water and land. Under IPC, strict controls on releases to any one medium (i.e. air) prevent emissions merely being diverted to another (i.e. water). Given the inherent logic of such an approach, the application of IPC can be expected to be introduced more widely, particularly within the EC's Integrated Pollution Prevention and Control Framework Directive. Since the UK was the first EC Member State to apply IPC, and the EC Framework Directive closely reflects the current structure of UK legislation, it is useful to outline the UK framework of pollution control.

UK ENVIRONMENTAL POLICY AND POLLUTION CONTROL

Environmental policy and law have a long history in the UK. Controls over air and water pollution are documented as far back as the fourteenth century. However, it was not until the industrial revolution that environmental protection as we know it today began to take shape. Controls on air pollution from industrial works were first developed in the 1860s and introduced the requirement that the 'best practicable means' should be applied to control the release of substances harmful to the environment. The concept of 'best practicable means' (BPM) formed the basis of environmental regulation of industrial emissions until replaced by the similar concept of 'best available techniques not entailing excessive cost' (BATNEEC) within the 1990 Environmental Protection Act.

While the UK Environmental Protection Act (EPA) builds on previous legislative measures, it is the key piece of environmental legislation which has drawn together and overhauled the regulatory structures and requirements of environmental protection in the UK. Much of the content of the EPA has been motivated by the activities of the EC, and will better enable the framework of UK pollution control to meet the demands of European environmental policy. However, in some areas, notably in the introduction of integrated pollution control, the UK EPA has provided the framework upon which future EC policy will be based, namely the forthcoming Integrated Pollution Prevention and Control Directive. This illustrates the extent of integration of EC and national environmental policies. The remainder of this chapter will discuss the demands that the EPA places upon industry, the institutional framework set up to administer it and its implications for industry.

The EPA introduces a range of new obligations for industry. While the Act includes measures in a number of areas, the two main sections of the Act which are of relevance to industry are Part 1 (Integrated Pollution Control and Air Pollution Control by Local Authorities) and Part 2 (Waste on Land). A full discussion of Part 2 of the EPA and the 'Duty of Care' obligations introduced for waste management can be found in Chapter 7.

The EPA details all processes which are subject to regulation and control in the UK. All 'prescribed processes' as defined by the Act must apply for authorisation to the relevant regulatory authorities in order to emit into the environment. If authorisation to emit is to be granted, the emitter must satisfy the relevant authority that the process for which they are responsible applies the 'best available techniques not entailing excessive cost' (BATNEEC) in emissions control. This is an important departure from past forms of control as it includes a management dimension in pollution control in addition to the technological criteria previously applied. The format of the application for authorisation is such that those companies who have developed environmental management techniques through a management system and have undertaken an environmental audit will be at a considerable advantage when gathering the information and applying the criteria of BATNEEC which are necessary for a successful application.

Part 1 of the EPA divides industrial and other emitters into two tiers of control. Part A prescribed processes are the most significant polluting processes in the country and all of their emissions are controlled under the EPA by the relevant pollution inspectorate. Part B processes are less significant but more common processes which are subject to air pollution control by local authorities.

Part A prescribed processes include around 5,000 of the most significant polluters in the UK. These processes are under the control of Her Majesty's Inspectorate of Pollution (HMIP) in England and Wales and Her Majesty's Industrial Pollution Inspectorate in Scotland. Under the terms of the EPA, Part A prescribed processes are obliged to apply the objectives of Integrated Pollution Control (IPC) whereby the total emissions to air, water and land are considered under one application for authorisation to emit. The firm is then required to apply the combination of inputs, processes and emissions control technologies and techniques which minimise the overall environmental impact of the facility. The aim of IPC is to minimise overall environmental impact and to ensure that the 'best practicable environmental option' (BPEO) is achieved. Authorisation to emit will only be granted should the regulatory authority be convinced that the BPEO has been reached.

The application for authorisation to emit under IPC regulations must offer a range of information including the following:

- a description of the plant and its physical characteristics and the flows of materials within it;
- descriptions of the nature of the product to be produced, the quantities of production and the time of that production;
- details of any neighbouring processes which could affect or be affected by the operation of the plant;
- an inventory of prescribed substances or other substances which are used which may be harmful if released;
- a description of any abatement technologies and techniques applied to prevent, reduce or render harmless any substances as described above into any environmental media;

- a description of any proposed releases and an assessment of the environmental consequences;
- a description of any monitoring facilities established;
- justification that the plant and its proposed activities meet with requirements for BATNEEC and BPEO;
- any other relevant information.

Compliance with UK environmental legislation therefore necessitates a considerable amount of information gathering and analysis. Depending on the condition of the plant, legislation may demand a high degree of capital expenditure and management reorganisation to ensure compliance with the demands of BATNEEC and BPEO. The information gathered within the application will be entered on a public register along with the decisions of HMIP relating to the application.

Part B processes, of which there are over 25,000 in England and Wales alone, are under the control of local authorities. While local authorities are only obliged to regulate emissions to air, Part B prescribed processes are still compelled to apply the principles of BATNEEC although they are exempt from the IPC demands placed upon larger polluters. This difference is reflected in the application for authorisation. Despite the direct absence of an IPC requirement for smaller polluters, solid wastes are regulated under Part 2 of the EPA and the Duty of Care (see Chapter 7) and liquid emissions are controlled either by the Water Authority or by the National Rivers Authority. Therefore, while the specific terms of the legislation affecting smaller companies may be slightly different, the range of legislative pressures facing them is broadly similar to those facing their larger counterparts.

For all companies it is useful to note the parallels between the needs of the application for authorisation as set out above and the benefits of undertaking process such as environmental impact assessment, environmental audits or the development of an environmental management system as discussed throughout this book. Once information has been gathered, skills developed, technologies incorporated and management systems designed, the costs of compliance or of adopting new environmental initiatives are significantly reduced. Indeed, the demands of legislation suggest that many of the elements of an integrated environmental management system must be assembled in order to reach compliance. The subsequent opportunities to move beyond compliance and to shift from a reactive to a proactive stance then become much more achievable. It is therefore evident that much of the effort and expense needed to compile a successful application under the EPA, if managed correctly, can also be utilised in order to work towards improved environmental performance in other areas.

One notable area where costs can be reduced through proactive responses to current and forthcoming environmental legislation is that of capital investment. As environmental legislation progresses, the environmental standards demanded from capital equipment will increase. This is particularly evident under the terms of the EPA which demands that the best available technologies and techniques are applied under BATNEEC. The interpretation of 'not entailing excessive cost' is unlikely to dictate that at short intervals companies must upgrade their capital equipment to remain within the law. However, at some point the application of BATNEEC will dictate that technology which, in terms of environmental performance, is out of date must be replaced even if it is still performing operationally. BATNEEC could therefore impose significant extra costs on some companies. These costs can be avoided if developments in environmental policy and technology are monitored and capital investments altered accordingly.

While reaching and maintaining compliance can be the first step in realising greater opportunities, the consequences of non-compliance under the EPA are significant. The regulatory authorities have the power to serve an enforcement notice if authorisations are breached. An enforcement notice will specify the necessary steps and the period within which they must be taken in order for compliance to be achieved. If a serious risk to the environment is posed, a prohibition notice may be served which may close the facility until the terms of the authorisation are met. Continued non-compliance can lead to prosecution, fines and potentially the imprisonment of the responsible person within the firm.

Of course the implications of non-compliance are wider than those of any direct action taken by the regulatory authorities. Re-application for authorisation is an unnecessary expense often demanding short-term crisis management measures which are more expensive to introduce and run than a better planned and more integrated solution. It will also divert management time from more positive aspects of business development. This will affect the relationship between the management of a company and its shareholders. Breaches of the law will add extra pressure and demotivate employees who are normally averse to working for badly managed, irresponsible companies. It is likely that insurance premiums for companies that have breached environmental legislation will be higher in the future than for companies that have always maintained compliance.

Surveys of public opinion reveal that the vast majority of people strongly object to the perceived irresponsibility of companies which pollute at all. For companies that pollute illegally the public relations stakes are very high indeed. The surrounding community do not like sharing the local environment with a company that illegally pollutes it. Customers are reluctant to buy from companies with a record of environmental non-compliance. The effects of non-compliance can be magnified by unwanted media or pressure group interest, particularly as the freedom of access to environmental information increases. All of these factors, whether they are driven by perception or reality, can represent extremely negative influences on the success of the firm and its management.

Therefore, companies included in the coverage of the EPA that do not view their emissions in a comprehensive and integrated way will be subject to refused authorisation and eventually higher costs, loss of reputation, fines, prosecution and closure. While environmental law may to some extent be open to interpretation and to some degree of subjectivity in relation to BATNEEC or BPEO, in the final analysis it is very clear – strategic decisions simply relate to compliance or closure.

CONCLUSION

The continued advance of environmental legislation poses a significant threat to many companies. As this chapter has discussed, it is most unlikely that the environmental policy agenda will relax in any way. It is the view of the European Commission that stringent environmental legislation drives industrial competitiveness. Therefore the views and influence of the EC relating to environmental policy in the Member States suggest that the threats and opportunities of environmental legislation will continue to mount.

Companies that focus on the opportunities offered through changing internal procedures and external markets will enhance their potential for success. Planning ahead and incorporating environmental legislation within all areas of the strategic decision-making process will be a necessary but not a sufficient condition of business success. Failure to do so will be a sufficient condition for business failure.

References

Commission of the European Communities (1992) 'Industrial Competitiveness and the Protection of the Environment', Communication of the Commission to the Council and to the European Parliament (SEC (92) 1986 final), November.

Haigh, N. (1992) *Manual of Environmental Policy: The EC and Britain*, Longman, Harlow.

CHAPTER 3

Environmental impact assessment: prevention is better than cure

A definitive element of any comprehensive environmental protection system must lie in its attempts to prevent rather than alleviate environmental damage. While much environmental legislation may in some way be seen to be preventative in outlook, few measures are explicitly preventative in their aims. Environmental impact assessment (EIA), also known as environmental assessment, however, is just this. It is a framework or methodology specifically developed to minimise the potential environmental impacts of new developments at the earliest stage possible – the design and development stage.

Environmental impact assessment is traditionally associated with procedures developed to aid decision-making by planning authorities responsible for granting or withholding planning permission. To this extent it is central to the planning of any business considering significant expansion of facilities or plant. In this traditional application, EIA can be defined as the formal and systematic collection and analysis of information relating to the possible environmental effects of a new or significantly altered project in relation to the physical, social and economic environment surrounding that development.

However, as will be illustrated below, even where an EIA is not required by law it is good business and environmental practice to undertake one anyway. It is hoped that through the information gathered and analysed under the EIA, internal management decisions can be taken on the basis of objective and more complete information. Thus, apart from facilitating environmental protection, EIA will help to ensure future compliance, increase efficiency and reduce the costs of a plant once it becomes operational. In order to achieve this potential, during the design stage management responsibilities must be assigned and procedures established to monitor, document, assess and improve the environmental impact of the development. These activities will form the basis of an environmental management system once the plant becomes operational. Environmental impact assessment offers the potential to incorporate the future needs of the environmental management system into the physical design of the plant at the very beginning of the design process.

The traditional procedures of EIA have been embodied within both EC and UK legislation. As will be discussed, applying the detail and depth of EIA as suggested by law can be a costly and time consuming exercise. However, for those developments for which EIA is not mandatory, the benefits of EIA can still be achieved without the imposition of such costs. The methodology of EIA can be applied in less detail than that required by law in order to highlight areas of potential environmental impact where particular attention is needed. The adoption and adaption of the EIA frameworks set out by EC and UK law should therefore be seen as the first step in the development of an environmental management system for new, extended, relocated or significantly altered production processes.

THE BACKGROUND TO EIA

Before moving on to discuss the application of EIA as a strategic management tool, it is important to understand the background of EIA and the legislative interpretation given to it by the European Community. Environmental impact assessment is now an established technique in environmental planning. Since 1988, the basis of EIA in Europe has been firmly based on the EC's Environmental Impact Assessment Directive, although as a process it had been fairly widely adopted since the early 1970s. Outside Europe, EIA has its origins in the United States, where in 1969 the adoption of the National Environmental Protection Act included requirements for the submission of an environmental impact statement (the document presenting the results of the assessment) for all major developments.

In the UK, prior to the implementation of the EC Environmental Impact Assessment Directive in 1988, there was no definite legislative requirement for new projects to consider formally their possible environmental effects. However, since the advent of widespread public concern for the environment in the late 1960s, opposition to developments which may have significant environmental impacts has grown. Prior to the EC Directive, such opposition was voiced through provisions for public participation made within the UK's land-use planning legislation. This provided a less explicit and often criticised screening process for the adverse social and environmental effects of proposed developments. These were subjected to an array of controls and guidelines, including environmental considerations, for many years prior to the adoption of an explicit requirement for an EIA. Only after 1988 has there been a mandatory requirement for an EIA to accompany applications for planning permission for many large-scale developments.

Despite the absence of a statutory requirement for environmental impact assessment prior to 1988, and the continuing absence of a mandatory EIA for small- and medium-scale developments, numerous studies of potential environmental impact were undertaken voluntarily. These were largely seen as a way of convincing the planning authorities of the suitability of a project and thus finding an easier passage through planning procedures. Such voluntary assessments often aim to satisfy a number of questions likely to arise as a matter of course in the planning process, for instance the need to illustrate that full consideration had been given to the potential effects on the surrounding environment of a project. Voluntary assessments thereby pre-empt potentially lengthy delays, bad publicity, heightened scrutiny from pressure groups and costly public enquiries.

THE EC ENVIRONMENTAL IMPACT ASSESSMENT DIRECTIVE

European experience of environmental impact assessment has been varied. The arrival in 1985 of EC Directive 85/337 on the assessment of certain public and private projects in the environment, more commonly known as the Environmental Impact Assessment Directive, seeks to harmonise efforts for a standard approach and to produce a 'level playing field' throughout the EC for all proposed developments likely to carry a significant environmental impact.

The importance of the preventative dimension in European environmental policy has been clear since the beginnings of environmental action at the Community level. Indeed, the first European Community environmental action plan in 1973 states that:

> The best environmental policy consists in preventing the creation of pollution or nuisances at source, rather than subsequently trying to counteract their effects ... Effects on the environment should be taken into account at the earliest possible stage in all the technical planning and decision making processes. (C112 20 December 1973, 6–7)

Despite the well-meant rhetoric, it took the Council of Ministers ten years from an initial proposal in 1975 to finally approve the EIA Directive. This became a central element in the EC's policy to avoid rather than alleviate environmental damage throughout the European Community once approved in July 1985. The Directive did not come into force for a further three years until July 1988 when each Member State had to build its aims into their own national legislation. Under the principle of subsidiarity, which states that all measures should be implemented at the most appropriate administrative level possible, it is up to each Member State to decide how the objectives of any directive are reached (see Chapter 2).

As a result of the EIA Directive, throughout the EC there is now a statutory requisite for a full appraisal of the nature of a range of major new developments and their potential environmental effects prior to planning approval being granted. The EIA Directive requires that before consent is given to a development that is likely to have substantial environmental effects, be it through the size, nature or location of the development, a thorough examination of those effects should take place. The developer, whether public or private, must present a study of the project and its potential environmental effects to the competent authority (i.e. that body which is responsible for taking the decision) on application for planning permission.

Due to the considerable costs and lengthy delays that can arise from the EIA procedure, the Directive offers a screening process to minimise the number of projects that must undertake a potentially costly EIA. It lists a range of projects of a significant scale where assessment is mandatory. These are built into UK legislation under Schedule 1 of the Town and Country Planning (Assessment of Environmental Effects) Regulations (1988) and are described in Table 3.1. The areas described are based upon the guidelines of the EC Directive and will be approximated within the national legislation of each Member State. While the Directive covers all 'major developments', that is those which are likely to cause significant environmental impacts, all planning applications not covered by the Directive remain subject to the existing planning procedures in each Member State. Experience has shown that although the costs of the assessment fall on the developer, throughout the study potential savings are realised which will ameliorate future costs. As will be discussed below, as part of good business and environmental practice, the application of an EIA must be undertaken on a wider scale than that set out by statute.

Each Member State can also select other developments where EIA is mandatory if they consider potential environmental effects to be significant. As with many environmental issues, the process of defining the boundaries of 'significant' is not an easy one. Subjective decisions must be taken regarding the project's categorisation into high or low, global or local significance. Outside those projects that fit under mandatory description, the boundaries for the UK have been determined under Schedule 2 of the Town and Country Planning (Assessment of Environmental Effects) Regulations 1988 and set out in Table 3.2.

Table 3.1 Developments where EIA is mandatory

- Crude oil refineries and installations for the gasification and liquefaction of 500 tonnes or more of coal or bituminous shale per day.
- Thermal power stations and other combustion installations with a heat output of 300 MW or more and nuclear power stations and other nuclear reactors.
- Installations for the storage and final disposal of radioactive waste.
- Steelworks for the initial smelting of cast iron and steel.
- Installations for the extraction of asbestos and for the processing and transformation of asbestos and products containing asbestos.
- Chemical installations.
- Construction of motorways, expressways, lines for long-distance railway traffic and airports.
- Trading ports and inland waterways which permit the passage of vessels of over 1,350 tonnes.
- Waste disposal installations for the incineration, chemical treatment or landfill of toxic and dangerous waste.

Table 3.2 Developments where EIA is discretionary

- Major projects which are of more than local importance.
- Occasionally for projects of a smaller scale which are proposed for potentially sensitive areas.
- In a small number of cases, where expert and detailed analysis of those effects would be desirable and would be relevant to the issue of principle as to whether or not the development should take place.

The growth of environmental awareness and concern about polluters has meant that all new industrial developments are likely to be questioned regarding their potential environmental impact before being given planning permission. Some degree of assessment of environmental impact will therefore be a requirement for the vast majority of new industrial developments whether they are covered by EIA legislation or not.

While traditionally environmental protection measures have been legislatively driven, increasingly it is recognised that good environmental performance is an essential element of business success. Reaching compliance, while essential, should not be seen as the final objective as there are real and tangible benefits in improving environmental performance in industry. The application of EIA outside the scope of the EC Directive is one example where moving beyond compliance can help to realise better business and environmental performance.

THE EIA PROCESS

If we study the general structure of EIA, then some of the benefits which are available to developers who apply its methodologies within their project planning procedures become apparent. While a more detailed methodology is considered below, the general structure of EIA is outlined in Figure 3.1. The structure of the EIA is displayed within Figure 3.1 and is discussed below.

Points 1 to 8 outline the general steps undertaken in the EIA which will be discussed in greater detail below. Once the EIS has been drafted, it should feedback directly to the proposed design in order to incorporate any scope for further improvement. It is then necessary to release the EIS and to invite public comment on the proposed development. These comments can then be incorporated into the proposed design and the EIS modified to better reflect the views of the public. This should be done before the EIS is submitted to the planning authorities. It may be necessary to repeat the process of modifying the proposed design until a compromise is reached if disagreements relating to the development are sustained. As the planning authority itself will invite public comment on the EIS, should the developer enter into consultation with the

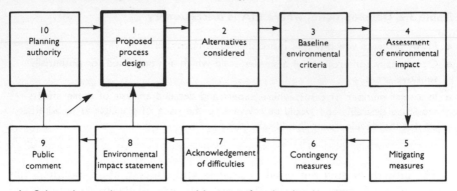

1. Select the product, process and location for the development.
2. Assess alternative products, processes and locations and justify the final selections.
3. Assess the nature of the environment within which the development will take place.
4. Identify and assess the impacts of the development upon that environment.
5. Select measures to minimise environmental impact, assess alternative mitigating measures and justify the final selections.
6. Plan and document emergency and contingency measures.
7. Discuss data collection and assessment difficulties.
8. Document the assessment within an Environmental Impact Statement (EIS).
9. Invite public and stakeholder comment on the EIS and identify any weaknesses or areas of particular concern.
10. Submit to planning authorities.
Revise and repeat where necessary.

Figure 3.1 The structure of environmental impact assessment

public and address their concerns prior to the EIS being submitted to the planning authorities, significant delays may be avoided.

Upon submission of the EIS, the planning authority will then accept or reject the application for planning permission. Should planning permission be awarded, it is normal that a number of revisions are requested and that a range of conditions are set in relation to the construction and operation of the facility. The design may therefore have to be altered to incorporate these conditions. If planning permission is withheld, a number of reasons will normally be given. If it is possible to alter the design in order to satisfy the reasons for withholding planning permission then the design should be revised, the appropriate areas of the EIA repeated and the EIS re-submitted.

As can be seen, EIA forces managers and designers to focus on the environmental impact of their proposals in great detail. It necessitates a full appraisal of the alternative processes and locations available. It demands an awareness of the environment in which the development will take place and provides a baseline for future comparison and compels a full appraisal of the environmental impacts of the development. It obliges the developer to work towards minimising those environmental impacts and encourages a systematic appraisal of pollution control technologies and techniques. It invites comments from all stakeholders which will enable the developers to address key areas of concern and to foster stakeholder commitment. Finally, it begins a process through which the future environmental impact of the development can be reduced and planning permission secured. These are the direct benefits of EIA; benefits which will then give rise to an array of internal management and external stakeholder advantages which are discussed below.

Of course the benefits of EIA must be offset against the costs of undertaking the study and incorporating its findings into the design of the development. As will be illustrated below, the process of EIA can require a wide range of scientific expertise which is unlikely to be available internally. Depending on the scale of the development and the depth of study undertaken, EIA can also be a lengthy process. Since all the costs of EIA fall on the developer, it is important that all parties involved in the planning stages of the project are committed to the application of EIA. Therefore, it is vital that the financiers, managers and designers of the development are conversant with the processes of EIA and what they can hope to achieve by applying them. Before moving on to discuss the potential benefits of EIA, a more detailed discussion of the stages of EIA and how it may be applied is necessary.

The format of EIA under EC and UK law

The process and methodology of EIA is extremely far reaching and encompasses a vast array of skills and analytical processes. The discussion below sets out the scope and format of the EIA according to the UK Department of the Environment in accordance with the EC Directive. It also begins to introduce some of the strategic elements of EIA that must be considered if the design of the facility is to fully incorporate the objectives of the environmental management system. While under UK legislation EIA is mandatory for a mixture of infrastructural and industrial developments, the discussion below relates to the adoption of EIA for all new business developments. It accepts the proposition that from a business as well as an environmental perspective prevention is better than cure. While the voluntary application of EIA may demand a less detailed analysis and allow a selective use of the format of EIA as set out by law, the general format should remain the same. The discussion below therefore incorporates the general principles and structures required for both statutory and voluntary approaches to EIA. The discussion relates to points 1 to 8 above.

1. Proposed process design

- Description of the purpose of the project
- General description of fixed physical attributes

- Operational characteristics
- Projected nature and level of all emissions

The first step in undertaking the EIA must be to decide upon and describe the exact nature of the proposed development and its purpose. This description should offer information relating to the purpose of the project and its physical characteristics in terms of size, the number of employees, the demands placed on the surrounding infrastructure and so on. A description of the operational attributes of the project is also required, and should include description of the production processes involved, the type and quantities of raw materials, energy and other resources consumed and the quantity and composition of any emissions generated. In line with the demands of Integrated Pollution Control set out under the 1990 Environmental Protection Act and the EC Integrated Pollution Prevention and Control Directive, the nature of the emissions considered should include liquid, gaseous and solid wastes, noise and any other legal nuisances which may be generated.

2. Alternatives considered

- Location
- Product design
- Process design
- Operational management

Discussion of any alternative sites and processes considered must be put forward along with the reasons for the final choice of location. For the purposes of obtaining planning permission and the statutory application of EIA, the choice of location is the primary consideration.

It is often the case that a production facility will be designed to produce a given product. However, as will be discussed in Chapter 7, the 'cradle to grave' environmental impact of a product can be significantly reduced through redesign and the application of life cycle assessment (LCA). While LCA is designed to expand the boundaries of environmental management outside the production facility, it very clearly includes study of the environmental impact of the production process. To minimise the overall environmental impact of a firm, it is necessary to integrate both product and process design. LCA will highlight those areas of the environmental profile of the product where particular attention is needed. The production facility should therefore be designed to produce a product which itself has been designed in order to minimise environmental impact.

Similarly, the EIA must also consider alternative plant designs and explain the motives for the final selection. The final choice of product and process should relate both to economic and environmental criteria. Managers and designers must therefore document and justify their decisions at all stages. Both for internal staff and for external stakeholders, it is useful to clarify and communicate the factors upon which the final product and process designs were chosen. This will foster understanding, commitment and support from all stakeholders.

3. The baseline environment

- Proximity and numbers of surrounding human population
- Present human use of the site
- Nature of flora, fauna and habitats
- Surface and groundwater quality
- Soil quality
- Landscape and topography
- Air quality and climatic factors
- Nature of the built environment
- Any other relevant environmental features

The next stage of the EIA is to undertake an ecological survey of the proposed site for the development and its surroundings. This stage clearly necessitates a wide range of expertise and will provide the baseline data which is needed in order to predict the environmental impact of various design scenarios and to establish exactly what the environmental impact of the facility is. While it may be necessary to bring in external consultants to undertake the baseline ecological study, it is important that their findings are fully disseminated to the project designers. This will highlight particularly sensitive issues and facilitate better decision-making.

4. Assessment of ecological impact

- Physical, social and economic
- Direct and indirect
- Cumulative
- Short-, medium- and long-term
- Temporary and permanent
- Positive and negative

It is necessary to assess the effects of the proposed development on the baseline data collected. Effects should be assessed not only in terms of the effects on buildings, flora, fauna and geology, land, air and water, but also in relation to the social and economic impacts of the development, the effects of the need for material and energy inputs and emissions during the production process, any wastes generated, the distribution of the output and so on.

Assessment should include not only a scientific assessment but also some assessment of the social and economic impacts of the proposal. Clearly this is an onerous task requiring a wide array of scientific and broader expertise. While the effects of the development on the natural environment may be relatively easily assessed through established monitoring and modelling techniques, any assessment of the social and economic effects of the development is much more difficult as they do not adhere to similarly 'hard' scientific facts and formulae. An assessment of socio-economic impact will require predictions relating to the positive impacts on the local economy through improved levels of income and employment as well as negative impacts such as the disruption caused during construction and the generation of nuisances such as noise and odour. The utilisation of cost-benefit analysis will be necessary to assess the socio-economic effects of the development.

The collection of baseline ecological data and consultation with the plant architects and engineers will enable the development to minimise its damage on its host site. Although industry's effect on the environment is normally assumed to be negative, it may also have a very positive role to play. In relation to EIA, in many cases it is possible to enhance the ecological characteristics of the site as a result of the development. This may be achieved in any number of ways, for instance by restoring or conserving a rare habitat as a feature of the development, by providing amenity services such as street lighting or sports facilities within the development or by landscaping a derelict site. It should not be assumed that the role of EIA is merely to minimise the negative impacts of a development, it is also to maximise the positive impacts.

5. Mitigating measures

- Technologies
- Techniques
- Alternatives
- Predicted effectiveness

Following on from the baseline survey and the assessment of the effects of the development, the EIA must analyse and describe the mitigating measures which have been considered and adopted where significant adverse effects are identified. These may be in terms of the site location and orientation, the type of process selected, any equipment incorporated in order to control, contain and treat wastes arising and any aesthetic and ecological measures taken to protect or enhance the surrounding areas. While it is easy to identify 'end of pipe' pollution containment measures, it is also important to describe any 'along the pipe' pollution avoidance measures. The EIA should also offer some predictions relating to the efficacy of the techniques as well as technologies applied in pollution reduction. A discussion of the alternatives considered and an assessment of the likely effectiveness of the mitigating measures adopted should also be provided.

6. Contingency measures

- Risk assessment
- Physical contingency measures
- Procedural contingency measures

The stages of EIA up to this point have analysed the impact of the proposed development on the surrounding social, economic and natural environment. However, it is all too apparent when studying major environmental incidents that many of them do not occur under normal operational circumstances. Thus the EIA should offer an assessment of the risks of accidents and an indication should be provided of the preventive measures to be adopted so that an accident is not likely to have a significant effect. Again, contingency measures should be assessed in terms of technologies and techniques.

7. Assessment difficulties

- Information collection
- Information assessment
- Prediction of effects
- Assessment of risk

Given the range of areas for assessment and the skills required to meet the complexity of the demands of the EIA, particularly as at the design stage it is a hypothetical development, some assessment of the difficulties in compiling information must be offered. It should be noted that this may not be seen as a weakness of the EIA itself, but as a strength on the part of the developer in recognising any shortfalls, especially if the developer undertakes to subject any areas of uncertainty to particular scrutiny should the project progress.

Where the EIA has been undertaken as a mandatory requirement, the results of the EIA are submitted to the planning authorities. Under UK planning law, the planning authorities can request further information relating to an application for planning permission at any time. Failure to supply sufficient information will thus result in planning permission being withheld and in the imposition of further costs and delays. It is therefore necessary that the structure and depth of the EIA are in accordance with the requirements of legislation.

Should the EIA be undertaken voluntarily, it is important that a systematic and thorough study is undertaken to ensure that all relevant factors are properly assessed. There will be areas of every development which have negligible environmental impact. In these areas, a less detailed analysis is required, and hence the costs of EIA may be reduced. However, it is vital that any decisions to omit or circumvent particular sections of the EIA process are taken objectively. Without this objectivity, potential environmental impacts that are not obvious will be overlooked. These decisions must be documented and justified and can only be taken on a case-by-case basis.

The environmental impact statement

The results of the EIA are then presented within an environmental impact statement (EIS). It must also include a non-technical summary of the processes and findings of the EIA in order to allow non-specialists to participate in the ensuing discussion regarding the acceptability or otherwise of the proposals.

It is a requirement of legislation that the EIS is open to scrutiny both from the competent authorities and from the public at large. Many of the EIAs undertaken voluntarily in the UK have also invited public comment as a way of identifying areas of public concern, making the necessary changes and communicating the results of the assessment, thus re-assuring public concerns and avoiding conflict. For some developments however, public participation can fuel local opposition to a development which may be of a wider social advantage; a common dilemma linked with the NIMBY (not in my backyard) syndrome. It is therefore important that a first draft of the EIS is revised to take in the views of all those involved in the consultation process. It is at this stage that the EIA draws in alternative views and approaches and ensures that the final EIS is as comprehensive a document as possible once it is submitted to the planning authorities and made available for public comment.

An open and cooperative stance on behalf of the firm at this stage can have significant benefits for the firm once the project is up and running. Such a stance is encouraged through the inclusion of a non-technical summary within the EIS which should be accessible to any interested party.

The costs of EIA and the scope for adaption

Should the guidelines of the EC and of the UK Department of Environment relating to the structure of the EIA be followed, then the costs of EIA procedures may be substantial. EIA could therefore increase the start-up costs for new developments and present a barrier to entry for new firms. While, as will be discussed below, there are economic benefits from EIA, it is unlikely that the substantial costs of undertaking EIA will be met if there is a significant risk that planning permission will be withheld and the returns on the investment not realised. For new market entrants without substantial capital resources the risk may simply be too great. The problem therefore is to encourage economic development while minimising the environmental impact of new developments.

In voluntary situations the solution may not necessitate the application of EIA in the same comprehensive and costly format suggested by EIA legislation. Accepting the principles of EIA and adapting it on a firm-by-firm basis so that the benefits of the process can be spread further than those areas explicitly included in EIA legislation is therefore necessary. The suggested format can be used selectively and in less depth to achieve the maximum environmental and financial benefits within the cost constraints of the firm involved. Certain elements of the format of EIA suggested by legislation that are not considered relevant (i.e. those areas where a company may have a marginal environmental impact) can potentially be omitted. However, it is important to note that EIA aims to identify and minimise impacts which are often not obvious. Decisions relating to the selective use of EIA procedures must therefore be taken objectively in relation to the particular circumstances facing the development. All aspects of the EIA procedure as set out above should be addressed, only those which after systematic assessment have marginal impact can be disregarded.

Even with the selective use of EIA in order to reduce its costs, the application of the cost-saving or revenue-generating measures revealed by EIA procedures must be seen in the same light as any other commercial investment. All commercial ventures compete for capital; those with minimum costs and maximum revenue are given the finance to proceed. As EIA is often a costly and time-consuming procedure with financial benefits arising throughout the lifetime of the development, the payback periods for the investment in EIA may be lengthy. As a result of the extra initial costs and the uncertain longer-term benefits, capital shortages and financial short-termism will negate the attractiveness of the improved environmental performance made possible through effective EIA. It is therefore vital that the benefits of EIA are communicated to developers and their stakeholders. It is to these which we now turn.

THE BENEFITS OF EIA

Business benefits

Apart from its use for external planning purposes, the process of EIA and the resulting EIS are of great internal relevance to the management of the company. Of course, the main internal benefit must be in relation to the lessons learned in the process of focusing the minds of management on the environmental effects of their activities and the reactions of the authorities and of the public to these potential effects. In undertaking such a process, direct changes will be made to the physical nature of the development, but perhaps more importantly, the managers will absorb knowledge that will change the nature of their decision-making so that it becomes more environmentally benign in the future.

Adding the environment to the priorities of a company can be a catalyst to a complete strategic overhaul and can protect the environment and the future of the company. However, these benefits are mainly available to companies which are proactive in their strategic response to the environmental challenge. Environmental impact assessment is the most proactive environmental management tool available to the business manager, although it is one which is seldom available as it is relatively rare to develop new or significantly altered production facilities. Thus when the opportunity arises to fully utilise EIA it is an opportunity which should be seized.

Many of the areas of study and the results gained will also be of direct use in other respects once the plant has been built, notably in applying to the regulatory agencies for authorisation to emit. There are also wider business benefits from the EIA which offer support to the proposition that regardless of any statutory requirement, many new developments should undertake some form of EIA as part of the strategic management planning process. It is accepted that as the statutory format of EIA is a very detailed and potentially very costly procedure, that an adapted and more selective form of EIA may therefore be appropriate. As has been mentioned above, adapting EIA procedures in order to reduce the associated costs will involve selecting areas with minimal environmental impact which may not demand detailed scrutiny. Those areas with minimal environmental impact must be identified objectively and can only be selected on a case-by-case basis.

Operational benefits

More specifically, there are clear business benefits associated with improved environmental performance in relation to improved efficiency, reduced waste, reduced risk and better stakeholder relationships. The process of EIA provides a forward planning framework through which these benefits can be realised. Environmental impact assessment seeks to build the management and stakeholder awareness and to develop the physical needs of environmental management which are necessary for these benefits to be secured.

It must be stressed that in order to translate the rhetoric of improved environmental performance into reality, top level managerial commitment must be secured and the need for and requirements of improved performance must be communicated throughout the company. This is particularly valid for business planners and product and process designers who will not build in measures to realise the full potential offered by the environment unless convinced of and conversant with the associated issues and solutions.

A committed participation in EIA will identify areas of the proposed development where alternative techniques and technology will reduce running costs once the project becomes operational. In many cases the payback periods for environmental investments are extremely short, the process of EIA will help to highlight such opportunities. Energy efficiency is perhaps the best documented example of investments which produce both financial and environmental benefits. Other facets of the EIA procedure, for instance the development of a projected waste inventory, may focus attention on any reuse or recycling opportunities within the firm or dormant markets for waste materials outside the firm.

The critical advantage of EIA is that it is at the design stage that the opportunities for improving environmental performance are most readily available. Setting environmental goals for the proposed development enables the founding of an environmental strategy at an early stage. It is under this overall strategy that the firm can design an integrated production process which utilises the most up-to-date and efficient technologies within a facility designed to encourage the best techniques in business and environmental management.

The development of the environmental strategy from the very beginnings of the project will ensure its acceptance at later stages. The introduction of effective environmental management systems involves designating new responsibilities, changing roles and having to overhaul management structures and accepted behaviour. Once the plant has been operational, adding these objectives will be considerably more difficult than allowing them to evolve throughout the development of the project. It is also likely that the add-on environmental management system will not be fully integrated into managerial decision-making and the day-to-day operations of the facility.

In physical terms, designing a new development with environmental considerations built in throughout the planning and development of the project will encourage proactive responses to anticipated negative effects and reveal more positive opportunities which may otherwise have gone unnoticed. Subsequent to the design stage, environmental technologies and techniques can only be incorporated by disrupting production and working within the confines of the existing plant or facility which is not to be renewed. Even where production facilities are renewed, it is rare that an entire process will be renewed at one time, rather it is more common that components will be renewed individually as they become obsolete. While each component may be the best environmental option, the existing components with which new plant must be compatible will limit the spread of integrated 'along the pipe' environmental technologies.

Thus, once the facility becomes operational the scope for introducing environmentally optimal production technology is limited even when the company invests in its own self-renewal. In essence, efforts will be confined to fine tuning any quality and waste management procedures which do exist rather than to embracing total quality and environmental management procedures which should be designed into the plant throughout the production process. The cost penalties of disrupting production once a facility is up-and-running suggest that business managers should seek the optimal design when they have the freedom to do so.

Although the frameworks of EIA traditionally address issues of process design, the design of the product is equally important in managing overall environmental impact. While life cycle assessment (LCA) is increasingly utilised as a product management tool, it is usually adopted within certain constraints regarding existing plant and facility. The most thorough forward planning will combine EIA and LCA to develop a comprehensive and integrated solution to the future business and environmental management of both process and product.

Legislative and stakeholder benefits

Aside from the internal benefits of EIA there are further benefits which may not be achieved without the level of forward planning which EIA encourages. In a climate of rapidly developing environmental legislation and other stakeholder pressures, forward planning which considers existing and forth-coming legislation and stakeholder pressure will pay dividends later by incor-porating best practice in the planning stages. As one example, systematic and comprehensive forward planning through EIA may avoid the high costs of replacing equipment rendered obsolete by legislative advances before its natural operational obsolescence.

This consideration is particularly evident in the UK where the application of 'best available control techniques not entailing excessive cost' (BATNEEC) as set out by the 1990 Environmental Protection Act may mean that capital stock will have to be replaced before its operational obsolescence because it does not match up to current environmental best practice. Of course this will depend on the interpretation of the economic criteria of environmental regulation (that is the 'not entailing excessive cost' consideration) which lacks a clear and practical definition. These influences will be replicated throughout the EC with the advent of the Integrated Pollution Prevention Control Directive.

As part of the incorporation of environmental concerns into the formative stages of a project and as a strategic response to the threat of legislative obsolescence, it would also be good practice to confer with the relevant regulatory authorities so that their demands can also be designed-in at the earliest possible stage. Consultation with regulators will highlight any short-comings that they may find with the proposed development and will establish a proactive relationship with future watch-dogs. It may also provide invaluable practical experience of the efficacy or otherwise of environmental technologies that have been applied in similar situations elsewhere. The role of the regulatory authorities in encouraging the adoption and spread of clean technologies relies on a cooperative relationship being established with industry. However, this in turn relies on sufficient resources being committed to environmental monitoring and enforcement by central and local government.

External benefits

In terms of the external relationship between business and the wider community, the attitude taken by the company to the concerns of the public regarding the development will form the basis of the corporate relationship when and if the project should become operational. In an age of heightening public pressure and accountability, the EIS, if managed correctly and seen to be balanced and credible, can have much wider benefit. A comprehensive EIS will reassure financiers, insurers, future employees and the surrounding communities of the integrity of the developer and of the development itself. An EIS which is perceived to be biased or less than comprehensive will have exactly the opposite effect.

It is hoped that the debate which follows the release of the statement will encourage a full understanding of the issues involved, allow representation from all interested parties within the decision-making process, and where appropriate incorporate the resulting considerations into the design of the development. The results of the discussion should take into account the views of all involved and as far as possible minimise the impact of a proposed development should it be allowed to proceed. Hence the role of the EIA incorporates socio-economic as well as environmental considerations into the debate regarding the acceptability of the proposal. The process of such a discussion can communicate the concern of the developer regarding the surrounding community and environment.

External perceptions of a company are a vital element of business success, and while a negative public image established through an environmental accident or a bad EIA may persist for many years, a positive public image established through a comprehensive and open EIA will foster external acceptance and a cooperative working relationship. As it is likely that the workforce will be drawn from the surrounding community, a positive external image will be reflected in a positive internal working environment and hence drive efficiency once the plant is operational.

While the developments covered by statute under the EIA Directive do not cover the majority of new business ventures, this should not be seen to indicate that the process of EIA has no relevance for smaller-scale developments. If treated as the first step in an ongoing commitment to good business and environmental performance, the investment of time, effort and resources in EIA at this stage will reveal many benefits for the firm as well as the environment once the proposed development begins its operational life. Future costs can be avoided and benefits realised with a strategic use of an extended EIA framework.

Although a comprehensive and advanced approach to EIA may initially require additional capital resources, savings in terms of process efficiency, management, present and future compliance and insurance coupled with new opportunities through marketing and the transfer of the technologies and techniques to less proactive companies will recoup the extra expenditure, well-documented practical examples abound of companies who have adopted such measures. Furthermore, the costs of not adopting such an approach to environmental management are also significant and in many cases will threaten the survival of the company at some point.

Managers should therefore view the EIA procedure as more than just a legislative requirement which must be undertaken before the plant becomes operational. It is a chance for the firm as well as the planning authorities, regulators, insurers, financiers and the surrounding community to ensure that the design of the proposed development is the best available option. The benefits which then accrue will be both financial and environmental.

THE EIA DEBATE

Environmental impact assessment is clearly a beneficial activity both for business and the environment as it ensures that full consideration is given to environmental concerns throughout the design of major developments. However, the application of EIA does have some scope for improvement, whether it is undertaken voluntarily or as a statutory requirement. The remainder of this chapter discusses the obstacles to the wider adoption of EIA both within the planning system and within the strategic management objectives of the firm.

For EIA to be at its most effective within the planning system it is essential that those developments which could reduce their environmental impact through redesign do in fact undertake EIA. For those that do, it is important that the appropriate information is collected, that the right techniques are used to analyse this information, that the results are interpreted correctly and that, if planning permission is granted, the design of the project is modified accordingly. Clearly, there is considerable scope for the application and methodology of EIA to be less than optimal in relation to the design of legislation, the way it is applied and the depth of coverage adopted within the EIA.

In relation to the nature of EIA legislation itself, some criticism has arisen surrounding the scope and extent of the legislation where it calls for mandatory EIA. By stating very clearly which developments require EIA, an equally clear message may be sent to other developers not specifically mentioned in the legislation that they are not required to undertake assessment. As discussed, it is certain that there are many benefits both for the firm and for the environment that may be achieved through the application of EIA as a strategic management tool during the design of new developments. These benefits would accrue to many developments outside those set down by statute. The formal incorporation of environmental considerations into the planning system for developments of a smaller scale and the communication of the business benefits of EIA are therefore necessary to encourage the wider adoption of EIA.

At the local level, the process of EIA can impose significant costs on developers who are applying to bring employment and economic growth to the area. However, the local authority which is responsible for granting planning permission will also be responsible for encouraging economic development. Consequently, it may not feel able to demand that EIA is carried out to its full potential or that costly modifications are made to the design of the project for fear of deterring investment. While EIA may protect the local environment, the fear of losing the development to other regions and discouraging economic expansion in the locality may prevent local authorities from encouraging its application. In such circumstances, it is necessary to communicate the benefits of EIA and therefore to encourage its voluntary application by developers.

To encourage local authorities to demand EIA, it is important to recognise that some proactive regions demand high environmental standards from their industry and create a 'clean and green' image which promotes a better local environment and therefore encourages new industry to locate in this area.

Through encouraging the integration of environmental management into business practice within their region, local authorities also facilitate sustained economic growth as the firms within their region are likely to be more competitive. Again, therefore, the threat of higher environmental standards can be turned into a significant market opportunity at the local level (the role of regional environmental management systems is discussed in Chapter 10).

Finally, in every aspect of good design the best results are obtained through a continuous cycle of improvement based on the monitoring and feedback of past performance. However, EIA legislation specifies that the EIS should be submitted with the planning application on a one-off basis, possibly followed with some recommended areas for improvement arising from the scrutiny of the statement. While planning permission is given with the condition that the plant is built according to the specifications put forward in the EIS, no provisions are made for the operational monitoring of the predictions made within the statement. It may be argued that the Directive therefore requires only one iteration in what should be a continuous cycle of improvement which minimises the overall environmental effects of the development. While it is not yet a legal requirement, planning permission is more likely to be granted if the developer undertakes to assess the environmental impact of the plant once it becomes operational through regular environmental auditing. As discussed in Chapters 5 and 6, there is also an incentive on the part of the management of the plant to continuously monitor and strive to minimise the environmental effects of the development through the adoption of environmental auditing and management systems.

CONCLUSION

Environmental impact assessment provides vital services both as a planning tool and as an internal management tool. The benefits that it offers are significant as it allows the flexibility to design in the best environmental option at all stages in the development of new facilities. This potential can be enhanced if EIA is used strategically in alliance with life cycle assessment to ensure that in terms of environmental performance the development will produce the best available product or service within the best available production facility. The benefits of the EIA process will then accrue both to the firm itself and to the local and wider environment.

For an optimal utilisation of EIA, a long-term view of the potential benefits must be taken in relation to the short-term costs to the firm associated with the EIA. This is also relevant for local authorities seeking to utilise EIA within their economic development objectives. In this respect, it is essential that business managers and their stakeholders are conversant with the need for high environmental standards and the role that EIA can play in helping their business to achieve these levels of performance.

Environmental impact assessment is an assessment of the potential environmental effects of a new development. It is an information gathering exercise through which predictions can be made and decisions can be taken objectively and design can be improved. It offers the opportunity to develop environmental awareness in management decision-making from the very beginning of an operation. In order to realise the full benefits of EIA once the plant becomes operational, the information which it collects must subsequently be incorporated through the environmental management system, the operational performance of the facility assessed through regular environmental auditing, and the environmental performance of the product improved through the continuing application of life cycle assessment. EIA is just the start of a never-ending search for improved environmental and business performance.

References

Department of Environment Circular 15/88 Environmental Assessment.

Environmental Assessment – A Guide to Procedures Department of Environment, HMSO, Norwich.

European Community Environmental Assessment Directive (85/337/EEC) (OJ L175 5 July 1985).

UK Town and Country Planning (Assessment of Environmental Effects) Regulations 1988 (SI 1988/1199).

CHAPTER 4

Making a start: environmental policies, environmental reviews and the measurement of environmental performance

The starting point for any organisation committed to improving its environmental performance must be to make a clear statement of that commitment through a policy. It needs to reflect its key objectives in a document and communicate that to as wide an audience as possible. However, once committed to environmental objectives, the company opens itself up to assessment and investigation. A hollow policy statement will soon be exposed by competitors and pressure groups. Therefore the firm needs to begin its journey down the path towards real environmental improvement. This must begin with a wide-ranging review of its current environmental impact which will establish its baseline for future improvements. Measurement of environmental performance is therefore important but this is an area where tremendous difficulties arise.

The environmental policy, the baseline review and the measurement of environmental performance therefore all go hand in hand. They cannot really be separated. For example, aspects of the environmental review may force the organisation to subsequently revise its policy and the policy itself will influence the way in which environmental performance is measured. This chapter therefore examines the key issues which firms must consider at the early stages of their environmental initiatives.

THE ENVIRONMENTAL POLICY

An environmental policy is an organisation-based statement of objectives which must clearly outline the firm's commitment to environmental improvement. In so doing it should be detailed enough to define future actions and provide information so that management and workers can clearly determine their areas of responsibility and authority, and so that workers, consumers, shareholders and the general public are aware of that commitment. It must relate enterprise functions to specific laws, national and EC environmental standards, society's perceived expectations and the degree and level of enforcement to be used. The ideal environmental policy will be proactive and commit the company to going beyond minimum legislative and regulatory requirements.

All aspects of a company's operations, from accounting and purchasing, to product design, manufacture, sales, marketing, distribution and the use and disposal of the product will have an impact on the environment and the environmental policy should reflect a recognition of this. The policy needs to be comprehensive and detailed but it should not contain statements or targets which the firm cannot hope to achieve. This will do more harm than good if exposed. The content of any policy will vary from firm to firm and be influenced by the activities of that organisation. However, there are some general principles which can be applied to the content of the policy statement:

- Adopt and aim to apply the principles of 'sustainable development' which meet the needs of the present, without compromising the abilities of future generations to meet their own needs.
- Strive to adopt the highest available environmental standards in all site locations and all countries and meet or exceed all applicable regulations.
- Adopt a total 'cradle to grave' environmental assessment and accept responsibility for all products and services, the raw materials you use and the disposal of the product after use.
- Aim to minimise the use of all materials, supplies and energy and wherever possible, use renewable or recyclable materials and components.
- Minimise waste produced in all parts of the business, aim for waste-free processes and where waste is produced avoid the use of terminal waste treatment, dealing with it, as far as possible, at source.
- Render any unavoidable wastes harmless and dispose of them in a way which has least impact on the environment.
- Expect high environmental standards from all parties involved in the business including suppliers, contractors and vendors and put pressure on these groups to improve their environmental performance in line with your own.
- Be committed to improving relations with the local community and the public at large and where necessary introduce education and liaison programmes.
- Adopt an environmentally sound transport strategy and assess the general infrastructure of the company.
- Assess on a continuous basis the environmental impact of all operations and procedures via an environmental audit.
- Assist in developing solutions to environmental problems and support the development of external environmental initiatives.
- Preserve nature, protect ecological habitats and create conservation schemes.
- Accept strict liability for environmental damage, not blaming others for environmental damage, accidents and incidents.

Environmental policies should identify key performance areas and form a sound basis for setting corporate objectives. They need to be detailed enough to demonstrate that the commitment of the company goes beyond lip-service. A clearly defined environmental policy should be implementable, practical and relate to the areas in which the company wishes to improve its environmental performance. In particular, when designing an environmental policy the organisation needs to think hard about how it is going to quantify its objectives and measure its environmental performance.

Many firms have already published detailed environmental policies. Outlines of the policies of National Power and The Body Shop are shown in Figures 4.1 and 4.2. Both policies are detailed, specific and implementable. Although they are written in rather different ways, they both convey the commitment of the organisation to environmental improvement.

Principles

1. To integrate environmental factors into business decisions.

2. To monitor compliance with environmental regulations and to perform better than they require, where appropriate.

3. To improve environmental performance continuously.

4. To review regularly at Board level, and to make public the company's environmental performance.

5. To establish a reputation for effective environmental management.

Implementation
National Power will implement these principles in ways which will:

- maintain an ability to understand the environmental implications of current and planned activities;

- lead to the adoption of technologies which contribute to future business development but which also reduce the company's environmental impacts;

- establish clear environmental targets across the company to enable performance to be measured;

- maintain an effective environmental management system throughout the company;

- raise employees' environmental awareness, and provide training so that they can effectively carry out their environmental responsibilities;

- minimise environmental incidents and complaints;

- provide information to aid consultation with all those interested in the environmental policies, plans and performance of the company;

- improve the efficiency of use of energy, materials and natural resources;

- reflect the company's commitment to sound ecological management;

- promote the adoption of environmental management practices by the company's contractors and suppliers.

Figure 4.1 Extracts from National Power's environmental policy

1. *Assessment of operations*
   The Body Shop itself will assume responsibility for the environmental impact of its operations. An annual environmental audit will take a life cycle approach and go beyond simple compliance auditing. The company strives to monitor environmental information, specifications and formulations from suppliers and the activities of service companies to ensure that their own operations are causing least damage.

2. *Sustainable resources*
   The Body Shop endeavours to make sustainable use of renewable natural resources. The company endeavours to conserve non-renewable natural resources through efficient use and careful planning. The Body Shop strives to obtain raw materials from communities wishing to use trade as a means of protecting their culture and traditional systems of land use which have a proven record of sustainability.

3. *Testing and marketing of safe products*
   The Body Shop sells products that have been designed to have minimal adverse environmental impact. The Body Shop ensures that they are tested for safety without using animals. The Body Shop provides information to consumers which will help them to assess the environmental impact of the company's products, practices and operations.

4. *Energy efficiency*
   The Body Shop strives to use the most energy-efficient systems operation. The Body Shop endeavours to reduce the use of non-renewable resources while actively seeking energy from alternative renewable sources.

5. *Waste management and pollution control*
   The Body Shop promotes an active policy of waste minimisation: waste is reduced, reused and recycled wherever possible. The Body Shop disposes of all waste through safe and responsible methods.

6. *Risk reduction*
   The Body Shop minimises the risk of damage to the environment and to the health and safety of all staff and customers by employing safe technologies and safe procedures.

7. *Communication and information*
   The Body Shop encourages regular interaction with environmental organisations and industry and thereby obtains a balanced view on environmental issues. The Body Shop ensures that information is provided on environmental practices and will publish its environmental audits.

8. *Land use*
   The Body Shop ensures that all sites due for development are fully assessed for environmental impact. Wherever possible, The Body Shop will use degraded land and improve conditions to stimulate biodiversity.

9. *Education*
   The key to environmental protection is understanding and making individuals responsible and accountable for their actions. The Body Shop strives to raise awareness on social and environmental issues among its staff, suppliers and customers.

Figure 4.2 Extracts from the environmental policy of The Body Shop

The environmental policy of National Power does contain many of the features of a comprehensive environmental policy. The organisation is committed to minimising the use of supplies and involving suppliers in their activities. It is committed to linkages with a range of organisations and aims to communicate its environmental performance to a wide range of stakeholders. The company appears to be aware of the advantages of pursuing a policy of cooperation with local communities, rather than one of confrontation. It also recognises the need for the constant monitoring of environmental impacts. Nevertheless there are some gaps. In particular, for an organisation which is involved in primary production processes involving the burning of non-renewable resources, there appears to be no statement on issues relating to sustainable development. Indeed, this raises the question of whether sustainable development is therefore attainable at all.

The policy of The Body Shop is very comprehensive. Sustainable development is at the centre of the Body Shop's environmental initiatives and the company puts great stress on the avoidance of non-renewable resources usage and has set itself a target to do so. It integrates its suppliers into its own environmental performance and is committed to regular assessment of that performance. It is committed to go beyond minimum requirements and has integrated environmental issues with health and safety and other commitments. The Body Shop is clearly committed to openness, education and access to information about their environmental performance. Surprisingly, for a company with so many retail outlets the policy itself does not stress issues concerned with transportation and distribution. However, the company does have a strict company car policy and staff are offered discounts on bicycle purchase.

In writing an environmental policy the firm needs, nevertheless, to be realistic in its objectives. No firm will be able to do everything which is required to reduce negative impacts on the environment to zero; it should nevertheless pinpoint priorities for action. These will vary from firm to firm and from industry to industry. The judgement relating to the choice of priorities for action may also be quite subjective but in the first instance will relate to compliance with the law. Subsequently the organisation will have to consider issues in relation to:

- its atmospheric emissions;
- its wastes and water discharges;
- its energy consumption;
- its impact on the natural environment;
- pressures from external agencies, its suppliers and competitors;
- the interface with health and safety issues;
- its accident and emergency procedures; and
- wider ethical considerations.

The introduction of environmental initiatives will often spur management on to consider wider aspects of the whole company performance. Arguably, the main focus of so many firms is the operation of the firm so as to minimise

Level	Operational objective	Examples of a strategic response
1.	Minimising costs	Identify the sources of costs in relation to existing products and existing markets and plan to reduce them.
2.	Maximising short-term profitability	Accurately identify costs and benefits and have a formula for attributing overheads. Identify areas where profit margins can be extended and concentrate on these.
3.	Maximising longer-term profitability	Begin to think about planning and strategic management. Recognise that a reduction in short-term profitability might be needed to ensure longer-term objectives, including survival.
4.	Innovation in products and strategies	Think in the long term about products, processes and business strategy, identify potential markets and undertake appropriate research. Take a close look at the strategies of competitors and think about strategic alliances. Invest in appropriate technology and innovations even though they may not be the cheapest available solutions.
5.	Recognising a total cost concept	Recognise that there are more than simple direct costs to consider, stop thinking of the environment as a free good and be committed to an ultimate aim of total pollution prevention (TPP). Implement waste management schemes and consider alternative sources of raw materials.
6.	Integrating the environment	Introduce environmental management systems into every facet of the organisation's activities, audit environmental performance and assess products from 'cradle to grave'. Be committed to improving environmental performance and commit the company to go beyond compliance with legislation and regulations.
7.	Widen the environmental base	Think about the total impact of the organisation on the environment at both a local and global level and introduce policies to reduce this. Insist that suppliers, contractors and vendors match your own environmental performance. Be open about the company's environmental impact and demonstrate how the company is improving its environmental performance. Work closely with pressure groups and the community on these issues.
8.	Planning for uncertainty and risk	Look forward in the organisation, introduce integrated planning procedures, be prepared for change, identify potential areas of legislation, be proactive and design management systems which can deal with uncertainty and shocks. Have systems in place to deal with accidents and emergencies and manage risk.
9.	Holistic management	Look at the company as a fully integrated system and create a culture which stresses the importance of all aspects of company performance. Revise the internal organisation of the firm removing demarcations and commit the company to wider ethical considerations. Introduce participatory arrangements and be a leader for other firms to follow.

Figure 4.3 A hierarchy of organisational objectives and responses

costs. Indeed, in the early 1990s when we observed the introduction of so many new environmental initiatives and much heightened interest in environmental management, the recession was forcing firms to focus on simple cost management. But increasingly firms are recognising the benefits of moving away from short-term, narrow objectives towards a more strategic, integrated and holistic management approach.

Not only do firms need to plan for the long term, consider wider definitions of costs and integrate environmental impacts, they also need to explore the problems associated with uncertainty. Many firms who have experienced accidents and spillages have been subjected to very high clean-up costs and many have also faced very heavy fines and legal costs, and considerable loss of reputation through such disasters. Firms therefore need to have proper systems in place to deal with the unexpected and unforeseen events.

Firms need therefore to go through a process of widening their view of the company and its objectives and progressing towards a fully integrated system. We might envisage a nine-level hierarchical model where firms begin with short-term objectives such as cost minimisation (level 1) and progress towards longer-term objectives such as planning for uncertainty (level 8) or a holistic approach (level 9). This model is illustrated in Figure 4.3. Not all firms begin at level 1, although many continue to be at that level and not all firms will necessarily want to move all the way to level 9. However, the aim of the environmentally conscious company must be to reach at least level 8 without missing any of the intermediate stages. Companies with wider ethical commitments will want to aim for level 9.

ENVIRONMENTAL REVIEWS

The process of environmental improvement must start with a measure of current performance. The review itself provides a broad picture of the environmental impact of the company's activities and gives management the information by which it can finalise its environmental policy and begin planning for the future.

The environmental review is sometimes referred to as a baseline environmental audit and follows many of the procedures of an audit. However, strictly speaking an audit measures the attainment or non-attainment of some target objectives whereas the environmental review simply provides an initial assessment of the environmental performance of the company on which to plan for improvement. Before starting on the design and implementation of the environmental management system (see Chapter 5) and the subsequent cycle of environmental audits (discussed in Chapter 6) companies need to carry out baseline environmental reviews in order to assess the present environmental performance of the company and help to formulate the company's objectives and environmental policy (see Figure 4.4). A very preliminary environmental

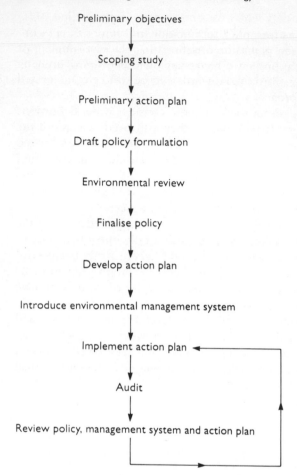

Preliminary objectives

Scoping study

Preliminary action plan

Draft policy formulation

Environmental review

Finalise policy

Develop action plan

Introduce environmental management system

Implement action plan

Audit

Review policy, management system and action plan

Figure 4.4 Pre-audit development stages

scoping study may also precede the review stage. Together these steps can be described as the pre-audit development stages.

Environmental reviews are also different to environmental audits because they are a one-off exercise whereas the audit cycle is periodic. An environmental review will present managers with a picture of the company from which it can plan its detailed environmental strategy. Standard terminology used to describe the environmental management process and its associated components is sometimes confused and the various terms used here such as scoping study, review and audit may be used slightly differently elsewhere.

Figure 4.4 shows the stages undertaken by many firms in preparing the company for the regular environmental audit. After making a commitment to environmental improvement and drafting general preliminary objectives the company undertakes a preliminary scoping study to assess the detailed needs of the organisation in relation to its environmental management programme. This will not only include plans for policy formulation and how this is to be facilitated but may also include plans for disseminating the environmental policy throughout the organisation and other issues such as training needs.

After the draft policy has been formulated an environmental review of the company is undertaken in order to provide a detailed snapshot of the company's present position. Given this information the company will need to revise and fine-tune its environmental policy to the particular needs and objectives identified in the review.

One of the major outcomes of the environmental review will be the development of an action plan on how to manage and ensure environmental improvement. This action plan must be implemented by the organisation through its environmental management system and the extent of environmental improvement will be measured and assessed regularly by means of an environmental audit. After each audit finding has been considered there will be a need to further consider the organisation's environmental policy, management system and action plan.

Environmental reviews are usually carried out by teams which include lawyers, management consultants, engineers, scientists and environmental generalists. Some larger firms often have the expertise to carry out reviews internally but others are likely to have to buy in at least some help. The environmental review has to be a systematic examination of a facility's processes and procedures and a measurement of the company's impact on the environment. It will therefore include analyses and testing in order to verify that legal requirements and internal policy and objectives are being met as well as an assessment of wider aspects of environmental performance. Ultimately the measurement and assessment of environmental performance must be a regular and ongoing task. A company's environmental audit programme, therefore, is a commitment to see the process as part of a continuous cycle of improvement and part of a company's wide range of assessment activities. Regular measurement of environmental performance will help the firm anticipate environmental damage and therefore prevent it from happening. However, before a company is in a position to conduct regular audits, it has to establish its baseline performance and this is achieved via the environmental review. A key element of this is the preparation of the assessment via the scoping study.

The scoping study

The scoping study is a pre-cursor to the full review programme and an important exercise in planning the review process. Once the company has decided to embark on a programme aimed at improving environmental performance and has considered its preliminary environmental objectives it will need to carefully consider the extent of the programme, to consider strategies available for the development of the programme and to establish a list of priorities. Although the formulation of an environmental policy has already been discussed it is likely that the scoping study will be an integral part of this process. The environmental policy will therefore only be formulated in an initial publishable form once the scoping study has been completed.

The first priority of the scoping study has to be to consider the preliminary environmental objectives set by the company or organisation. These specific objectives must be addressed, added to and where necessary modified. There is also a need to consider the exact scope of the environmental management programme. In most cases the whole organisation should be included but sometimes there may be advantages in dealing with different sectors at different times. In addition, reviews will normally be carried out on a site-specific basis and so multi-site organisations will have to consider logistics as part of the scoping study exercise.

As with the formulation of the environmental policy, there is a need to consider any particular priorities for action. These priorities may have been set out by management or arise as a result of the type of industry in which the company operates. For example, a key priority for a metal finishing firm might be the minimisation of hazardous wastes such as cyanide.

A major part of the scoping study will be to plan the baseline environmental review. A review team must be selected which has expert knowledge both of environmental issues and the industry in which the company operates. Key issues of selection are the same as those involved in selecting the audit team (indeed this team may be used to carry out subsequent audits) and this is dealt with below. Usually a team leader will also be selected and it will be his/her responsibility to communicate the results of the review to management. Where external consultants are to be used in the review process there is also a need to identify a key individual within the organisation (who may also be a member of the team itself) to help to resolve difficult issues and act as a mediator and 'door' into the organisation.

No plan of action will be possible without reviewing the performance of the organisation in terms of compliance with current and prospective legal standards at local, national, EC and international levels. Detailed consideration of these issues will be part of the review process but some consideration of them is necessary at an early stage as part of the scoping study. In particular, there may be specific regulations which apply to certain industries or processes and these need to be researched.

Eventually, the review process will have to draw heavily on information and data and the scoping study will need to consider what data might be required and the availability of that data and the ways in which it might be collected. Without such data, meaningful assessment is not possible. At this stage another important consideration is what aspects of environmental performance are to be measured and how they will be measured. These issues are discussed towards the end of this chapter.

One of the major elements of the scoping study will be to begin work on realistic plans, targets and performance indicators for environmental management. A final action plan will be developed when the findings of the environmental review have been studied. Nevertheless a project plan outline will be required which will clearly define the objectives, priorities, extent of the review and where the review fits into the broader environmental management programme.

In summary, the scoping study agenda is likely to be as follows:

1. The scope and coverage of the overall environmental programme
2. Particular priorities for action
3. The environmental review:
   - formulation of review team
   - selection of review team leader
   - selection of link person into the organisation
4. Consideration of current and prospective legal standards
5. Data requirements and measurement methodology
6. Environmental action plan:
   - specific project plan
   - environmental targets
   - performance indicators
7. Other issues.

The key aim of the scoping study will be to prepare the ground for the environmental review but it may go further and consider some of the following issues.

1. Training needs for management and the workforce

It may be the case that a key priority for the organisation may be raising the awareness of the environmental challenge among those working in the organisation. The dissemination of policy may also require training. In both cases the scope and nature of training programmes need to be identified. In particular, however, there may be a need to involve senior management via a training or briefing seminar at a very early stage. Commitment of management is vital for the successful implementation of the environmental management programme and it is therefore important to actively involve management sooner rather than later. Management may also have significant contributions to make to the process.

2. The methods used to formulate the final environmental policy

The formulation of the environmental policy is important and therefore the way in which it is done is a key issue. Management needs to be fully involved in the formulation of the policy so that its commitment towards it is strong. A tried and tested model of policy formulation is to get management to develop that policy in a seminar situation, facilitated by an individual or team who can work well with management and has knowledge concerning the important environmental issues to be addressed.

3. Dissemination of the environmental policy

Eventually the policy in its preliminary publishable form (which is likely to be after the environmental review has been carried out) has to be disseminated. One task of the scoping study may be to consider the general form in which the policy might be published and disseminated to all interested parties.

The review stage

The environmental review, sometimes called the baseline audit, is considered by some to be the first environmental audit and is the first major investment the firm will make in its environmental programme. However, this has led to some confusion. It should be stressed that the review is not really an audit in the sense of checking and verifying environmental performance, but rather defines the starting point and measures basic environmental performance upon which the environmental action plan must build. The audit measures performance against a basic standard established by the review. It is important therefore that the review is conducted properly, comprehensively and systematically. Like the scoping study the environmental review may be done internally but it is likely that some external expertise will have to be brought into the organisation.

If conducted properly, the benefits of the environmental review are wide ranging and include:

- the establishment of a basis upon which to build effective environmental management;
- the identification of current and forthcoming demands from environmental legislation;
- the identification of potential cost savings;
- the identification and development of market opportunities;
- the identification and prioritisation of areas of significant environmental damage;
- the provision of management information relating to significant strategic problems;
- the provision of information which will enable the company to fine-tune its environmental policy and focus its response;
- the provision of information needed to establish the basis for the constant appraisal of environmental performance via the environmental audit; and
- the provision of a basis of risk evaluation which is increasingly needed by insurers and investors.

The environmental review will also provide shareholders, workers, customers, suppliers, the media and the general public with a message that the organisation is serious about its commitment to environmental improvement. This, along with the publication of the company's environmental policy, will be the first stage in the important public relations exercise linked to the environmental initiatives.

The environmental review may be undertaken as an internal exercise or conducted by external consultants. This will necessarily impose a cost in terms of fees and management time. Increasingly however, this cost, along with the costs of the regular environmental audit, is becoming unavoidable and must be considered as a fixed cost of the company's activities. The benefits associated with the improved environmental performance of the firm are less quantifiable but significant. Even in the short term, however, they include a lower chance of litigation, lower waste disposal costs and cheaper insurance. The costs of not undertaking some sort of environmental review will certainly increase over time.

The environmental review is essentially an overview of the environmental situation facing the firm and is usually divided into profiling the firm from three standpoints:

1. **Scientific and technical**: The measurement of environmental impacts, an assessment of the appropriateness of technology and processes and an evaluation of products, their procurement, distribution and disposal.
2. **Legal**: An assessment as to the compliance of the company or site with national laws and EC Regulations and Directives, an identification of areas of potential litigation and a study of future legislative requirements.
3. **Managerial**: An evaluation of the effectiveness of present management systems in reducing the likelihood of environmental damage and accidents and recommendations for the design of an environmental management system.

In effect the environmental review is what the British Standard on Environmental Management Systems (BS7750) calls an Environmental Effects Inventory. The topics covered in the initial report will include the following.

- An historical review of the site.
- An outline of specific environmental issues relevant to the organisation in terms of the impact on air, water and land and an assessment of other nuisances including noise, odours and landscape.
- Waste management, recycling and disposal.
- Raw materials management and storage.
- Transportation.
- Product design, planning and management.
- Prevention and mitigation of accidents, gradual pollution, sudden, unexpected and unforeseen pollution.
- An assessment of legal liability exposure.
- A review of the practices of competitors.
- Staff information, training and involvement.
- Relationship with the local community, customers and the public in general.

- Suggestions for the development of an environmental policy.
- Recommendations for the implementation of an environmental management system.

Once the environmental profile of the firm has been established, the overall environmental policy of the firm can be finalised and subsequent audits take place as described in Chapter 6.

Increasingly environmental reviews are also being used in pre-acquisition situations. For example, where a potential purchaser has little knowledge or information about a particular plant which it may be interested in buying a review can provide valuable information, which in a climate of increasing environmental pressures, could alter a decision or at least the offer price considerably. Indeed, in most instances it would be foolish not to have some sort of environmental review in this situation.

This risk can be highlighted by the case of the Maryland Bank and Trust Company in the USA, who at the end of 1991 had a $335,000 loan go into default. At first they were not unduly worried. The loan was for $335,000 and they had the titles to a piece of land with a book value of $335,000 as collateral. The bank acquired the land in settlement of the debt. At that point, however, the land was visited by the US Environmental Protection Agency and as a result the Maryland Bank and Trust Company subsequently had to pay out $500,000 in clean-up costs before it could re-sell the land. No environmental assessment of the land had ever been carried out.

As more institutions and firms realise that many of their current assets could turn out to be major financial liabilities because of environmental damage, we will see much more care being taken over the purchase of new assets and the protection and care of existing ones. In the case of companies purchasing other companies or plants, a pre-acquisition review or audit is increasingly common.

Having outlined the organisation's priorities and objectives in the scoping study, there is a need to prepare for the process of gathering and evaluating the relevant information and data. Time spent on preparation will always make the later stages of the review easier and should not be rushed. It is important that each member of the selected review team understands the terms of reference of the process and their own role in achieving a useful outcome. The particular responsibilities of each person therefore need to be clearly defined and agreed before any on-site review begins. Team members may have particular aptitudes (e.g. for interviewing, data analysis, report writing, etc.) and these need to be identified.

Each team member will need copies of the report which followed the scoping study and be aware of the company's objectives and draft environmental policy if it exists. A workplan will need to be constructed and the methodology, quality assurance procedures and communication and reporting procedures carefully defined. Although the review team may only consist of a very small number of people, nevertheless key responsibilities need to be identified so that gaps in the process do not occur.

Conducting the environmental review

The outcome of the environmental review will depend on the cooperation of all staff in the organisation. They should therefore be informed that the review will take place and asked to cooperate where requested. It is important that staff realise that the review is being undertaken for positive reasons. The review itself will also have to be clearly timetabled, with projected target dates for the completion of each stage.

The key people with which the review team need to communicate need to be identified early on in the review process. That communication may be via interviews or via written questionnaires. In either case carefully structured questions need to be prepared which will ensure collection of the information required.

The central aim of the review will be the collection of information and data and the subsequent analysis of that information and data. There are two key areas to address:

● information about the organisation's environmental performance; and
● information about external environmental pressures and opportunities.

The key areas which will have to be examined at the review stage (and subsequently re-examined by the environmental audit) include:

1. **Sites and buildings management.** Offices, plants and other company sites should be safe and energy efficient. Where a company is using hazardous materials or processes, efficient and effective site management should be assessed. The land on which a plant is built should also be considered in terms of potential contamination.
2. **Raw materials.** Some raw materials may make lower overall demands on the environment than those currently in use in the company. Wastage of materials should be examined along with recycling opportunities. The use of non-renewable resources should, if possible, be replaced by using sustainable resources.
3. **Energy:** There should be a policy on energy efficiency and on the reduction of energy use. A manager with responsibility for energy efficiency needs to be appointed with a remit which includes internal energy use and energy use in distribution systems. Energy sources should also be examined and consideration should be given to the option of producing energy on-site, for example, with waste to energy incineration.
4. **Products and services.** The products and services offered by the company should incorporate the most effective design and technologies to achieve the minimum impact on the environment. Their procurement, use, reuse and disposal needs to be considered in relation to their performance, measured in terms of fitness for the task for which they are intended.
5. **Processes.** Efficient technologies should be used, properly maintained and carefully controlled to optimise production and minimise waste.

6. **Wastes and discharges.** All wastes and discharges resulting from the operations of the organisation need to be properly evaluated, their sources identified and their disposal costs highlighted. Air emissions, water discharges, solid wastes, noise and odours should all be included in the assessment to see what reductions are possible.

7. **Transport and distribution systems.** Distribution of goods, inwards and outwards, should be as efficient as possible, avoiding one-way loads where possible and paying particular attention to routing and timing. Special precautions have to be taken for the transportation of dangerous goods, toxic substances and waste. Reducing vehicle usage and vehicle emissions should be examined.

8. **Paper and packaging.** Opportunities for improving environmental performance through the use of recycled paper and packaging materials should be examined. Unnecessary packaging should be eliminated and polyvinylchloride (PVC) should be avoided.

9. **Accidents and emergencies.** There should be well-designed and tested systems in place for dealing with accidents and emergencies, including having effective communication links with the local community and with the press and media.

10. **Health and safety.** Health and safety is intrinsically linked to environmental improvement and the performance of health and safety procedures should also be assessed.

11. **Recycling.** Recycling systems should be tested and potential recycling schemes investigated. This should focus on both in-company recycling and the recycling of products, components and packaging after use.

Having collected the relevant information there is a need to evaluate it and prepare a report which will outline the findings of the review. The degree of analysis required will depend on the type and format of the information collected. An important consideration, however, is to think about how the information will ultimately be used and by whom. There is a need to produce accurate information in a way that is readily understood and easily accessible.

The key findings of the review must be summarised along with recommended actions and targets. It is usually useful to present the available data and findings for each part or division of the organisation. These findings can then be compared with defined company policies. They will also help in the preparation of an action plan which may define priority areas by division or process in the organisation. It is also important to quantify the costs and the benefits to the business of each area of improvement. For that reason it is important to highlight both the strengths and the weaknesses in the review findings.

After the information has been fully considered there is a need to determine recommended actions. Recommendations will need to be related to the company's original objectives and appropriate targets with timescales need to be set. Recommendations may be prioritised in terms of actions requiring short-term, medium-term and long-term implementation. Targets need to be ambitious but achievable and should be measurable in absolute terms and subject to periodic review.

MEASURING ENVIRONMENTAL PERFORMANCE

Early on in the process of environmental management the company or organisation needs to think carefully about how it is going to measure environmental performance. This needs to be integrated into the environmental policy since it is useless having meaningless objectives which cannot be quantified in some way and the measurement of baseline performance is, of course, central to the environmental review. In order to report to the stakeholders of any organisation (both internally and externally), performance measurement and reporting systems will be required. The measurement of environmental performance is also important in further developing and extending environmental performance and objectives.

Environmental policies and objectives will have to cover a range of performance areas and not just those prescribed by legislation and regulations. In addition to measuring waste discharges, emissions and energy usage, performance areas such as product and process design, raw materials usage and linkage along the supply chain might also be identified for action. However, environmental performance needs to be measured alongside other aspects of business performance. Shareholders, for example, may not be impressed with environmental improvements which reduce their dividends significantly.

There are no absolute rules concerning what to measure. Each company needs to decide on measurement areas, levels and priorities based on the formal environmental review or simply good judgement. However, setting priorities and targets is important in order that objectives can be translated into workable programmes and those programmes become manageable. Furthermore, there are few absolute standards for what constitutes good performance. However, in addition to legislatory requirements there may be current norms established within industries and the aim of the environmentally aware organisation must be to do better than these norms. A general principle to bear in mind when setting performance targets is that they should be realistic and attainable and at the same time challenging, but they should not be so ambitious as to make them unattainable since then they will be discouraging and may have a negative rather than a positive impact.

Deciding on performance measures

The crucial first step in the measurement of environmental performance must be to identify the areas in which to measure the environmental performance of your organisation. Preliminary consideration should take place at the time of drawing up the environmental policy and undertaking the scoping study and the initial environmental review. However, it is not until after the review has been done that there will be sufficient information to make a real choice. The areas of environmental performance chosen should match the environmental policy of the organisation and in some circumstances, following the environmental review and the choice of performance measures, the policy will require some amendment.

We can identify four key performance areas and organisations need to think about the appropriateness of measures of environmental performance within the following broad categories.

1. The company and its product:
   ● processes, procedures and operations;
   ● the involvement and integration of the supply chain;
   ● the appropriate use of materials; and
   ● product use and disposal.

2. Direct environmental impacts:
   ● the treatment and disposal of waste;
   ● emissions to air and effluent to water;
   ● energy usage;
   ● noise;
   ● the use of and impact on natural resource depletion; and
   ● impacts on nature and ecosystems.

3. Infrastructure:
   ● the use of equipment and technology;
   ● transportation;
   ● storage;
   ● buildings;
   ● communications; and
   ● management systems.

4. External relations:
   ● local community involvement and public relations;
   ● education;
   ● customer relations; and
   ● wider support for environmental initiatives.

Deciding on priorities for action is always important. It is simply the case that no organisation can do everything it wants tomorrow and therefore a hierarchy of priorities will help companies decide on an action plan and where best to allocate resources. Priorities clearly need to reflect the main sources of environmental impact. There is also the important issue of environmental information to consider. In the early stages of developing environmental management strategies there is likely to be very little information about environmental impacts. The environmental review will begin the process of developing and understanding this area but it may take a long time to fully develop useful environmental information systems.

Some areas, such as supplier performance, are inevitably more difficult to measure than more quantifiable areas such as waste generation. There may be a need to look at more qualitative information in some areas, but the general principle of setting appropriate targets still remains. Areas where the organisation does not have direct control pose additional problems. Once again, supplier performance initiatives may be difficult to control in the short run but over time reasonable objectives should be achieved.

Having identified areas for action the next step must be to select appropriate measures of environmental performance. There are a few basic principles for choosing appropriate measures which are worth considering before embarking on this activity.

- The areas identified must be capable of being measured.
- Measures need to be consistent with environmental policy objectives.
- Too many measures might confuse issues and be costly to implement.
- The measures need to be appropriate and understandable to those who have to act upon them.
- Measures must be transparent and not reflect a hidden agenda; they should be clear to all involved and encourage participation and commitment.
- Measures must be appropriate over time so that significant improvements or deteriorations can be mapped out and results can be communicated to stakeholders.

Measurement

There are many different measures which may be adopted by the firm. The choice will depend in part on measurability but consideration of how the measures are to be used and communicated will also be fundamental. In many cases the measurement of environmental performance is not an easy task, especially when issues are not directly quantifiable, and it is not only the negative aspects of environmental performance (e.g. discharges) which need to be examined but successes and positive attributes also need to be considered. Measures should also always relate to some base so that comparisons can be made over time, between sites and between activities.

Quantitative measures are obviously the easiest to deal with. They will relate to physical things where objective measures are possible. However, subjective judgements will also often need to be made and here some sort of qualitative measure will have to be undertaken. Nevertheless, qualitative judgements can be translated into useful information by the use of rankings or some sort of scoring methodology. Although financial measures alone provide limited information relating to environmental performance, measures of expenditure on environmental protection can provide a useful indicator in conjunction with other measures.

As well as assessing environmental impacts at the company level through the measurement of waste, effluent, discharge and energy usage, it is also important to design contributor measures. Contributor measures examine measures of performance which include the appropriate use of technology and materials, product and supplier performance and the effectiveness of environmental management systems. Such measures are outlined in Table 4.1. External relations measures also need to be adopted and these will include the assessment of risk (see Table 4.2).

Developing performance measures

The development of environmental performance measures is an iterative procedure. Over time the measures will be easier to collect and to analyse and the most useful measures will be determined. Some measures may prove to be less effective and so it is useful not to lay too much stress on any one measure of environmental performance.

Much information needed in the analysis of performance may already be available. The main task is then to analyse and present this information in a format useful for monitoring and control. Additional information is also likely to be needed however, and this may require the installation of monitoring equipment. For supplier measures, information will be required from the suppliers themselves, often collected through questionnaires. However, a

Table 4.1 Contributor measures

Performance area	Examples of measure
Technology	Level of investment in new technology
	Substitution of clean technology
	Effectiveness of new systems
Materials	Utilisation of process materials
	Use of renewable resources
Products	Implementation of design changes
	Level of investment to meet higher environmental standards
	Level of rejects and direct waste
Suppliers	Achievement of supplier survey
	Implementation of supplier awareness initiatives
	New procurement procedures
Management systems	Level of implementation of system
	Effectiveness of new procedures
	Performance against audit
	Level of organisational commitment and participation
	Existence of training programmes

Table 4.2 External relations measures

Area	Examples of measures
Impact measures	Numbers of prosecutions Levels of complaints Positive and negative exposure resulting from pressure groups Number of complimentary or adverse media reports Falls or increases in sales related to environmental impact
Positive measures	Level of public disclosure Availability of environmental impact information Level of consultation with outside agencies Public awareness programmes Level of support for external environmental programmes
Risk measures	Measures of the probability of accidents Existence and understanding of emergency plan Speed and effectiveness of emergency plan Communication with emergency services Public disclosure of likely impact of accidents

means of verifying this information will be needed and in part this can be provided by adherence to written environmental standards. The ultimate test of any performance measure clearly lies in whether it is effective in informing the appropriate target groups and providing information of such a quality as to aid the achievement of set targets.

Performance measures need to be developed in line with the development of an organisation's own environmental management system and it is important therefore to see measures of environmental performance as consistent with overall business policy and objectives. The information systems must be able to support management and staff and must be seen as an aid to the development of the business rather than a tool primarily aimed at pin-pointing deficiencies. The integration of environmental performance measures will introduce change in the organisation and therefore careful management is required to overcome barriers to change. In this respect good communications, participation and rewards for good performance need to be developed which should aim to generate enthusiasm and commitment.

CONCLUSION

The three issues of policy development, environmental reviews and the measurement of environmental performance have been put together in this chapter because it is so hard to separate them. We need an environmental policy in order to decide what to measure, but we also need to think about that measurement so that meaningless things are not put into the policy statement. We clearly need to be able to measure environmental performance within the review, but the review itself will suggest the most appropriate areas for future measurement. The environmental policy of the firm is the starting point, but at the same time managers are likely to want to re-examine the policy after the environmental review has been done. The three issues cannot really be separated and it must therefore be recognised that the three issues must be developed simultaneously. Finally, we must recognise that environmental management is a relatively new area of development and the learning curve for most firms will be steep. We should expect changes in the environmental initiatives and approaches within firms. Like the environment itself, firms will need to respond to change in a dynamic and progressive way.

A key theme which has run through this chapter is a need to establish and set priorities for action. We cannot expect firms to do everything tomorrow or in most cases ever reach the ultimate goal of zero negative impact on the environment. However, we can expect them to introduce systems which will improve environmental performance over time. It is to this issue which we turn in the next chapter.

CHAPTER 5

Linking quality and the environment: creating environmental management systems

MANAGEMENT SYSTEMS

The investigations into many accidents and disasters have concluded that the event could have been avoided had there been an effective system in place which could adequately deal with the event or alternatively, that although there was a system in place, there were gaps in it which allowed the event to happen. Moreover, it is often the lack of a comprehensive and effective management system which has caused accidental damage and has cost firms and organisations heavily in terms of clean-up costs and damaged reputations. When we think of key disasters such as the Exxon Valdez oil spill, the Three Mile Island explosion and the Chemical Spills in Tours, France, it was the environment which became irreparably damaged due, at least in part, to inadequacies in systems which were supposed to prevent such disasters.

Management systems aim to pull a potentially disparate system into an integrated and organised one. To that end the system covers not only management's responsibilities but the responsibility and tasks of every individual in an organisation. An integrated system which covers the totality of operations helps management and workers to clearly see their place in the organisation and recognise the interdependence of all aspects of an organisation. Through establishing clear communications and reporting channels it should pull a potentially tangled web of structures and tasks into a clearly defined matrix of relationships with clear horizontal and vertical links. This means that functions are less likely to be lost in a maze of mini organisations and that a key aspect of an organisation's tasks are not forever lost in a black box labelled 'nobody's responsibility' until it is revealed by a mistake, accident or disaster.

Building an effective management system

An effective management system is therefore central to the avoidance of disasters and accidents in so much as it pulls together all the other tools and strategies for the avoidance of risks. Quite simply, a management system should be developed and implemented for the purpose of accomplishing the objectives set out in a company's or organisation's policies. Each element of the system will vary in importance from one type of activity to another and from one product or service to another. However, there are some general characteristics which every management system needs to embody. In short, the system needs to be:

- comprehensive
- understandable
- open.

Without these attributes gaps may occur in the system which will allow mistakes to happen and the system will not be flexible enough to develop and improve over time. Let us deal with each of these issues in turn:

1. The system needs to be comprehensive, covering all the activities of the organisation. Gaps must not occur in the coverage of the system since this is where errors and mistakes will occur and where accidents and disasters may happen. Every part of an organisation must be involved in the implementation of the system and every person must recognise his or her responsibility for putting the system into practice.
2. The system and procedures within that system therefore need to be understandable to everybody involved. If roles and duties are not specified in an understandable way they may not be carried out. This will usually involve documenting the system, training people fully in their tasks and responsibilities and reviewing or auditing what is actually happening periodically. It requires that the system and all its elements are monitored and if the system breaks down it must be rectified quickly.
3. The system must be open to review and there must be a commitment to a continuous cycle of improvement in the operations of the firm and in the quality of products or services it will produce. This continuous cycle of improvement can also be applied to the environment where firms should aim for an ultimate goal of zero negative impact on the environment. Everybody has a role in the system and therefore participatory styles of management are usually superior to hierarchical ones. Management pyramids often need to be flattened to allow for a freer flow of information from both top to bottom and bottom to top.

An effective organisational structure of any management system is vital and should be clearly established within the organisation. Clear lines of authority and communication channels need to be defined. The following are typical organisational aspects which need to be considered.

- All activities of an organisation should be identified and defined and appropriately documented.
- General and specific responsibilities and authorities should be defined to particular groups and individuals and where these are assigned to individuals somebody else should be made responsible in their absence.

- A management representative, preferably independent of other functions, should be appointed to resolve disputes and problems.
- The interface and coordination between different activities needs to be clearly defined.
- Emphasis should be placed on the identification of actual or potential problems and risks along with the initiation of remedial or preventive measures.

The importance of various aspects of organisational structure to the effectiveness of a process or organisation and the minimisation of risks associated with those have been highlighted by the numerous documents, essays and books on the subject. The conclusion can be put quite simply as 'everything matters'. Although case studies of organisations and disasters can provide useful information, it is dangerous to imagine that success stories or accounts of disasters are universally applicable, as organisational culture, operating conditions, people, history, processes, products and services are rarely exactly comparable. In making these types of comparison, management needs to fully appreciate the critical nature of some of the differing factors involved and decide what reliance can be placed upon assumptions made. There is no real alternative to taking a good hard look at every aspect of ones own organisation and systems. Moreover, this is not a once and for all process but an ongoing requirement if risks of failure are to be minimised.

A central aspect of any management system will revolve around decision-making. Senior management is ultimately responsible for making balanced judgements. But modern management methods highlight the need for flexibility and participation and this usually involves decisions being taken further down the hierarchy. In arriving at decisions the calibre and personal integrity of staff are of fundamental importance and management needs to ensure that each person in the organisation understands his or her role in decision-making and the consequences of his or her actions. Decisions are often of a higher quality when they are participative and systems need to avoid giving single individuals too much power. The quality of decisions is also closely linked to the availability of adequate education and training programmes for all employees and such programmes need to be built into organisation-wide systems.

Documenting the system

There is no substitute to the documentation of management systems. This provides a means of clarification for staff, an introduction to the system for new staff and the process of being forced to write the system down makes it more systematic and less susceptible to something being missed. All the elements, requirements and provisions adopted by an organisation for the management of operations should be documented in an orderly manner in the form of written policies and procedures. It is management's responsibility to establish and maintain control over all the documentation including control procedures, checklists, drawings, specifications, procedures, process control methods and deviation and accident procedures. These documents should not only be created and brought up to a satisfactory and useful standard, but should also be implemented as written and subject to continuous evaluation for effectiveness and adjusted where necessary. They provide a basis for control evaluation and review and without them, differences in policy and procedures can arise and variations may occur leading to confusion, uncertainty and the ubiquitous gaps in the system which can be so dangerous.

In addition, adequate records also need to be kept and retained in order to demonstrate the effective operation of the management system. All changes to the system need to be in writing and processed in a manner which would ensure prompt action at the specified point, indicating whether the changes are retrospective, immediate or to be carried out at some future specified date. Provision should be made for the prompt removal of all documents from points of issue as they become obsolete.

Documents are best collected into a system manual which is the rule book by which the organisation works. Its primary purpose is to provide an adequate description of the system while serving as a permanent reference in the implementation and maintenance of that system. Such a manual is useful for a number of reasons.

- It will provide an aid for training and will help complement work instructions and designated tasks and assignments.
- It will give an indication of the responsibilities and interrelated activities of personnel and functional groups.
- It will provide a basis for auditing, reviewing and evaluating the system.
- It provides information from which customers may derive confidence in the supplier's organisation.

The manual should contain checklists and clear procedural guidelines so that in the event of an accident a systematic approach can be taken.

ENVIRONMENTAL MANAGEMENT SYSTEMS AND TOTAL QUALITY MANAGEMENT SYSTEMS

The areas which are most highly developed in the context of management systems are in the area of quality. It is therefore worth examining these in detail since they do provide a powerful model for the implementation of comprehensive, understandable and open environmental management systems. Environmental management systems have drawn heavily on the lessons to be learned from quality and are important in their own right because so many disasters have emanated from or resulted in accidental pollution.

Companies and managers who take the environment seriously change not only their processes and products but also their organisation. The ability to do this effectively, profitably and in an environmentally friendly way depends on the qualities of management itself and the effectiveness of systems in place. For many organisations, the 1980s were a time when the benefits of quality management were recognised and where for many, new work practices, flexible arrangements and even the abandonment of production line technology were introduced. At the forefront of such innovations was the development of total quality management (TQM), which ultimately aims for zero defects, that is, preventing defects occurring in the first place. For many forward-looking organisations environmental responsibility has become an aspect of the search for total quality and as such zero defects also mean zero negative impact on the environment.

Competitiveness is often measured by three things: quality, price and delivery. It is often a misconception that quality costs extra money in terms of inputs. The theory behind a TQM system is that as quality improves costs actually fall through lower failure and appraisal costs and less waste. The concept that defects in the production process cost most to remedy if a product has left the factory gates seems obvious. But TQM is much more than assuring product or service quality; it is a system of dealing with quality at every stage of the production process, both internally and externally. Total quality management is a system requiring the commitment of senior managers, effective leadership and teamwork and this is also true of any system which aims for environmental improvements.

While the force behind a TQM system has to come from senior management, the responsibility for quality itself belongs to everybody in the organisation. The TQM system requires that every single part of the organisation is integrated and must be able to work together. This is exactly the ethos which is needed for an environmental management system to be successful; the push must come from the top but everyone has a role. For firms with a TQM system in place or considering one, the next steps towards an integrated and effective environmental management system are not hard to make.

The elements of the TQM system

The main elements of the TQM system therefore need to be reflected in any environmental management system and these are:

- **Teamwork**: This is central to many parts of the system where workers have to feel they are part of an organisation. In addition, teams of workers will often be brought together into problem-solving groups, quality circles and process improvement teams.
- **Commitment**: To be successful, systems need to be truly company-wide and therefore commitment is required from the Chief Executive as well as from the whole workforce. Middle management has an important role to play in not only grasping the concepts themselves but also in explaining them to the people for whom they are responsible.

- **Communications**: Poor communications can result in organisational problems, information being lost and gaps occurring in the system. Gaps lead to failure of processes and therefore lead to quality and environmental defects. A good flow of accurate information, instructions and feedback is vital in maintaining the cohesion needed by the system.
- **Organisation**: A cohesive system needs to be an organised one with clear channels of responsibility and clearly defined reporting procedures. Quality and environment-related errors can be quickly rectified if an efficient organisational structure is in place.
- **Control and monitoring**: Systems will not remove the need to monitor processes and sample outputs and waste. Monitoring is vital as a check on the performance of the system. But many organisations only use after-the-fact controls causing managers to take a reactive rather than a proactive position. Systems need a more anticipative style of control.
- **Planning**: Processes need to be planned carefully if they are to be efficient. This usually requires recording activities, stages and decisions in a form which is communicable to all. A clearly defined process reduces the scope for error and provides the basis of an analysis into possible improvements that might be made.
- **Inventory control system**: It is in the storage of raw materials, components or the finished product that quality can diminish and energy usage is high. The keeping of stocks is also physically expensive and can lead to cash flow problems. An inventory control system is therefore required to keep stocks to a minimum while ensuring that supplies never dry up. One such system is the just-in-time system (see below).

A breakdown in any part of the TQM or environmental management system can lead to organisational gaps where wastage may occur or quality be over-looked. Errors have a habit of becoming multiplied and failure to meet the requirements of one part of the organisation creates problems elsewhere. The correction of errors is time consuming and costly. Total quality management can provide a company with a competitive edge which will be important given the increases in competition which the Single European Market implies. This means that managers must plan strategically both externally and internally and that internal strategic planning has to involve everyone in the workplace. Total quality management is an approach aimed at improving the effectiveness and flexibility of business as a whole and is aimed at eliminating wasted effort as well as physical waste by involving everyone in the process of improvement; improving the effectiveness of work so that results are achieved in less time and at less cost.

Close parallels may be drawn between aiming for total quality and the concept of 'cradle to grave' environmental management. For example, just as remedying errors and defects is more expensive once a product has left the factory, so cleaning up after an environmental accident is much more expensive in terms of physical costs and reputation, than preventing the damage in the first place. Cheapest in the long run is total pollution prevention (TPP) which means removing toxins used in production processes and substituting environmentally damaging materials and processes with environmentally neutral ones.

An important aspect of quality of a manufactured product is the total loss caused by that product to society as a whole. One key strategy is therefore to aim to minimise loss to society. Losses include the consumption of any non-renewable resources in the production process as well as the costs of any environmental damage subsequently created. These have to be weighed against the satisfaction of the consumer. When one considers time though, given that the effects of environmental damage and the impact of the depletion of a non-renewable resource are unknown into the future and given that consumption satisfaction is likely to be bounded by time, then the former is likely always to be greater than the latter. In other words, the true cost of environmentally damaging consumption is always greater than the benefits it brings. The traditional price mechanism, however, cannot achieve such sophistication or reckoning and therefore the commitment and responsibility of companies is paramount.

The achievement of environmental improvement and ultimately of TPP requires many of the characteristics needed in the TQM system including, teamwork, commitment, communication, organisation, monitoring and a proper stock control system. If the system breaks down then, like the TQM system, gaps emerge and deterioration may occur. When dealing with the environment though, it might be something rather more harmful than lost quality which escapes from the production process. Total quality management systems aim for the achievement of zero defects and ultimately the pursuit of environmental quality means a search for products and processes which result in zero harmful emissions (the green equivalent of zero defects). It may be that zero defects are never achievable and equally zero harmful emissions may be unachievable even in a sustainable society. But at issue here is the so-called 'threshold effect', in other words the acceptance that limited pollution can be dealt with up to a certain threshold (which we far exceed at the moment). The important point is, however, that aiming for zero defects or zero harmful emissions creates a corporate culture and a clear target which will guarantee environmental improvement.

Planning an environmental management system

Using some general principles from the practice of total quality management, it is possible to build up a picture of what the environmental management system (EMS) may look like. There has to be commitment at all levels of the organisation but particularly from senior management and this means that the system is top-down. However, information and communication must also be able to flow up the organisation and participatory arrangements needs to be encouraged. Figure 5.1 represents a typical environmental management

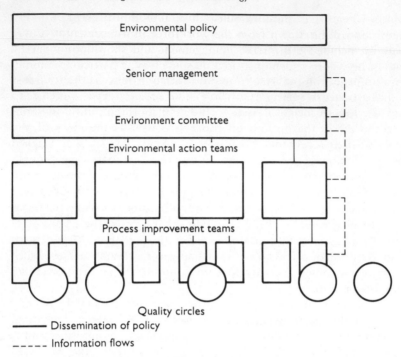

Quality circles
——— Dissemination of policy
– – – – Information flows

Figure 5.1 The structure of a typical environmental management system

system. This shows that the environmental policy is disseminated throughout the organisation from senior management via the environment committee. It also demonstrates the need for bottom-up information flows. Let us deal with each stage in turn.

Commitment of senior management

Commitment towards environmental improvement needs to come from the top of the organisation and the Chief Executive has to be seen to be fully supportive of plans for environmental improvement. Upon the design and implementation of a company's environmental policy there needs to be appointed a board director either solely or, depending on the size of the organisation, partly responsible for the implementation of that policy and the improvement of processes which will improve environmental performance.

The environment committee

The environment committee will be made up of a small number of people (around eight) and chaired by either the Chief Executive or the Environment Director. Key individuals also on the team will include the health and safety officer and the director with responsibility for quality improvement. The rest of the committee will be drawn from the workforce in a representative way and is likely to include both middle management and shop-floor workers. Those people who will have demonstrated, in some way, a particular commitment to environmental improvement are vital for two reasons. Firstly, they demonstrate to the workforce at large that environmental improvement is a firm-wide approach requiring a participative, collaborative and committed approach at all levels of the organisation. Secondly, it provides senior management with a quick source of information about what is actually happening in the depths of the organisation. Those chosen to be on the environment committee therefore need to be effective communicators.

The environment committee will not be there to solve problems. That must be done where the problems occur. It is there to organise the implementation of the environmental management system, monitor progress towards environmental improvement and ensure proper lines of communication. The detailed work involved in achieving environmental improvement will be done by environmental action teams.

Environmental action teams

An environmental action team will be led by one or more members of the environment committee. Its task will be to examine, in depth, a particular part of an organisation's activities. This might include, for example, transportation, office procedures and paper usage, packaging, storage, production, waste management, marketing systems or any other part of the internal functions of the organisation.

Process improvement teams

There are potential environmental improvements to be made in every activity and every process of the organisation. Everybody working on a particular process has a responsibility to try to improve that activity in environmental terms and to ensure that waste and energy usage are minimised. A process improvement team might be made up of all the workers associated with a process, where this is small, or alternatively, a small group of those workers. Their aim is to critically examine the particular process and suggest ways in which it can be improved. At an administrative level this may manifest itself in the reduction of paper usage, in a warehouse it might mean energy usage reduction and elsewhere, other environmental improvements.

Process improvement teams will be closely linked with quality circles and in some cases the two may be the same. As shown in Figure 5.1, in many cases these teams are likely to overlap considerably. Within the depths of the organisation therefore, environmental improvement and quality once again become closely related.

ty circles and environment circles

lity circle, which might be extended to include an environmental brief, is usually defined as a group of workers doing similar work who meet together regularly under the leadership of their supervisor in order to identify and solve work-related problems and recommend solutions to management and implement those solutions once they are agreed. An important feature of quality circles is that people must be invited to join them and not forced to do so. In general, there are no formal rules governing the size of quality circles but very large groups are difficult to manage and become unproductive. Groups usually range from three to fifteen people but an optimum number is probably eight to ten. Commonly, such circles could meet typically for one hour per week. The impact of the circles is to make workers feel needed as well as acting as a monitor on quality and a forum in which new working arrangements can be discussed. Many firms offer bonuses to individuals or groups who can come up with new systems or new practices in their work area which will ultimately save the company money.

It is within a tight and cooperative quality circle that advances on the environmental front can also be achieved. Not only can innovation based on environmental improvement be encouraged and achieved at this level, but recycling, care with respect to waste and better monitoring of processes can also be achieved. Indeed, there may be considerable overlap between suggestions made by quality circles and the work of process improvement teams. This overlap can be encouraged.

Employees themselves can make a major contribution to environmental improvement simply by taking care and being committed to the idea. Quality circles can also provide the means to disseminate environmental information and policy to the whole workforce and many firms in the USA ask a representative of each quality circle to join an environmental committee convened by the member of senior management responsible for environmental issues.

Although quality circles can be linked with particular jobs and with production-line technology, often their use has been associated with a move away from the production line towards team-based production where several tasks in the production of a good, rather than one task, is done by a group of people. The best example of this is the movement away from producing a car on a production line to a system where a group of people receive the shell of a car and assemble the whole product to an exact specification to meet the needs of the customer. Such a system was implemented by Volvo in Sweden and is being increasingly adopted by other manufacturers in Europe in the 1990s. In this way large-scale production has been disaggregated.

It is precisely the production processes based on large-scale technology which are the most difficult to control and where gaps can be found in the system. For a long time, large-scale production had been justified by reference to economies of scale. That is, the idea that as output capacity expands, so per unit costs are reduced. But typically that notion measures only private costs and not the costs of environmental degradation so commonly caused by large-scale production. Advocates of total quality have often argued for the disaggregation of production processes and if one considers the huge environmental costs of large-scale production, the whole notion of economies of scale becomes flawed.

Inventory control systems

Inventory control is a very important aspect of environmental improvement. Storage of finished or unfinished goods take up land space and consume energy involved in that storage. In an attempt to avoid a loss of quality, inventory control systems are also central to total quality management systems. One such system is just-in-time.

Just-in-time (JIT) management systems are credited to the Japanese who developed and began to use them in the 1950s. Such management techniques have been adopted but many European firms have been relatively slow to recognise the benefits of such systems. Just-in-time is a programme directed towards ensuring that the correct quantities of materials are purchased or produced at the right time and that there is no waste. Just-in-time fits well under a TQM umbrella and is essentially one type of inventory control system. But even more importantly, JIT systems cut down the need for storage. They also cut down the need for as much protective packaging around items that may be stored and it reduces the potential for hazards with respect to warehouse accidents. Therefore, JIT has a role to play in improving environmental performance.

Within the JIT system, materials and/or services are purchased or generated in exact quantities and just at the time they are needed. The primary objective is therefore to improve quality through the elimination of waste and, in turn, the system demands that stocks or inventories of raw materials, semi-finished and finished products are kept to a minimum. This results in cost savings for the following reasons:

- less capital has to be invested in inventories;
- inventory items do not become obsolescent or deteriorate;
- less space is required to keep inventories;
- the risks associated with the storage of hazardous substances is reduced;
- stock control costs are minimised.

The JIT system is not purely about inventory reduction though. It is essentially good management with problem-solving, planning and decision-making taken further down the ladder of authority. The whole system is often linked with worker incentives, staged promotion systems, performance-related payments, regular retraining and often, in Japan, guaranteed lifetime employment.

The benefits of JIT management systems and techniques are evident in many Japanese firms and increasingly in American and European ones as well. For example, Nissan's automobile assembly plant in Murayama, Japan schedules its supplies by computer link and updates the schedule every 15–20 minutes. Suppliers deliver between 4 and 16 times a day with an on-time delivery performance of 99.9 per cent. This allows Nissan to keep only one day's stock throughout its whole system.

An important outcome of the JIT technique is a programme for improving overall productivity and reducing waste. This leads to cost effective production or operation and delivery of goods or services, in the correct quantity, at the right time and which exactly meet the requirements of the customer. This is achieved with a minimum amount of equipment, materials, people and warehousing. Once again a key operational concept is that of flexibility. But the reduction of waste and the lower levels of equipment, materials and warehousing required also represent an environmental improvement.

In Europe JIT systems are becoming more popular. Companies like Massey-Ferguson, GKN, IBM, 3M and Lucas have introduced JIT management. In addition there are many Japanese firms operating JIT systems in their plants in Europe. Just-in-time is therefore becoming recognised as being able to provide another competitive edge and for this reason we are likely to see its implementation even more widespread in Europe over time. Linked to environmental concerns it provides a workable strategy not only to reduce costs and to ensure quality but also to improve environmental performance.

ENVIRONMENTAL MANAGEMENT SYSTEMS AND STANDARDS

Once they are in place, management systems should satisfy the objectives for which they were introduced. Increasingly, firms will wish to tell their customers and suppliers about their management system and achieve recognised levels of management practice. For this reason and others, as outlined below, firms are often building their own management system to conform with some pre-determined standards laid down by outside agencies. Responsible Care, BS5750 and BS7750 are three such standards.

The Responsible Care programme

The Responsible Care programme can be seen as one of the earliest environmental management systems used across companies. It is a voluntary programme where performance is measured in terms of continuous improvement. Responsible Care is unique to the chemical industry and originated in Canada in 1984. Launched in 1989 in the UK by the Chemical Industries Association, the cornerstone of the system is commitment. Chief Executives of member companies are invited to sign a set of guiding principles pledging their company to make health, safety and environmental performance an integral part of overall business policy. Adherence to the principles and objectives of

Responsible Care is a condition of membership of the Chemical Indu
Association. All employees and company contractors have to be made ;
of these principles. The guiding principles also require companies to:

- conform to statutory regulations;
- operate to the best practices of the industry;
- assess the actual and potential health, safety and environmental impacts of their activities and products;
- work closely with the authorities and the community in achieving the required levels of performance;
- ·be open about activities and give relevant information to interested parties.

The Responsible Care programme's approach is firmly based on the principles of total quality management and many companies operating the Responsible Care programme have been able to design their systems so as to be compatible with ISO 9000 requirements. Responsible Care is designed to cover all operational functions and the Chemical Industries Authority (CIA) provides codes of practice and guidance notes for firms implementing the system. The system requires ongoing assessment to ensure ongoing improvements are achieved.

A company operating the Responsible Care programme is required to have a clear company policy and the communication of this is seen as vital. The CIA provides questionnaires which help to identify inconsistencies between policy and practice and enables companies to develop action plans to bring about improvements. Such questionnaires are also used to monitor progress. The key principle being used in the Responsible Care programme is therefore self-assessment and this has led to some criticism of the approach of some chemical firms.

However, the CIA does assess the effectiveness of the programme across all firms by collecting indicators of performance from the firms. Companies are encouraged to submit six classes of data to the Association. Individual company data are not published but a national aggregate figure is published annually. This shows industrial trends and enables individual companies to assess their own placing accordingly. The six indicators of performance are:

1. Environmental protection spending.
2. Safety and Health (lost time accidents for employees and contractors).
3. Waste and emissions:
   - discharges of 'red list' substances;
   - waste disposal;
   - an environmental index of five key discharges by site.
4. Distribution (all incidents).
5. Energy consumption (total on-site).
6. All complaints.

A key element of the Responsible Care programme is the sharing of infor-mation and participation of employees and the local community. Local

Responsible Care 'cells' operate for the exchange of information and experience between firms. Employee involvement is also encouraged and the CIA has established training programmes which set targets for appraisal. Firms are encouraged also to have community liaison groups and initiatives, recognising the continuing need to forge improved relationships with the public.

Responsible Care goes some way to meeting the needs of an integrated environmental management system. The CIA suggest that the system is compatible with BS7750 and in some cases this may be the case. However, for many chemical firms operating Responsible Care, BS7750 would provide a much more stringent standard to adhere to.

Improvement through standards

Like the measurement and specification of materials and products, the standardisation of quality systems has become increasingly important. In the last decade, one British Standard has attracted overwhelming attention. BS5750 was the world's first published national standard dealing with a complete approach to quality management. Internationally, BS5750 is the basis of the European Quality Standard EN29000 and of the ISO 9000 series. Following the philosophy of BS5750, environmental management systems will also become standardised, measured and accredited via BS7750. Such standards set down technical and sometimes organisational criteria which help to:

- ensure that goods and services are fit for the purpose and meet a customer's needs;
- rationalise, simplify and harmonise manufacturing techniques thus reducing needless variety and duplication misuse of resources;
- provide a means of communication and measurement which can be used in the specification of contracts;
- provide a means of communication and identification to customers and suppliers;
- ensure safety and good health.

BS5750

Organisations produce a product or service which is intended to satisfy consumers' needs or requirements. Such requirements are often specified in contracts but this alone will not guarantee that the specifications will be met. In today's competitive markets, major purchasers of goods and services increasingly demand proof of a company's ability to produce quality products and quality services. This has led to the development of quality system standards (for example, the Ministry of Defence DEF STAN 05–21 to 05–29 series, the NATO Allied Quality Assurance Publications AQAP–1 to AQAP–9 series and BS5750). The series of international standards (ISO 9000 to ISO

9004) embodies a rationalisation of a number of national specifications but is heavily based on BS5750. The lowering of European trade barriers has given increased importance to ISO 9000. The ISO 9000 series has now been adopted by CEN–CENELEC (the joint European Standards Institution) as the EN29000 series.

The quality system of an organisation is influenced by the objectives of the organisation, by the product or service and by the practices specific to the organisation. Therefore it will vary from one organisation to another. The quality system should include the objectives, policies, organisational structure, responsibilities, procedures, processes and resources for beginning and developing a process of quality improvement. The organisation must provide confidence to the purchaser that the intended quality is being, or will be met in the delivered product or service required.

As a quality system BS5750 involves all phases from initial identification to final satisfaction of requirements and customer expectations. These phases and activities will include:

- marketing and market research;
- product design and development;
- procurement;
- production preparation and process planning;
- production;
- inspection and testing;
- packaging and storage;
- sales and distribution;
- installation and operation;
- technical assistance and maintenance; and
- disposal after use.

This represents an approach near to a 'cradle to grave' system based on the maintenance of quality. That same 'cradle to grave' approach is common in the assessment of environmental improvement and an environmental improvement programme can be layered on top of a quality based system such as BS5750.

The essence of BS5750 is shown in Figure 5.2 where it can be seen in terms of a continuous cycle of improvement. The key is to document the quality management system in operation and to justify that system. There is a requirement to adhere to that system. In other words, to do what has been documented. What actually happened in the organisation needs subsequently to be recorded and reviewed in order that the system can be improved and revised accordingly and new documentation prepared.

There are a number of benefits for an organisation if it can obtain BS5750 registration:

- it is a first class marketing tool;
- major purchasers accept BS5750 certification and registration as proof of quality and technical expertise;

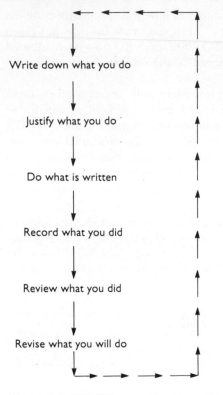

Write down what you do

Justify what you do

Do what is written

Record what you did

Review what you did

Revise what you will do

Figure 5.2 BS5750: a continuous cycle of improvement

- customers are much less likely to ask for their own special assessments, and the number and extent of quality audits and assessments can be minimised, thus saving time and money;
- confidence for the organisation resulting from the quality system being under independent surveillance;
- improvement in quality performance and company morale;
- the cost of lost orders, reworking, extra handling, scrapped production, wastage and senior executive time will be reduced;
- improved customer satisfaction, leading to increased sales, competitiveness and profitability.

BS5750 is nevertheless simply a base on which an organisation can build and develop its approach to TQM. Total quality management does require a major change in attitude and behaviour within an organisation and may take a number of years to achieve. However, BS5750 provides a model to move towards and it is important to remember that in the context of organisations that quality is all-encompassing. If procedures in a number of accidents and disasters had been followed as specified then they would never have happened.

BS7750

BS7750, the British Standards Institution's (BSI) standard on environmental management systems, was launched in 1992 after over a year's discussion with industry and practitioners. In many respects the BSI provided a management tool requirement increasingly demanded by a range of stakeholders from consumers to shareholders. It is the first of a new generation of standards covering every aspect of environmental management.

The introduction of a standard for environmental management is a significant milestone. As the standard is increasingly adopted it will cease to be part of a company's strategy for creating a 'competitive edge' and will become a minimum standard for good practice. The British Standards Institute's Environmental Management System Standard is designed to aid industry by providing a generic model that will help organisations to establish, develop and maintain their own purpose-built environmental management system.

The standard does not attempt to outline expected levels of performance, indeed the whole issue of the measurement of environmental performance is an area where considerable research is required. Compliance with the standard is centred on the ability of management to meet its own stated objectives and working towards those objectives may be an intricate process in itself. Those objectives are likely also to change and be modified over time. Central to the system is the recognition of the need for regular auditing and a continuous cycle of improvement which in itself will lead to redefinition of the environmental policy and objectives.

The starting point for the organisation adopting the standard is a commitment to control its environmental performance and the first step is therefore to undertake a positioning review and formulate a coherent policy statement. All activities have to be recorded, assessed and audited and product development has to be examined in terms of a life cycle assessment.

Like BS5750, the system adopted by the organisation has to be documented and subsequent activities have to adhere to that system and performance has to be measured. In the light of experience the stated policy has to be reconsidered and the whole process repeats itself.

Experience in the use of quality systems shows that an appropriately designed management system can ensure that requirements of any kind can be met and the system certified accordingly. Companies which have been through a BS5750 development process will find BS7750 relatively easy to implement to the extent that much of the system documentation required is parallel to that required under BS5750. Nevertheless, like BS5750, the documentation requirements for BS7750 can be formidable.

The standard is applicable to a wide range of industries from manufacturing to service organisations. Central to its requirement is the need to consider the total organisation and the total process which means that the environmental management system can borrow many of the techniques and principles of total quality management. In addition, organisations should also be seen as being involved in a wider process flow where they will have impacts beyond the boundaries of their own production process. For example, the use of raw materials and the disposal of products after use are, to some extent, influenced by the organisation and life-cycle assessment represents an appropriate tool for the analysis of wider product impacts.

The standard is fully compatible with EC initiatives on eco-auditing and eco-labelling and has its own system for certification for compliance. The key requirements of BS7750 are as follows:

1. **Environmental policy.** BS7750 requires that the environmental management system (EMS) should aim to ensure compliance with the environmental policy and objectives of the firm. At an early stage therefore there is a need for a clear and detailed consideration of what that policy should be. It must be seen as an integral part of the EMS and stress the need for a continuous cycle of environmental improvement. The policy must nevertheless be understandable and communicated widely to ensure implementation at every level of the organisation.

2. **Commitment**. The standard requires commitment at the highest level in the company. By adopting the standard an organisation will have to accept the changes which this implies and support for change is therefore required at Board level. Management needs to publicly declare its whole-hearted support for the adoption of the standard.

3. **Environmental review**. There is a need for organisations to carry out an initial environmental review which will provide the information required to design the organisation's environmental management system. The standard's document lays out a whole range of suggested areas for investigation.

4. **Organisation**. Personnel are central to the success of any management system and jobs and roles within the organisation must be clearly defined and their links with each other made apparent. People must be clear about their own role, the authority with which to act and their lines of demarcation, responsibility and reporting. The organisation must therefore be tight. Gaps in an organisational structure are often the source of mistakes and problems.

5. **Registers of environmental effects**. Organisations are required to keep registers of environmental legislation, regulations, planning requirements and discharge consents relevant to their operations. They must also develop an effects register which evaluates the environmental impacts of their operations based on a life-cycle approach from procurement to disposal of products after use.

6. **Objectives and targets**. Organisations should specify attainable and achievable targets which nevertheless go beyond minimum legislatory requirements. The targets can be staged over predefined time scales to achieve a continuous cycle of improvement.

7. **Environmental management programme, records and documentation.**

Plans and strategies to achieve environmental improvement must be clearly defined and documented. Procedures and responsibilities must be defined in detail and there must be procedures for adapting and changing the plan in the light of changing requirements, results of the environmental audit and experience. There must be systems in place for maintaining records relevant to the environmental strategy. These must include records of any failure of compliance and information concerning suppliers and contractors. More detailed consideration of documentation is provided below.

8. **Operational controls and records**. There must be measurement and verification of the organisation's activities and the effectiveness of its strategies for environmental improvement. If measurement discovers the failure to meet specific targets then procedures for corrective action must be defined.

9. **Environmental audits**. Organisations must carry out periodic audits of the operations and systems based on a detailed and documented plan setting out the auditing methodology and the procedures for reporting and publishing findings.

10. **System reviews**. Management systems should be open to adaptation and refinement based on the results of the auditing exercise and experience and there must be a commitment to periodic reviews of the environmental management system and its operation.

Designing the environmental management system

The environmental management system itself must be designed by the company around the general requirements above. In effect, this means that the organisation must design, implement and continuously improve processes aimed at achieving the objectives and targets laid out in the environmental policy. BS7750 does provide a generic model on which to build the specific design which requires processes to be put in place to ensure that:

- a policy exists and is properly communicated;
- management responsibilities are clearly defined, properly organised and have appropriate resources allocated to them;
- education and training programmes exist;
- inventories exist of the environmental effects of the organisation;
- inventories exist of the legal requirements;
- the objectives and specific targets to be attained are clearly stated and that these are drawn from the results of the environmental review and the organisation's stated policy;
- a plan of how the targets are to be met is established;
- appropriate quality control systems are in place to ensure compliance with the plans;
- appropriate records are kept; and that

- regular audits are carried out to ensure that the system works and continuous improvement can be achieved.

The actual design of the system will have to be periodically reviewed by management based on the information supplied by the audit, changing legislative requirements and stakeholder pressure. The approach must at all times be systematic and documented.

Documenting the environmental management system

There are four key components of an environmental management system:

1. The environmental review
2. The environmental policy
3. System design and implementation
4. The environmental audit

Each of these components is distinct but all need to be comprehensively documented.

The environmental review

BS7750 requires that environmental effects inventories are kept. One of these should record the actual impact of an organisation's activities on the environment. The initial environmental review is therefore the baseline for establishing this and will be the level against which improvements are measured. It is critical that the results of the review are documented. Much of the documentation at this early stage will simply represent an inventory of the organisation's activities. If we build on this idea of inventory analysis the documentation might include the following.

1. **Consumption inventory**. This would record all materials consumed by the organisation over a particular time period often broken down into generalised categories with particular attention paid to natural resources and hazardous substances.
2. **Product inventory**. A listing of all products produced by the company over the same time period which might include some analysis of the life-cycle impact of the products.
3. **Releases inventory**. A listing of all releases to the air and water including particulate releases and an assessment of the impact of these activities.
4. **Disposal inventory**. All materials which are disposed of should be recorded along with details of how they are disposed of with particular attention being paid to the ratio between on-site disposal and off-site disposal.

5. **Stocks inventory.** A listing of stocks kept over the period paying particular attention to hazardous substances and the potential risks of the stock-holding and any warehousing entailed.
6. **Reconciliation.** The first five inventories should be capable of reconciliation in terms of mass balance. This exercise helps to discover undetected waste and emissions.
7. **Impacts inventory.** An assessment of the overall impact on the environment should be made. This should cover site-specific, local, regional and global impacts and pay particular attention to impacts on local communities.
8. **Impact mechanisms.** The routes by which impacts occur are important and should be identified and recorded. The analysis should cover procurement, life-cycle impact of products, processes, storage, transport, waste disposal and emissions and accidents. A clear understanding of impact mechanisms is required in order to attempt to reduce the level of such impacts.
9. **Regulatory and legislative requirements register.** A record of all regulations, legislation, planning requirements, etc., pertinent to the operation of the organisation should be kept. These will be treated as a minimum level of compliance and suggestions may be made for going beyond these minimum requirements.
10. **The existing management system.** The review needs to identify the extent to which a systematic management system already exists within the organisation and the good and bad practices which arise from this. Where a recognised standard such as BS5750 has been implemented some consideration of how BS7750 might be implemented in parallel needs to be undertaken.

The environmental policy

The organisation must have a clear and detailed policy with respect to environmental improvement. This should be widely available and at least a summary of it should be available to the public. The method by which the policy is to be made available to the whole organisation, along with measures taken to ensure that the policy has been understood and is being acted upon must be documented. Where a policy sets specific objectives for each of its general impacts then these should be explained and justified and shown to be realistic, yet ambitious and attainable.

System design and implementation

The plan of the environmental system needs to be set out in considerable detail and both its design (in terms of structure) and its implementation strategy needs to be considered. It must be made clear how the environmental management system sets out to achieve the objectives set out in the policy statement.

The documentation for the EMS needs to lay out how it proposes to achieve its objectives and would typically cover the following.

- Staff responsibilities, standard lines of reporting and procedures for unforeseen circumstances such as accidents.
- The resources to be devoted to the EMS, a justification of these and a demonstration of how these resources will bring about environmental improvement.
- Specific actions to be undertaken by the organisation to meet specific environmental objectives along with a timescale for implementation.
- A timetable of anticipated environmental achievements and details of how these are to be measured and assessed, and procedures for action should the targets not be met.
- The way in which staff are to be informed of their specific tasks in the organisation which may include the production and distribution of manuals and other documentation setting out roles and responsibilities.
- The way in which staff are to be trained in new working practices, new procedures or general environmental awareness, the content of the training programmes and what they seek to achieve.
- The coordination and management of all the organisation's activities related to its environmental performance.
- A clear mechanism by which environmental performance will be monitored and a justification of that system.
- A schedule, protocol and methodology for regularly auditing the performance of the environmental management system and the environmental performance of the organisation.
- The mechanism by which all results and assessments will be verified.
- A schedule for regular strategic reviews of the organisation's policy and environmental management system.
- The way in which the organisation will communicate its environmental performance to its stakeholders.

The environmental audit

The environmental audit should compare the organisation's actual environmental performance against basic standards set by legislation and regulations, the organisation's own stated objectives and by best practice elsewhere (for example by a company's competitors). The documentation for the EMS needs to establish a clear auditing methodology including the timing of the auditing procedure.

IMPLEMENTING THE MANAGEMENT SYSTEM

Putting an effective environmental management system or indeed any management system in place in an organisation is not easy, is time consuming and as a process itself will never end. An intellectual understanding of environmental issues provides the basis of the environmental management system but this has to be translated into commitment, policies, organisation, plans and actions for environmental improvement. The commitment to the system needs to be kept up and members of the organisation need to have the importance of the management system reinforced periodically. Without this ongoing commitment the whole initiative will eventually be marginalised and disappear and, as with any culture change programme, the whole workforce needs to realise that the strategy is a continual process. There is therefore a key, ongoing need for training and help with the implementation process and development of the environmental management system over time. Much of this implies a change in corporate culture but it should be remembered that organisations which try to change their environmental culture, without effectively communicating their objectives and reasons to everyone involved in that organisation, will not succeed.

It is often a good idea to identify a team who will drive the initiative and coordinate the strategies. That team, which is likely to be the environment committee, discussed above, will have to ensure that the implementation of the system remains high on the agenda. Having a clear target to aim for will often help to focus efforts and therefore the ultimate aim of attaining accreditation with a standard such as BS7750 can act as a very positive impetus.

Figure 5.3 lays out ten stages central to the implementation of an environmental management system. Essentially this involves senior management undertaking and developing the following ideas.

1. Understand the environmental challenge in relation to its global, national and local contexts and particularly in relation to your own organisation.
2. Be committed to environmental improvement and communicate that commitment to the whole workforce and, indeed, to all stakeholders and move environmental issues up the environmental agenda.
3. Establish an environmental policy and any associated objectives and publish them widely. Consider the appointment of a person with a brief for environmental initiatives who will be responsible to the chief executive.
4. Assess and measure the extent of environmental damage within the organisation, in other words undertake an initial environmental review and subsequent, regular environmental audits.
5. Organise and structure the environmental management system so that it is efficient, effective and can be understood by the workforce. Identify any gaps which emerge in the system and take steps to rectify them.
6. Decide on the organisation's environmental priorities and structure plans to improve environmental performance.
7. Introduce training in order to make all members of the organisation aware of relevant environmental issues, to help them understand the plans and to facilitate the environmental management system.

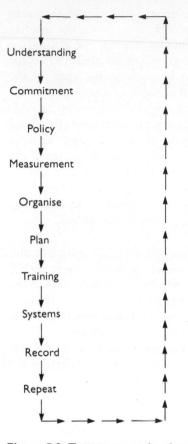

Figure 5.3 Ten stages to implementing an environmental management system

8. Carefully introduce and continually develop your environmental management system in order to achieve environmental improvement. Make sure that the system is properly understood and communicated to all relevant parties.
9. Record achievements and impediments to improvement and act on them ensuring that gaps are plugged.
10. Do it all again ensuring that the message is reinforced and that systems and environmental performance are continually improved.

Following these ten stages can, but will not necessarily, lead to a successful environmental management system. Neither do they imply a mechanistic or narrow technologically-based approach which looks at only one issue at a time. Such an approach will be hampered by the limitations of current scientific knowledge, competing demands on capital expenditure and management time, conflicts between competing organisational objectives and the power of technical expertise in decision-making. What is needed is a complete and holistic approach which implies that an evolutionary, integrated and proactive approach needs to be taken to environmental issues. This would mirror the total quality management approach which has proved so successful in many organisations. Environmental problems will clearly not be solved overnight but what we can expect is continual improvement over time.

The precise order of the ten stages identified may be changed to suit the particular operation or organisation but it should be stressed that they are not one-off or discrete tasks. They have to be approached in an integrated way and will need to be repeated aiming for a continuous cycle of improvement. However, the ten stages do provide the building blocks of the system and provide a structured path to be followed and repeated. It cannot be stressed too much that an environmental culture or philosophy which creates corporate commitment to environmental improvement needs to be developed. Underlying this ten-point strategy there is, therefore, a need to adopt an overall approach encompassing the following ten requirements for achieving environmental improvement.

1. Recognise the importance of environmental improvement and record this in the organisation's mission statement.
2. Adopt a new philosophy towards your organisation's operations which sees environmental damage as a quality defect.
3. Ensure that environmental improvement is endogenous to all systems and processes and develop teams to improve those processes.
4. When assessing production possibilities, measure total costs, not just internalised private costs, and identify and cost potential environmental problems.
5. Make it clear that management is committed to environmental improvement and sees that as a key element of corporate performance.
6. Institute modern methods of management which will promote motivation, participatory arrangements, improved information and communication flows and adequate and high-quality training and retraining.
7. Measure and identify environmental improvement and record and act on impediments to that improvement.
8. Aim for proper waste management, recycling and reduced dependency on non-renewable resources.
9. Value the workforce, involve them in process development, encourage them to establish their own environmental goals and reward them accordingly.
10. Do it all over again, aiming for a continuous cycle of improvement, regularly audited and reported to shareholders, suppliers and customers.

Where quality systems such as BS5750 or ISO 9000 already exist in an organisation these can be built on to embrace the environment as well. Many of the structures, improvement teams and the central need for commitment will already be in place. Indeed, as has been suggested previously, if environmental damage is considered as a quality defect then the systems in place may be sufficient. But it is important to stress the role of every person in the organisation and the need to adopt a participatory style of management where the workforce is involved and valued and not treated as a discrete factor of production. Where there is no quality system in place the task is obviously more difficult. But it is likely to be in the interests of the organisation to pursue the ultimate objectives of zero defects and zero harmful emissions in parallel.

CONCLUSION

For most organisations the ultimate aim of zero negative impact on the environment, widely defined, simply cannot be met. The only way to ensure such a position would be to have virtually no industry at all. What we can expect is improved environmental performance over time and therefore a never-ending or continuous cycle of improvement is an achievable goal. The environmental management system has to be firmly tied to a regular assessment of company performance and audit of environmental damage. The central importance of commitment must not be lost, if it is, the system will collapse. The never-ending improvement cycle will mean that the organisation learns from its successes and failures and improves operations and outputs. This has to be done in a planned, systematic and documented way in order to create an organisational culture which protects the environment and the reputation of the company, that permeates the whole organisation.

It is no longer sufficient to see environmental strategy as an add-on to other corporate policies. Environmental improvement and the avoidance of accidental damage, like the culture of total quality management, needs to be firmly embedded at all levels of the organisation. Of central importance here is a need for a proactive stance and an evolutionary approach to the improvement of environmental performance. This can be achieved by adopting the type of environmental management system outlined in this chapter. Moreover, environmental management is no longer an option. Increased legislation, the European eco-management and audit system, consumer pressure and pressure on suppliers from organisations with their own environmental policies mean that the establishment of environmental management systems cannot be seen simply as a 'competitive edge'; they will in time become a means of survival.

CHAPTER 6

Environmental auditing: monitoring continuous improvement

Environmental auditing is not a particularly new discipline. However, its popularity as a means of assessing environmental performance has increased substantially recently. Indeed, the first environmental audits can be traced back to the United States of America, where US corporations adopted this methodology during the 1970s in response to their domestic liability laws. During the 1980s these audits were extended beyond simply adhering to legislation and regulations. For example, proactive audits which went beyond pure compliance were introduced by Shell Oil in 1981. Such audits are now common among US industry and rapidly growing in importance in Europe. In general, environmental auditing is a series of activities initiated, by management, to evaluate environmental performance, to check compliance with environmental legislation and to assess whether the systems in place to manage environmental improvement are effective. Audits are done at regular intervals to assess the environmental performance of the company in relation to the company's stated objectives and environmental policy. The environmental audit is therefore an integral part of the environmental management system discussed in the previous chapter.

Like environmental reviews, audits are carried out by interdisciplinary teams which will include lawyers, management systems experts, engineers, scientists and environmental generalists. The US Environmental Protection Agency (EPA) has been instrumental in promoting environmental audits in the USA and has published policy guidelines which recommend going beyond the minimum legal requirements to identify actual and potential environmental problems. The International Chamber of Commerce has also drawn up audit guidelines which promote the need for self-regulation by the business community in the spirit of responsible care. In Europe the European Commission has been promoting environmental audits and its eco-management and audit scheme is discussed later in this chapter.

The definition of an environmental audit provided by the International Chamber of Commerce (ICC) (1989) is:

> A management tool comprising a systematic, documented, periodic and objective evaluation of how well environmental organisation, management and equipment are performing with the aim of helping to safeguard the environment by: (i) facilitating management and control of environmental practices; and (ii) assessing compliance with company policies, which include meeting regulatory requirements.

While this definition is rather 'management' oriented and the full role for everyone in the organisation should be recognised, it gives an idea of its basic approach. Much stress should be laid on the words systematic, documented, periodic and objective. In other words, the audit must be an ongoing and thorough assessment of environmental performance which is documented and at the very least verified by an objective third party. This definition of the environmental audit has become standard but there is still some confusion over the term and some environmental consultancy firms still seem to want to call any kind of environmental assessment an audit.

An environmental audit is central to a company committed to the implementation of the type of environmental management system. Indeed, it would be wrong for the environmental audit to be seen in isolation, it is one very important component of a comprehensive approach to environmental management and is recognised as such in standards such as BS7750. As with much of environmental management the role of senior management in the audit process is crucial. Without top management support an internal environmental audit programme will not succeed. Moreover, management needs to be fully committed to environmental compliance and to correcting any deficiencies uncovered by the audit programme. The ICC paper on environmental auditing includes the following statement on full management commitment:

> It is important that management from the highest levels overtly supports a purposeful and systematic environmental auditing programme. Such commitment is demonstrated by, for example, personal interest and concern, the adoption of high standards, the allocation of appropriate manpower and resources, and the active follow-up of recommendations.

An environmental audit is more than a simple inspection or assessment which offers an opinion based primarily on professional judgement. It has to be a methodological examination of a facility and its procedures which will include analyses and testing in order to verify that legal requirements and internal policies are being met. In this context, auditors will base their judgements of compliance on evidence gathered during the audit. An audit can look at particular issues facing the company or it can be a wide-ranging audit which includes a full assessment of the effectiveness of an environmental management system as well as compliance, safety and quality control. The ICC approach clearly promotes the latter.

Neither is the audit a one-off activity. It needs to be seen as an ongoing programme where the audit is not only repeated periodically but also developed in terms of scope and sophistication over time. Seeing a single audit as a panacea would not only be wrong but is likely to lead to more problems than it solves. Central to the audit programme therefore, is a commitment to see the process as continuous and part of a company's wide range of assessment activities. In effect, an auditing system helps the firm anticipate environmental damage and therefore prevent it from happening. However, before a company is even in a position to audit, it needs firstly, to establish its baseline performance which is achieved via the environmental review and secondly, to begin to implement an action plan through a clearly structured environmental management system.

AIMS AND OBJECTIVES OF THE ENVIRONMENTAL AUDIT

Once the environmental review has been completed and the management system is in place there will be a need to regularly assess that system and to further measure the environmental performance of the firm. There will also be a need to verify that any actions being implemented as the result of any previous report are effective. This is the role of the regular environmental audit. The overall aim of environmental auditing is therefore to provide an ongoing status check which will enable environmental improvement within the organisation to continue and in so doing, will help to safeguard the environment and minimise the risks to human health. Although auditing alone cannot achieve environmental improvement, it is a powerful managerial tool. The key objectives of the environmental audit are:

● to determine the extent to which environmental management systems in a company are performing adequately;
● to verify compliance with local, national and European environmental and health and safety legislation;
● to verify compliance with a company's own stated corporate policy;
● to develop and promulgate internal procedures needed to achieve the organisation's environmental objectives;
● to minimise human exposure to risks from the environment and ensure adequate health and safety provision;
● to identify and assess company risk resulting from environmental failure;
● to assess the impact on the local environment of a particular plant or process by means of air, water and soil sampling; and
● to advise a company on environmental improvements it can make.

There are a number of benefits available to firms which undertake an environmental audit. These include assurances that legislation is being adhered to and the consequent prevention of fines and litigation, an improved public image which can be built into a public relations campaign, a reduction in costs (particularly in the area of energy usage and waste minimisation), an improvement in environmental awareness at all levels of the firm and an improvement in overall quality. Many environmental audit programmes are established on the direct orders of top management for the purpose of identifying the compliance status of individual facilities and thereby providing management with a sense of security that environmental requirements are being met. Increasingly, ignorance will not be tolerated as an excuse when environmental litigation is being pursued.

On the other hand there are some potential disbenefits of the audit. These include the initial costs of the audit and the cost of compliance with it and the temporary disruption of plant operations. It is also vital that management sees that the recommendations of the environmental auditor are adhered to otherwise an audit report could be incriminating in a court case or insurance claim. An audit report is a 'discoverable' document and may therefore be used in any legal proceedings which may follow. Before an audit is undertaken, therefore, management must recognise that the audit may recommend changes which require immediate action because they are either illegal or hazardous to human health. There is a need to establish a contingency budget to cover expenditure which may be required in response to such recommendations.

There is also often a natural reluctance on the part of management and workers to see outsiders entering the organisation and assessing their own performance. In particular, management can become unhappy about its line of responsibility being invaded. The legitimacy of any auditing team, which may not have the same level of knowledge of an industry as do internal personnel, will often be challenged. In these respects, therefore, it is vital that senior management are seen to be supportive of both the audit team and the process of auditing.

As has already been made clear, the primary benefits of environmental auditing are to indicate in good time whether environmental measures are satisfactory and to assist with the subsequent compliance with legislation, company policy and the public's demands. Experience of auditing in a number of companies has, however, highlighted a range of less tangible benefits. These include for example:

- increasing awareness of environmental policies and responsibilities among the whole workforce;
- providing an opportunity for management to give credit for good environmental performance;
- identifying new working practices which can significantly aid waste minimisation and energy usage;
- providing an up-to-date environmental database which can be drawn on when making decisions on plant modifications or for use in emergencies;
- evaluating training programmes and providing information for the training of staff.

INCENTIVES TO UNDERTAKE THE AUDIT

Over the last decade, as public attitudes towards environmental degradation have changed, as insurance markets have become more aware of the potential risks associated with pollution and as more national and transnational legislation has come onto the statute book, the incentives to undertake an environmental audit have increased. The particular reasons for undertaking a regular environmental audit are therefore likely to include the following considerations.

1. **Insurance**. Costs of remediation following pollution incidents have been increasing dramatically. Consequently, premiums have increased and the number of exclusions from policies has been extended. While it is still possible to find insurance cover for pollution which is sudden, accidental and unforeseen, there are very few insurance companies which will cover general pollution risks unless regular environmental audits are carried out.
2. **Market forces and competition**. One of the consequences of public interest is that consumers are increasingly willing to switch to products which are in some way more environmentally friendly than their normal purchase. Companies need therefore to demonstrate that their product and their processes cause minimum harm to the environment. In the past the marketing of 'green' products has often been misleading and sometimes dishonest. Some firms have had their 'green' products exposed as not being environmentally friendly at all. With the growing strength of pressure groups, dishonesty will be exposed and it is therefore necessary for firms, who wish to tell their consumers about their environmental improvements, to undertake independent and regular environmental audits of their processes. With the introduction of an eco-label for some products across Europe, which will assess not only the product but the production process before an award is made, the role of the audit becomes crucial.
3. **Acquisitions**. Major organisations are becoming increasingly aware of the massive potential risks involved in acquiring land which has already been contaminated or acquiring a business which has poor environmental performance. Costs associated with ground remediation, the capital cost associated with introducing or upgrading pollution control plant and the cost of potential litigation and compensation claims for past mistakes can easily outweigh any financial advantage of an acquisition. It has increasingly become standard practice, therefore, for purchasers to commission a pre-acquisition environmental assessment or to want to examine the reports from an organisation's environmental audits.
4. **Legislation**. The Environmental Protection Act (1990) in the UK requires organisations to reduce emissions to the atmosphere and discharges to rivers and sewers using methods which present the 'best practicable environmental option' (BPEO) and the 'best available techniques not entailing excessive cost' (BATNEEC). Specific industries involved in the processing of toxic materials have, in addition, to apply to Her Majesty's Inspectorate of Pollution (HMIP) for an authorisation to operate. For smaller units there is commonly a need to gain an 'authorisation to operate' from the Local Authority Air Pollution Control. Applications for such authorisation, which are likely to be expanded in the future, require the completion of a complex questionnaire and this is often not possible

without the information which results from an environmental audit. In addition, there are mounting European directives and legislation to be considered so that part of the audit needs not only to verify compliance but also to look forward to future legislative and regulatory demands.

AUDIT PRINCIPLES

An increasing number of consultancies have been established during the late 1980s and 1990s which aim to undertake environmental audits. Some of these have grown out of quality assurance operations and others out of the expertise developed through environmental impact assessment. However, environmental auditing requires skills and attributes which go beyond both of these frameworks and entails a much more interdisciplinary approach. Increasingly some degree of external help and consultancy will be needed by business for four reasons:

1. All but the largest of firms are unlikely to have the necessary expertise to cover the legal, scientific and technical, and management-related requirements of the audit process.
2. Increasingly, companies are looking for third-party verification of their audit results. This is required, for example, by the EC eco-management and audit scheme. External consultants can bring a degree of objectivity to the process and introduce fresh ideas.
3. Traditionally many audits have been strictly site-specific and have not sought to assess linkages along the supply chain and the external environmental effects of operations. There is, however, a clear trend towards an assessment of external environmental effects such as pollution, and disamenities where expertise and measurement beyond a single plant or operation are required.
4. The findings of audits were traditionally for internal company consumption but there is now a move by some companies, reacting to demands from pressure groups and encouragement from industry itself, government and the EC, to publish the results more widely and to consider the provision of public information. Thus the information resulting from the audit needs to be comprehensible to the public and believed by them. This can be better achieved with external impartial advice and third-party verification.

However, in using external advice organisations need to assure themselves that they will be getting value for money and a quality service. It is possible to identify ten key elements necessary for the conduct of effective and reliable environmental audits. Unless these can be adhered to by auditors, companies cannot be assured of the quality and objectivity of the auditing procedure and will need to take their business elsewhere.

1. Clear and explicit objectives need to be formulated before the commencement of the environmental audit. In addition, there needs to be a clearly defined benchmark in terms of environmental legislation, standards and the best practice of other companies in order that the audit results can be assessed.
2. The audit team needs to be proficient and expert with appropriate knowledge of the issues under consideration and an appropriate environmental understanding with respect to scientific, technical, legislative and management issues. Each audit member needs to be able to demonstrate his/her particular expertise.
3. Auditors need to be independent and to work in a confidential manner and due professional care should be exercised at all times.
4. Firms specialising in environmental auditing and individual consultants should be able to demonstrate their own adherence to general principles of environmental improvement.
5. The on-site audit should be planned, managed and supervised so as to ensure minimum disbenefit to the company and appropriate security and safety to the individual auditor.
6. Environmental audits should include the proper study of management systems in operation and an assessment of the reliability of internal environmental controls. Tests should be devised so as to ensure the effectiveness of management structures.
7. Sufficient, reliable evidence should be gathered through inquiry, observation and tests to ensure that the audit findings are objective.
8. Audit reports should be clear, concise and confidential. They should ensure full and formal communication of audit findings and recommendations.
9. Auditors should ensure that strategies for the implementation of the recommendations of the audit are practicable and possible and should contribute to the implementation of corrections.
10. Auditors should clearly indicate to companies the consequences of not correcting deficiencies, particularly where they may result in litigation being taken against the firm. If this is not done then auditors should accept their own negligence.

PARTIAL ENVIRONMENTAL AUDITS

The environmental audit has to be systematic and comprehensive. However, some firms have carried out narrower assessments of part of their activities for specific purposes. In effect these are partial audits and although their general methodology may be similar, they do not adhere to the main task of the audit which is to assess the environmental management system and to measure environmental performance. A partial environmental audit will be specific to a particular task, process or issue. These narrower types of audit continue to exist and for that reason are briefly reviewed here.

Compliance audit

Compliance auditing has, until recently, been the most common form of environmental auditing. The audit regularly checks the extent to which an organisation is complying with existing environmental laws and company policies. A more progressive compliance audit will examine areas not yet covered by legislation and other standards in an attempt to be more proactive in its environmental strategy.

Process safety audit

A periodic process safety audit will seek to identify the hazards and quantify the risks arising from the production process. It will look closely at procedures for accidents and emergencies and may be combined with a compliance audit to cover health and safety legislation. Accident reporting and investigation systems will be checked along with emergency response preparedness and the appropriateness of training in the areas of health and safety, accident prevention and accident response.

Occupational health audit

Occupational health auditing examines the exposure of the workforce to pollution and physical disamenities (e.g. noise and temperature) and is measured and recorded periodically. The availability, quality and usage of protective equipment and clothing, training and information will be assessed.

Product audit

At companies such as The Body Shop an analysis, which they have called a product audit, has been carried out. The Body Shop's approach is to analyse a particular product line examining most aspects of sourcing production, packaging and waste disposal. In effect, this sort of approach is equivalent to a life-cycle assessment of the product.

Product quality audit

Quality auditing is increasingly being linked to quality standards such as BS5750. Here auditing is focused on product or operational quality systems. Existing safety and product control systems would be analysed, quality assurance programmes assessed, consumer information appraised and labelling, packaging and safety data examined.

Issues audits

At British Petroleum (BP) audits have been conducted which are neither site, organisation or product specific. They have introduced the concept of an issue audit which focuses on how the whole Group is dealing with specific environmental issues of key concern, such as the loss of tropical rainforest habitat. This audit involves an evaluation of policy, guidelines, operating procedures and actual practice within all businesses.

Pre-acquisition audits

This sort of audit or review (strictly speaking that is what it is more likely to be) are associated with merger or acquisition activities. We have already seen that it is risky not to have some sort of environmental assessment in such situations. Such investigations concern the assessment of significant environmental liabilities (past, present and future) associated with an installation or organisation about to be acquired. These liabilities may be associated with contaminated land or ground water, existing or potential litigation and the need to install new pollution control technologies. Pre-acquisition audits are sometimes referred to as due diligence investigations.

While the general principles for conducting any type of environmental audit are generally similar, for the remainder of this chapter we assume that we are dealing with a comprehensive audit of a site or organisation after an environmental review has been conducted.

IMPLEMENTING THE AUDIT

All environmental audits involve gathering information, analysing that information, making objective judgements based on evidence and a knowledge of the industry and of relevant environmental legislation and standards. There is also the need to report the results of the audit to senior management with recommendations and possible strategies for the implementation of the findings. This all needs considerable preparatory work as well as follow-up time in order that the findings are accurate and comprehensive. Ideally, there needs to be three clear stages to an audit (see Figure 6.1).

The first, the pre-audit stage will aim to minimise the time spent at the site and to maximise the audit team's productivity and will involve the following.

1. Planning the nature and scope of the audit and providing a framework for setting goals and objectives, developing strategies for their achievement and specifying accountability for accomplishing the work, and scheduling the audit process.
2. Selecting members of the audit team and allocating resources to the strategies and policies determined in 1. The audit team will consist of people chosen for their expertise not only in environmental matters but

Pre-audit
stage

Audit
stage

Post-audit
stage

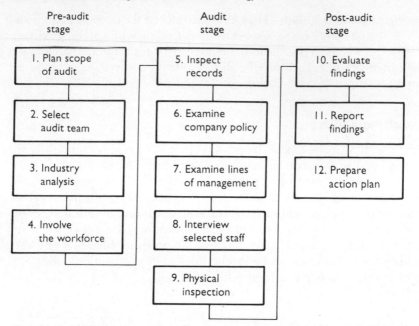

Figure 6.1 Stages of an environmental audit

also having knowledge of the industry in which a company operates. An assignment of audit responsibilities should be made according to the competencies and experience of the team.

3. Getting to know the industry and company to be audited. A useful strategy here is to use pre-survey questionnaires submitted to management in order for the audit team to familiarise themselves with the type of instalment, the site and the location. It will also focus the minds of management on what will be required of them during the audit.

4. Questionnaires may also be sent to a representative sample of the workforce (to be filled out in confidence) asking about key issues such as communications, planning, health and safety and working conditions.

The second stage is the on-site audit itself. This will include the following.

5. An inspection of records kept by the company, certificates of compliance, discharge consents, waste licenses, etc.

6. The examination of inspection and maintenance programmes and the company's own policy on what to do in the event of spills and other accidents. Auditors will have to assess the soundness of the facility's internal controls and assess the risks associated with the failure of those controls. Such controls will include management procedures and the equipment and engineering controls that affect environmental performance.

7. Examining lines of management and responsibility, competer personnel and systems of authorisation. There needs to be a w understanding of the facility's internal management system and effectiveness.

8. A confidential interview of selected staff at all levels of operation with a view to collecting information, particularly in the area of the effectiveness of systems and waste management.

9. A physical inspection of the plant, working practices, office management systems and surrounding areas including a check on safety equipment, verifying the company's own sampling and monitoring procedures, investigating energy management systems and where necessary taking measurements of waste, liquids, soil, air and noise.

The final stage of the audit will involve the following.

10. Confirming that there is sufficient evidence on which to base and justify a set of findings and evaluating the audit information and observations. Such evaluation will involve the audit team meeting to discuss all facets of the environmental audit.

11. Reporting the audit findings in written form and in discussion with the management of the audited company. This entails a formal review of the audit findings to avoid misinterpretation and discussion about how to improve the environmental performance of the firm based on the audit report. Management is thus provided with information about compliance status and recommendations regarding action which should be taken.

12. This will often result in the development of an action plan to address deficiencies. This will include assigning responsibilities for corrective action, determining potential solutions and establishing timetables. Recommendations for the next audit may also be made.

The environmental audit is more likely to be successful if the general ethos of the firm is supportive to the success of the programme and the welfare of the company. To this extent it is useful to consider some key characteristics which will provide the foundation for a successful programme. These factors will include:

- comprehensive support for the programme throughout management and particularly by senior management;
- acceptance that an auditing programme is for the benefit of management rather than a tool of individual performance assessment and is a function which, in time, will improve management effectiveness;
- the recognition that useful information will come out of the audit programme and that information needs to be shared and acted upon;
- the commitment to consider the comments and suggestions at each level of the organisation's management and workforce and to encourage responsible participation;
- a commitment to establish systems for managing and following-up results;

- clearly defined roles and responsibilities and clear operational systems; and
- the recognition of an integrated approach where the auditing system is linked to a wider environmental management system which in turn is linked to all the other systems in use in the company.

Much stress needs to be placed on the idea that audits should be seen by management as positive help rather than a threatening or hostile exercise. The company must create a culture led by its main board directors which recognises the positive benefits of the audit and sees it as good day-to-day management practice. Management must feel that they own the audit and even though some external expertise may be used, it is an activity which is promoted and driven internally rather than externally.

THE SCOPE OF THE AUDIT

It is clear that the environmental audit must be defined within some boundaries. If possible, the audit should use the same boundaries as the environmental management system since one of its key tasks is to assess the performance of this. However, in large companies with integrated environmental management systems the scope and coverage of them may be too wide and too unwieldy to assess using one single audit. In addition, the measurement of environmental performance needs to be done within manageable parameters. It is often necessary to break down the assessment of the system and environmental performance into parts based on the following sorts of considerations.

1. Geographical scope

Most audits are considered as site specific, but even if we take that as a norm the geographical scope of the actual environmental assessment and measurement needs to be clearly defined. Ultimately any organisation will have an impact upon the environmental situation in the whole world but while reference to these factors is valid, measurement is clearly impossible. Equally, most organisations will in some way pollute the community around them, but again the definition of the community is difficult and measurement equally problematic.

It is most appropriate to keep the geographical scope small – to begin with familiar territory – and then to expand that scope as the programme matures. Within a multi-plant firm for example, one site may be chosen initially. If the geographical coverage is to be expanded over time then a plan for this expansion needs to be drawn up and communicated.

Cultural differences and language barriers will make auditing in unfamiliar settings more difficult and this will have a clear impact on the planning stage. It may mean that extra personnel are taken on by the auditing team to cover such problems but there are benefits in using the same core auditing team so that consistency and comparability in assessing the overall 'picture' can be achieved.

2. Subject scope

The precise scope of the subjects to be audited will depend on the particular company or facility under consideration. It is vital, however, to recognise the interdependence between environmental issues and other key elements of a company's activities. Environmental audits often include some assessment of the following broader areas:

- occupational health;
- safety in the workplace;
- product safety;
- security;
- employment practices;
- transportation safety;
- transportation to and from the workplace;
- inventory control;
- production methodology;
- corporate culture;
- industrial relations; and
- participatory arrangements.

Since environmental considerations need to be integrated, at least some comment on these areas might be expected. However, the extent to which they are properly assessed will have an impact on the cost and length of the audit and so some boundaries are clearly necessary.

3. Scope within the organisation

In large companies senior management will have to decide which operations and business units are to be covered by the audit programme and there will need to be a step-by-step or gradualist approach. The environmental impact and significance of different business units will be quite disparate. Once again though, there is a need to identify priorities and in many companies, at least initially, there is a need to target segments of company activity which are perceived as being the most likely to cause environmental damage. Top of the list here tends to be central production processes and research laboratories. More extensive audits will include warehouses, administration systems, and empty premises. In time, the scope of the audit should be expanded to include joint ventures, suppliers, contractors, vendors and distributors. There are already some large companies committed to the environmental auditing process who are expressing a preference for buying from companies which have an auditing system in place themselves.

4. The scope and development of the audit over time

As corporate audit programmes mature, they will be conducted against an evolving set of criteria. The environmental review will have concentrated on investigating the broad environmental context in which the firm operates, identifying problems so that they can be corrected, and are likely to put stress on verifying compliance status. At first audits will replicate this procedure and will include an assessment of the impact of any materials and energy used and the measurement of polluting emissions and deposits. In time, however, more sophisticated audits will have to assess the effectiveness of the environmental management control systems and will be expected to gradually extend their scope. The more sophisticated the audit, the more it will help the company control its overall environmental performance and provide assurance that environmental functions are operating satisfactorily and eliminating the gaps or 'blind spots' that may exist. Over time the audit should help to develop a uniform approach to managing environmental activities and further develop the integrated environmental management system.

Environmental management effectiveness should be so defined as to be measurable over time. Basic measures which are quantitatively measurable will include an improved compliance record, reduced number and size of fines, improved accident and incident statistics and a reduced volume or potentiality of environmental hazards. There will be other measures, more difficult to quantify but nevertheless important. These include improved reputation, favourable publicity and being cited as an example of good practice.

THE NEED FOR OBJECTIVITY AND INDEPENDENCE IN THE AUDIT PROCEDURE

Environmental auditing, like financial auditing requires independence and objectivity if the results of the activity are to be credible. In time, just as with financial auditing, such independence will not only be desirable but will become mandatory. Auditors need to be able to carry out their work freely and objectively, so that they are in a position to provide management with an honest, impartial and unbiased view of the environmental status of the subject under assessment. No auditor of any value will take on a contract unless independence can be guaranteed since interference will lead to competing objectives, compromise and incomplete conclusions. The auditing system requires that any assessment should be based on facts and that those facts should be documented.

Post-audit there may be a need to weigh up the audit findings against other objectives and imperatives but this is beyond the scope of the auditor and is a task which clearly returns to senior management and policy-makers. The auditor should not be influenced by outside factors such as the impact on profitability, market share or production schedules. Optimum strategies to assure objectivity and independence include the following requirements.

- Auditors should not be employed by the company in any other capacity than as an external consultant, neither should they have a vested interest in the ownership of the company.
- In the first instance the audit report should be presented to senior management and where necessary only to those who do not have day-to-day responsibility for the business units being audited.
- The audit team itself should be brought together from a range of backgrounds and disciplines and put into a situation where there is little potential for bias. Companies wishing to undertake an environmental audit should be wary of using consultancy firms which claim that they can offer a complete package without the use of any external personnel brought in for specific reasons. In this way bias may often be introduced by the wish to gain repeat business.

There are, however, cost implications to bear in mind here. Using only external consultants will not be cheap and may seem to be wasteful of the considerable expertise which may exist within the organisation. Many large organisations may wish to develop their own internal auditing unit but, at the very least, some form of third-party independent verification should be seen as essential.

USING QUESTIONNAIRES FOR ENVIRONMENTAL REVIEWS AND AUDITS

One very efficient and relatively cost-effective way of collecting data on a company's environmental performance is by the use of questionnaires. A well-designed questionnaire will save auditors time both in data collection and in subsequent analysis. Questionnaires may either be sent to key personnel to be completed by them or administered by an interviewer.

When a pre-audit questionnaire is used there are three major objectives which should be taken into consideration. Firstly, it should prepare management for the type and detail of the information which will be required for the audit, helping them to put the audit requirements into perspective. Secondly, the questionnaire should collect basic information, such as plans and records, to be gathered and forwarded to the audit team in advance of the site visit thus saving on on-site time. Thirdly, a key role of the questionnaire will be to help in the identification of the key individuals at the facility responsible for managing key areas of the facility's activities and who will be required for interview at the time of the site visit. This information will ensure that the audit team are familiar with operations on-site prior to visiting.

To be effective, however, questionnaires have to be systematic and provide for a full coverage of environmental issues. The following common principles should therefore be adopted in the design of questionnaires.

- They should be easy to understand and unambiguous.
- They should be as simple and brief as possible without losing any of the information required.
- Questionnaires should be designed with measurement and analysis in mind and most responses should be quantifiable in some way.
- They should minimise the potential for errors during completion.

These four principles together mean that a commonly used and successful approach is to design the questionnaire with as many tick boxes as possible and encourage a graded response where appropriate. It is useful to invite whoever is completing the form to use rating scales and ranking procedures. This structured approach using closed questions will be easy to analyse. However, such a structured approach will require a detailed knowledge of the organisation's activities in order to prepare, and it may sometimes limit the respondent's replies.

Therefore there will also be a need for some more open questions on the questionnaire, where an unconstrained response is encouraged. If attitudes or opinions about issues or policies are being sought, space should be provided for respondents to express themselves more freely and an introductory letter with the questionnaire should make it clear that any criticism of the company will not be seen as disloyalty but as a constructive attempt at aiding the company's environmental improvement programme.

The way in which specific questions are worded will also be an important factor in determining the quality of information obtained. Questions should only ask for one piece of information at a time and complicated questions should be broken down into parts. Ambiguous questions and ambiguous terminology should be avoided. For example the word 'efficient', although important in determining the environmental performance of the firm, should be avoided in questionnaires because it may mean different things to different people. In circumstances like these the question must be precise in asking for information.

Where a questionnaire is to be given to a respondent to complete, the presentation and layout of the questionnaire is important. A professional-looking document which explains the purpose of the study is likely to be treated with more respect and, consequently, answers should be of a higher quality.

The questionnaire should contain an introductory page which outlines:

- the purpose of the questionnaire;
- the likely benefits of the survey to the organisation and the respondent;
- the confidentiality of the respondent's answers where opinions are being sought;
- the fact that the questionnaire and information gathering process has the support of senior management; and
- a contact name and contact point, should further information or clarification be required.

The questionnaire is not easy to compile and will often contain hundreds rather than tens of questions. Consultants usually guard their questionnaires with much care since they are valuable resources which will have taken a long time to compile if they are comprehensive. It is nevertheless possible to provide the broad headings under which detailed questions will be asked. They are:

1. General information about the company, its ownership, activities, products, production processes, markets and suppliers.
2. A site history including the length of time the process has been operated, modifications of the site, earlier uses of the site, drainage and water sources and whether there have been any accidents or spillages on the site.
3. External factors such as local amenities, information about the local geography and infrastructure and other industries in the area.
4. The environmental management system and environmental policy of the organisation, contacts and relationships with local authorities, accident and emergency procedures and statutory regulations applying to the site.
5. Legal compliance and relevant consents in relation to the discharge of gases and effluent, air emissions, waste management and noise nuisance.
6. Storage of raw materials, semi-finished and finished products, the storage of hazardous materials and construction details.
7. Transport and transport policies including the number and type of vehicles operated from the site.
8. Special substances.
9. Relationships with the local community, local authority, regulatory bodies and pressure groups.
10. Accident and emergency procedures and communications with emergency services.
11. Other issues which may be relevant to the environmental performance of the organisation and/or site.

Questionnaires may also be used to identify the environmental performance of suppliers, contractors and vendors. Increasingly there is a need to integrate their performance into your own assessment and this is particularly the case where organisations are committed to 'cradle to grave' responsibility for their products. Confidentiality is at the heart of such questionnaires although they are likely to be more general and less extensive than pre-audit questionnaires. They will enquire about environmental policies, environmental management systems and the results of environmental reviews and audits carried out. Although they will be somewhat different in their scope and coverage, the general principles relating to questionnaire design and delivery outlined here remain the same.

AUDIT REPORTS

After the practical part of an environmental review or environmental audit has been completed there is a need to prepare the final report and to present this to senior management. The report should begin with an executive summary which lists the key findings, the priority areas for action and highlights achievements which have been made.

In the main body of the report, findings and recommended actions need to be prioritised and this should be done by reference to the original objectives and environmental policy of the firm. If the findings indicate that the organisation is failing to meet required standards or not adhering to legislation then this should be a top priority. Recommended actions should be defined in terms of short-term, medium-term and long-term time scales and details should be provided as to how these actions should be implemented.

With the agreement of senior management, the report, or a summary of it, should be published and distributed to employees and shareholders and any interested parties external to the firm (consumers, local residents, the media, etc.). Although very few companies have, as yet, published their environmental audits, there are some notable exceptions which include the Norwegian firm Norsk Hydro, Noranda of Canada, the Dutch company BSO/Origin, The Body Shop and British Airways.

The format of the report is likely to be as follows:

1. Executive summary
   - General issues
   - Positive and negative factors
   - General risk assessment and identification of high-risk activities
   - Recommendations

2. Introduction
   - Site description
   - Operating history
   - Process description

3. General environmental factors
   (a) Air
      - Emissions
      - Monitoring
      - Dispersion
   (b) Water
      - Supply source and quality
      - Water reuse
      - Sampling
      - Waste water
      - Collection and discharge
      - Stormwater
      - Ground water

   (c) Land
      - Storage

- Spill control measures
- Waste disposal (see also waste management)

(d) Noise
- Measurement
- Control
- Complaints
- Protection

4. Waste Management
- Sources
- Disposal methods
- On-site treatment
- Off-site disposal and reclamation
- Waste storage
- Analysis and monitoring
- Paper and packaging policies
- Recycling

5. Energy Efficiency
- Sources of energy
- Potential energy savings
- Alternative energy sources

6. Technology
- Description of technology and processes
- Clean technology
- Maintenance programmes

7. Health and safety

8. Fire control and emergency procedures

9. Special substances

10. Non-adherence to standards or legal deficiencies

11. Recommendations and costings
    Priority 1 Factors where there is a strong probability of an incident which requires urgent and effective action or where the company is acting illegally.
    Priority 2 Factors where there is a more remote probability of an environmental incident but which needs to be addressed in the course of new spending by the company.
    Priority 3 Factors which will not have immediate consequences for the firm but where the company will benefit in taking action either through reduced costs or through employee, customer and public relations.

THE EC FRAMEWORK FOR ENVIRONMENTAL AUDITING

Within the European Community countries, the environment has been protected by environmental impact legislation for a number of years but the European Commission only became actively involved in preparing a Directive on environmental auditing in the early 1990s. Commission discussion papers suggested Directives covering the following requirements:

- ensuring that companies carry out periodic environmental audits of industrial activities which have a potentially significant impact on the environment;
- verification of the audits by independent registered organisations; and
- the disclosure of audit information to relevant authorities and to the public.

In the Netherlands, the concept of environmental auditing has been known since 1984, although Dutch subsidiaries of American-owned firms had used the technique before then. The Confederation of Dutch Industries promotes environmental management within companies, encouraging interaction between government and industry and providing guidelines. Environmental auditing in the Netherlands is largely confined to the largest of industries but the Dutch expect that good practice by large, successful firms will be emulated by small and medium-sized firms. In the Dutch Shell group, the requirements for environmental auditing vary but the general principles have been published. Shell regularly conducts health, safety and environmental audits worldwide for agrochemicals formulation and environmental audits of oil and gas explorations take place every three years. Partial internal audits of plants takes place annually with a full external audit taking place every three to five years.

In Norway, factories are required to establish and maintain an internal environmental control system, supervised by a government agency. Environmental auditing is not legally required but a number of companies practise environmental auditing on a voluntary basis. Within the Norwegian company Norsk Hydro, every major installation is audited once every two years, lasting between three and five days in each case. Norsk Hydro is well known for its policy of publishing the results of its environmental audits.

In the UK, the CBI has published a set of environmental auditing guidelines. These stress the practicalities of undertaking an environmental audit and stress the need to implement audit recommendations and continue monitoring processes. The UK Labour Party has stated in its programme for a greener environment that it believes that environmental auditing should be made compulsory within EC company law.

The number of companies operating audit programmes in the European Community will grow whether or not environmental auditing legislation is implemented. Demands from groups such as environmentalists or local communities will lead to pressure on companies not only to undertake environmental audits but also to disclose the results of those audits. The increase in auditing activity is also likely to lead to more standardisation of auditing practice and environmental standards. However, without the development of an overall integrated environmental management system, environmental auditing will be a mere palliative.

The European eco-management and audit scheme

While the first stance of the Environment Directorate of the EC has always been to encourage firms to improve standards of environmental performance without waiting for regulation there is nevertheless a growing amount of European environmental legislation. Moreover, the EC has been keen to establish common environmental standards and systems for environmental reporting. One such system is embedded in the eco-management and audit regulation.

At the end of 1991 the European Commission approved a proposal for a Council Regulation to establish a European Community eco-management and audit scheme which would be open for voluntary participation by industrial companies. The Regulation was published in March 1992. The eco-management and audit scheme provides a framework for companies to think ahead, assess their own environmental impacts and commit themselves to a policy of reducing them. It also encourages firms to keep the public informed by regularly making statements and reporting progress. At the present time the eco-management and audit scheme is voluntary and administered by individual Member States but many expect the scheme to become compulsory for larger firms in time and the Council has retained the right to introduce compulsory registration. Member States themselves also have the right to adopt a compulsory registration scheme for certain industrial categories if they feel this is beneficial.

The objective of the eco-management and audit scheme is to promote improvements in the environmental performance of industry by encouraging companies to:

● establish and implement environmental protection schemes;
● carry out regular, systematic and objective evaluations of the environmental performance of these systems;
● provide information about environmental performance to the public.

The purpose of the scheme is not to confirm compliance with legislative requirements (although this must be achieved), nor is it aimed at awarding best practice or performance. The scheme aims to recognise efforts to improve environmental performance over time given a baseline established by an environmental review of the firm. The scheme highlights the need for a continuous cycle of improvement.

In order to join the eco-management and audit scheme a firm has to adopt and adhere to an eco-audit cycle (see Figure 6.2). Essentially this requires the firm to:

● define an environmental policy, based on an overall review of the environmental impacts of its activities;

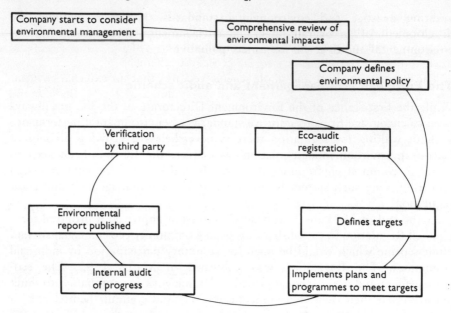

Figure 6.2 The European eco-audit cycle

- set targets for achievement within a set time;
- put into place plans and systems to achieve these targets and include provisions for the constant monitoring of these;
- periodically audit to assess progress;
- report the audit findings to the public and have these findings verified by a third party; and
- set new targets for further progress and repeat the procedure.

There is a need to establish systems based on the environmental review which:

- assess and manage the environmental impact of the activities;
- manage the use of energy, raw materials and water;
- minimise waste;
- consider the selection and design of products and processes;
- prevent accidents;
- include staff in consultation and provide motivation and training;
- inform and involve the public.

Essentially, the audit assesses this system and evaluates performance in relation to the environmental review and the operation of the system as defined and documented. The results of the audit have to be considered by senior management and any necessary revisions to the company policy, objectives, targets, action plans and systems made. All of these steps can be internal to the company if there is sufficient expertise available to perform the various tasks adequately. Indeed, the intention of the eco-management and audit scheme is that the discipline of having to follow these steps should help the company better manage its own environmental performance. However, there are important external aspects to the eco-audit scheme.

The eco-management and audit scheme requires that an external environmental statement is prepared based on the findings of the audit or initial review. Validation of this statement must be made by an external accredited environmental verifier (AEV). The validation will confirm that the statement has covered all of the environmental issues relevant to the site in enough detail and that the information presented is reliable. The validation process involves the examination of relevant documentation, including information about the site, its activities, a description of the environmental management system and details and findings of the environmental review or audit. This would normally be followed by an inspection visit to the site and preparation of a verifiers report.

In order to join the eco-management and audit scheme a company has to be able to demonstrate that this sequence of events has taken place, and that sensible targets have been set towards which the firm should make progress. The approved independent and accredited environmental verifier will have checked that the audit process was carried out properly and that the environmental report is a true and fair view of the company's environmental performance. Application can subsequently be made for inclusion in the eco-audit register of companies. On submission of the validated external statement and supporting documentation, the company is entitled to use an eco-management and audit logo in relation to all its participating sites.

In order to continue to be eco-management and audit registered companies have to continue the eco-management and audit cycle and maintain commitment to improving environmental performance. Any lapse will result in the removal of a company's name from the register.

CONCLUSION

In the early 1990s when we experienced a rapid growth in environmental awareness in industry, it was the environmental audit which was seen as the first great step towards improving environmental performance. Many companies boasted about the fact that they had had an environmental audit. Because of developments such as the introduction of BS7750, businesses are coming to realise that it is the environmental management system which should be at the centre of the organisation and that environmental auditing is an integral part of that system. The environmental audit checks not only compliance and measures environmental improvements, but also checks the effectiveness of the system itself. What we mean by an environmental audit and how it is implemented is also becoming clearer and the key difference between a review and an audit needs to be clearly recognised.

There are still too many firms, however, who having undertaken an environmental review, call it an environmental audit (as their consultants may have told them) and then claim to be an environmentally conscious firm. Conscious, they might be but effective they will not be. As with so much of environmental management, the audit has to be an ongoing process which never ends. The key role of the audit must be to check and assess all the other activities of the firm in relation to environmental improvement. European Community moves to standardise the auditing process and an encouragement to publish audit reports is to be welcomed, but auditing is a technique which is still in its infancy and there is much scope for experimentation. This is particularly so in the area of measuring environmental performance.

CHAPTER 7

Waste minimisation and life-cycle assessment: issues for product and process design

The links between the disposal or emission of the by-products of industrial production and environmental damage are fundamental; waste and environmental degradation are synonymous. The challenge to industry, as set out by mounting social and environmental pressures and ever more stringent legislation, is to minimise its impact on the environment through changes in its products and how they are produced. At all stages, the design of products and processes must incorporate the environmental perspective to work towards the goal of waste minimisation.

The by-products of production which constitute waste can take many forms, whether as gaseous, liquid or solid wastes. However, they have a wider dimension than the tangible measures of waste which are normally reported. It is not only the losses of materials and energy that occur as a result of production and use, but also that waste which comes about through the inefficient utilisation of materials and energy.

Increases in efficiency and the associated decreases in waste output are key factors which conspire to encourage industry to minimise its environmental impact. Waste is not only an environmental problem but also a very significant business problem. Whether due to the inherent value of resources which may be under utilised, sent up a chimney or down a pipe, or due to the costs and liabilities imposed by legislation seeking to address the environmental problem, the formulation of a company-level waste management strategy is central to efficient business management. Effective waste management not only avoids significant input and disposal costs and liabilities, but through the creation of new market opportunities can offer notable revenue generating potential.

Approaches to waste management are therefore of the utmost importance for the continuing viability of both business and the environment. However, it is important to define exactly what waste is, who produces it and how it can be managed in order to develop strategies to minimise its effects. The management of waste within the productive unit and up and down the supply chain through the application of life-cycle assessment is therefore a fundamental prerequisite of environmental protection.

HE WASTE PROBLEM

Waste presents a fundamental challenge to the quality of the environment. This challenge is manifested in a number of ways: through the unsustainable depletion of natural resources, the by-products of the production process and the waste created by consumers during and after the use of the output of industrial activity.

It cannot be denied that in some cases the environment is capable of providing renewable resources and accepting large quantities of waste and rendering them harmless without itself being affected. In relation to sustainability it is therefore acceptable to use resources and to dispose of waste to the environment in some circumstances. However, the level of demand for non-renewable resources and the impact of waste emissions on the assimilative capacity of the environment indicate that we have exceeded the levels of consumption and waste generation that the global environment can sustain. Throughout the world, due to the escalating demand for natural resources and the production of waste, mineral, agricultural, forest and marine resources are being more rapidly depleted than ever before and habitats are being contaminated or destroyed. The pressure to maximise the efficiency of production and to minimise the level of waste generation is mounting.

Throughout western economies, the shift away from volume towards value production has decreased the level of raw material consumption and waste production per unit of income generated. However, overall increases in income and consumption have negated any environmental benefits that this increase in relative efficiency may have produced. Furthermore, structural change in the global economy has included a flow of manufacturing industry from the First World to the Third World. It is therefore clear that any increases in environmental efficiency in western economies has not been sufficient and that greater effort is needed.

At the company level, companies can work to further break down the relationship between the scale of their production and the environmental impact of their activities. In order to achieve sustainability, the emphasis of industrial activity must be directed towards providing the services that are demanded from their goods and not necessarily the goods themselves. To offer an example, when purchasing a car, the consumer demands a mode of transport with a combination of characteristics such as convenience, speed, safety and style. The consumer does not demand the car itself, but the services which it provides, and these services could be offered with a considerably lower environmental impact.

Such a subtle change in outlook would encourage the provision of the services demanded by the consumer with the minimum environmental impact at all stages in a product's life. Products and the ways in which they are produced must become environmentally benign through the application of waste minimisation techniques. Such an approach to the waste problem has significant financial as well as environmental advantages. The challenge that faces industrialists, environmentalists and legislators alike is to ensure that such mutual interests are translated into action.

THE LAW RELATING TO WASTE

Before moving on to discuss the practicalities of the waste management strategy, it is important to understand the legal framework of waste management within which companies must operate. Such legislation, whether explicitly or implicitly relating to waste, increases the costs and liabilities of waste disposal and hence drives the need for effective waste management. Legislation relating to the handling, transportation and treatment of waste has a long history and has emanated both from the EC and the governments of the Member States for many years.

European Community policies on waste are founded on the 1975 Framework Directive on Waste (EC Directive 75/442). Very generally, the Directive requires that waste is disposed of in a way that does not present a risk to human health or the environment. The original Directive has now been replaced by the 1991 Framework Directive on Waste (EC Directive 91/156) which is based on the 1989 EC policy document 'A Community Strategy for Waste Management'. This sets out two main aims, namely to encourage waste minimisation (waste avoidance, reduction, reuse and recycling) through the adoption of clean technologies, and to encourage national and EC self-sufficiency in waste management.

Under the general objectives of the 1991 Framework Directive on Waste, the EC has developed a number of more specific Directives which affect company waste management procedures. These include Directives on integrated pollution prevention and control, hazardous waste and its incineration, liability for damage caused by waste, recycling of packaging wastes and freedom of access to environmental information. These measures are addressed within the following discussion of waste management legislation.

In the UK, the adoption of the 1991 EC Framework Directive on Waste had largely been anticipated under the 1990 Environmental Protection Act (EPA). Under the terms of subsidiarity, the aims of EC Directives are made more specific within the national legislation of each Member State. Thus the EPA and its associated regulations provide the mechanisms and definitions through which the EC's aims are applied in the UK.

Before moving on to discuss UK waste management policy, it is important to discuss the legislative definitions of waste. While waste is generally perceived as an unwanted by-product disposed of to some environmental medium (i.e. land, water or air), it can take many forms. Generally, however, the term waste in relation to legislation refers to solid wastes. For all but the largest polluters, other forms of waste (i.e. emissions to air and water) in the UK are dealt with in separate sections of legislation and at present by different regulatory authorities. However, under the demands of Integrated Pollution Control currently set out by the UK EPA, large industrial producers are required to view waste in terms of all three environmental media. They are then obliged to pick the 'best practicable environmental option' (BPEO) to minimise the overall environmental impact. The UK system of IPC will be replicated in coming years by the EC's Integrated Pollution Prevention Control Directive; the principles of BPEO are therefore likely to be more widely applied throughout Europe in the future.

Even under the narrower heading of solid wastes, legislation offers a range of definitions for the different natures of waste arising. In general terms, the UK EPA defines (solid) waste as:

> any substance which constitutes a scrap material or an effluent, or other unwanted surplus substance arising from the application of a process and any substance or article which requires to be disposed of as being broken, worn out, contaminated or otherwise spoiled.

In the UK there are three main classifications of waste which fall under this more general definition, namely controlled waste (as defined by the EPA), special waste and hazardous waste (as defined by the 1974 Control of Pollution Act).

- Controlled waste constitutes any household, commercial and industrial solid waste with the exception of explosives, agricultural and mining wastes.
- Special waste relates to any waste which is dangerous or difficult to handle, transport or treat so that special provisions are needed for its management if human life is not to be threatened. Assessment of special waste is founded on measures of toxicity, corrosiveness and flashpoint, and is based on a list of substances which meet certain measures of these criteria.
- Hazardous waste characteristics relate very closely to those of special wastes, and often refer to wastes which are transported across national boundaries and are thus subject to international conventions such as Basel Convention on the Control of the Transfrontier Movements of Hazardous Wastes and their Disposal.

Under the 'Duty of Care' regulations introduced by the EPA, any individual or company which produces, holds or is otherwise concerned with controlled waste (with the exception of household waste produced from the home) is responsible for its safe passage through the waste disposal chain to its ultimate safe disposal. Each party must ensure that all reasonable measures are taken to prevent any unauthorised or harmful deposit, treatment or disposal of the waste for which they are responsible.

Under the requirements of the Duty of Care, companies and managers within them are liable to fines and prison sentences should they fail to fulfil their legal obligations in the waste disposal chain. Penalties are considerably greater should the waste in question be classified as special waste. Such criminal liabilities are applied by the state to those who illegally damage the welfare of society. However, the law goes further than the application of criminal liability alone. The EPA imposes civil liability in respect of any person who deposits, causes or permits unlicensed waste disposal or if the waste for which they are responsible causes damage to the environment or to human health. The imposition of civil liability establishes a system whereby those responsible for waste will be liable to bear the costs of any damage caused by that waste. Any affected civil party (which may be an individual or a group of individuals rather than the state or its representative as under criminal law) can then claim in Court for the costs inflicted upon them by the illegal management of waste under the terms of the EPA. This is in line with the proposed EC Directive on Civil Liability for Damage Caused by Waste. This Directive imposes strict liability for damage caused by waste where liabilities are assigned regardless of fault. It is therefore considerably more potent than current UK legislation. The legal (and hence financial) penalties for mistakes in the waste management chain are therefore becoming ever more significant.

The application of civil liability for damage caused by waste is a clear attempt to pass back some of the costs of the environmental damage caused by waste to those responsible for creating that waste. The increased use of financial instruments, such as regulatory charges, landfill levies, fines and the application of strict liability to some extent are all practical manifestations of the 'polluter pays' principle.

In the UK, the inception of the EPA and the Duty of Care, coupled with the application of civil liability for damage caused by waste, imposes a considerable responsibility on all parties in the waste disposal chain. As a result, the enforcement of these laws throughout the waste management chain in alliance with the decreasing availability of waste disposal routes will ensure that the costs of waste disposal will continue to rise. Future legislative developments, such as the wider adoption of the German Packaging Ordinance (see Chapter 8), are likely to supplement current laws to increase these obligations still further.

Additionally, the EC Directive on Freedom of Access to Environmental Information and the requirements included under the EPA for public registers of polluters will enable greater public and media scrutiny of a firm's waste management performance. Clear links have been established between environmental incidents and the associated loss of reputation, reductions in market share and sharp falls in share price values. Greater access to information on the environmental performance of companies will aid the enforcement of criminal and civil liabilities now in place and will magnify the consequences of inadequacies in waste management.

Consequently, managers with environmental responsibilities are now responsible for the entire reputation of their firm. Those companies which are most able to minimise the amount of waste that is subject to the array of waste management legislation will avoid significant costs, liabilities and threats to their reputation. An effective waste management strategy is a clear way of addressing these fundamental environmental and therefore business issues.

THE BENEFITS OF THE WASTE MANAGEMENT STRATEGY

In recent years many companies have revealed a clear change in behaviour relating to the issue of waste. In general, the emphasis of dealing with the by-products of industrial activity has changed from one of waste disposal to one of waste management and waste minimisation. The view of waste as something to be discarded has shifted to one where by-products should be reduced, reused and recycled through a variety of means designed to minimise both the financial losses to the company and the environmental risk and impact of its activities. This philosophy forms the basis of the waste management strategy.

Such a change in outlook has been driven by two central pressures. Firstly, increasing legislative demands relating to waste disposal and liability for damage caused to the environment by waste have ensured that higher standards of waste disposal and risk management are more widely adopted. Secondly, there has been an increasing realisation of the escalating disposal costs and of the loss of potentially valuable resources in waste. These factors have driven increased waste management efficiency for purely economic reasons.

It is important to recognise that waste management is not a new field. In the majority of manufacturing processes, reduction, reuse and recycling have taken place automatically for many years. This has been an activity linked more with common sense than with any desire for improved environmental performance. It is only recently that such measures have been recognised as having concomitant environmental benefits. The boundaries between established practice in product design and process engineering and environmental management strategies are therefore far from distinct.

A closer look at the benefits of effective waste management reveals a range of reasons why firms should integrate waste minimisation measures into their more traditional business strategies. Of course the primary reason must be that there are clear environmental, health and safety benefits associated with reduced waste flows. However, there are also a range of financial benefits which will accrue through the waste management strategy.

As energy and raw materials become more expensive, waste minimisation incentives increase accordingly. However, while the last decade or so has seen generally low or falling energy and primary product prices, incentives to reduce raw material usage have also decreased. Even so, the spread of waste minimisation programmes such as 3M's PPP (Pollution Prevention Pays) programme, or Dow's WRAP (Waste Reduction Always Pays) scheme, suggest that the benefits of effective waste management remain even while industrial inputs are relatively inexpensive. A general long-term, upward trend in energy and raw materials prices can, however, be expected, a trend which will be reflected in the associated benefits of efficient waste management.

As has been discussed, as acceptable waste disposal routes decline due to legislative, social and environmental pressures, disposal costs will increase. A waste management strategy will minimise the impact of these rising costs on the financial performance of the firm. Proactively addressing the increasing legislative pressures will integrate present and future compliance levels into the design of the technologies and techniques applied. This will be less expensive than a reactive approach where technologies and techniques will have to be revised in order to comply with legal obligations.

Apart from the costs of raw materials, waste disposal and legislative compliance, there are a number of less obvious costs of waste management within the firm. These include those costs relating to the identification, separation, collection, monitoring, handling, storage, transportation and administration of the waste stream, the necessary health and safety measures and the associated environmental risks and liabilities. As legal obligations extend, so will the costs of resources such as these which will be needed to comply with waste management laws. This is particularly evident under the Duty of Care obligations set out under the UK 1990 Environmental Protection Act.

In addition to minimising the costs of waste management, the waste management strategy will reveal areas of revenue generating potential. A systematic assessment of the wastes generated, for instance by drawing up a waste inventory, may reveal opportunities to reuse or recycle waste materials within the company or may identify external markets for the waste. Particularly for larger companies with a diversity of production interests, many of the wastes which cannot be reused in one plant or process may be used in other existing processes. The waste management strategy may therefore suggest new areas of utilisation for waste materials within other areas of the company or may reveal the potential for selling waste products as a raw material to other industries. This may not be the case for small- and medium-sized enterprises, although a local authority waste inventory will aid both economic and environmental development at a regional level.

In the process of developing waste minimisation solutions in one company, lessons will be learned and technologies developed which may have potential for transfer to other companies in a similar position. The increased costs and expenditures of environmental protection in one company are reflected by increased revenues in another – environmental protection is a zero-sum game. The scale of the market for clean technologies and environmental protection skills throughout the world is such that the transfer of clean technologies and techniques may be a very considerable benefit arising through the adoption of an effective waste management strategy.

It is important to recognise that it is not only the day-to-day reductions in impact that are important but also the reduction of risks and liabilities. The main environmental impacts associated with particular companies have come about due to accidents rather than the overall impact of their activities (for example Union Carbide in Bhopal, Exxon in Alaska, Sandoz in Basel). While these incidents were publicised around the world, at the local level most areas also have a perceived 'environmental ogre'. For companies involved in an environmental accident, the costs of clean up, fines and compensation are frequently considerable. Following an environmental accident, regardless of the response of the company, once an irresponsible image has been established, the first impression associated with a company judged to have caused an environmental accident will be negative. This will affect the behaviour of customers, suppliers, employees, financiers, regulators and the surrounding communities. Apart from the health, safety and environmental benefits therefore, the entire company stakeholder and marketing image may rely on the achievements of the waste management strategy.

Finally, it should be recognised that generally the financial benefits of good waste management accrue within the firm and that until recently the marketing benefits of being a 'clean and green' company were marginal. As industry and consumer awareness of environmental issues and the opportunities to communicate good environmental performance increase, for instance through BS7750, the EC's eco-management and audit and eco-label schemes (see Chapter 8), then the marketing and stakeholder benefits of the waste management strategy become more available. The range of benefits that are available to firms which develop effective waste management strategies is displayed in Figure 7.1.

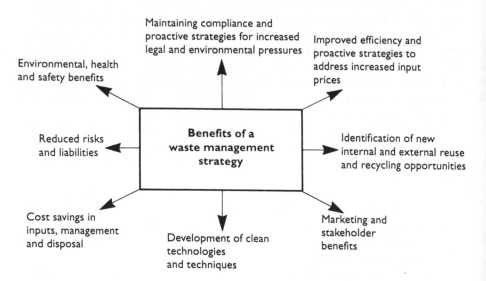

Figure 7.1 The benefits of a waste management strategy

IMPLEMENTING THE WASTE MANAGEMENT STRATEGY

In order for the benefits of the waste management strategy to be achieved, it is important that general objectives are set, that current levels of performance are established through a waste management review and that strategies are formulated through which performance can be improved and the objectives realised. The company must commit itself to an ongoing process of improvement in waste management, the performance of both production systems and waste management systems must be periodically measured through a waste management audit to aid a continuous cycle of improvement.

It is important to stress that the waste management strategy is just one component of the wider environmental management strategy. An integrated approach to environmental management within the firm is vital if the full benefits of the exercise are to be achieved, both in terms of increased business performance and improved environmental performance. However, as the generation of waste is such a fundamental component of the overall strategy, particular attention is necessary. While offering greater detail in this area, the waste management strategy as discussed below should be developed in parallel with the more general environmental management strategy.

Waste reduction may be in terms of process, product or packaging wastes. However, as the benefits of waste reduction in product and packaging waste are at present external to most companies, the objectives of the waste management strategy usually focus on process and internal (plant) waste management. It is certain in some areas, at least, that life-cycle assessment, product stewardship and packaging legislation will change the horizons of the waste management strategy to include the environmental impacts of the firm's activities outside of the factory gate.

The objectives of waste management

The ultimate aim of the waste management strategy must be to avoid the generation of any waste products. So that this may be achieved, in order of priority, the objectives of the waste management strategy should be to reduce the creation of waste, to reuse the waste products generated in their current form or to recycle them into a form where they are reusable. It is only after all technically and economically feasible options in these areas have been exhausted that the strategy should resort to recovering any value from the waste, for instance through waste-to-energy schemes, and finally rendering the waste safe before ultimate disposal. The general objectives of the waste management strategy are illustrated in Figure 7.2.

The waste management review

To achieve the objectives of waste management, it is necessary to adopt a holistic approach to the apparently unwanted or unrecoverable by-products of

Figure 7.2 Ranking waste management objectives

production. This will require a restructuring of both production and management systems. It is therefore vital that senior managers are conversant with the potential benefits of waste management and offer their support to the general objectives displayed in Figure 7.2. Given that managers are able to work toward medium- to long-term objectives in the absence of short-term performance or cash flow pressures, then securing managerial commitment should not be difficult. This may necessitate an educational phase which reveals the tangible benefits of waste management to the decision-makers within the company.

The process of waste minimisation must begin with a review of the current performance of the company. An initial review of waste management procedures should highlight areas with potential for waste reduction and will provide a baseline against which future performance can be measured.

Undertaking a review of current waste management performance has both internal and external applications. For regulatory reasons alone, many companies must make detailed assessments of their waste generation and the measures adopted to improve their performance in this area. Undertaking a review of waste management will thus assist in the achievement of regulatory requirements and will offer security of knowledge to managers that compliance is being achieved. The review should also include an assessment of the financial implications of waste management, both in relation to operational costs and exposure to risk. This aspect of the review may be used to secure the commitment of management and other stakeholders to the specific measures which are necessary components of an ongoing programme for waste minimisation.

The waste management review will follow a similar methodology to that of the more general environmental review as discussed in Chapter 4. It will, however, offer greater depth of study, and to this end it should include two specific stages: namely, the analysis of the inputs to the production process, of the process itself, and of its outputs.

Inputs

In order to develop a comprehensive waste management review, it is necessary to assess the nature of the raw material and energy inputs utilised in the production process. A number of elements should be considered. Establishing an inventory of inputs will facilitate the development of baseline data in relation to the efficiency with which inputs are converted to outputs. The use of such conversion efficiencies will indicate the level of waste generated and can therefore act as a performance measure for specific inputs. It will also provide a baseline against which alternative inputs can be assessed.

In relation to the nature of inputs, a number of criteria must be addressed. These criteria are displayed in Table 7.1.

It therefore becomes clear that when assessing the inputs to a production process, an integrated approach is necessary whereby the impact of the input at all stages throughout the production facility is considered. It also becomes apparent that it is impossible to separate product and process design. The choice of raw material is a key component of both process and product design, and should be assessed in relation to wider horizons than the production facility alone. Ideally, raw materials should be assessed from 'cradle to grave' through the application of life-cycle assessment as discussed below.

Table 7.1 Criteria for the assessment of raw materials

- Is the raw material renewable?
- Is the raw material recycled?
- Is the raw material ultimately reusable?
- Is the raw material ultimately recyclable?
- Is it possible to substitute high-quality raw materials for lower grade inputs which meet the desired performance standards?
- Is the input supplied in a form which is instantly usable?
- Has the quality of inputs been assessed in relation to output defects and therefore waste generation?
- Are toxic or hazardous inputs only used where there are no alternatives?
- Are inputs which produce toxic or hazardous wastes only used where there are no alternatives?
- If the quality of raw materials degrades with time, can the ordering schedule be altered to minimise waste?
- Does the company practise stock rotation in order to minimise wastage?
- If the nature of the output varies with time, can the ordering schedule be altered to minimise waste?
- Are local suppliers used wherever possible?
- Can the packaging of the raw material be reduced and returned to the supplier?

Inputs should be chosen in relation to their environmental impact, to the renewability of their extraction, and their ability to be reused and recycled. Both financial and environmental benefits may be realised if lower grade raw materials can be used without affecting the quality of the end product. Inputs should also be assessed in relation to the form in which they are supplied. If changes are necessary, for instance to alter the shape of the input in order to feed it into the production process, then it will be necessary to commit resources to carry out this transformation. From both a financial and environmental point of view, it may be beneficial if the supplier can be persuaded to supply the raw material in a form in which it can be used without any transformation.

It is necessary to assess the quality of inputs so that suppliers can be encouraged to reduce defects and therefore wastage. It is important to establish quality control measures for raw material inputs as any defects in raw materials will be the source of product defects later in the production process when extra time, energy and resources have been added. For quality and hence environmental management to be at their most effective, all defects must be identified and removed at source.

Wherever possible, the use of hazardous or toxic inputs should be avoided, as should inputs which generate hazardous or toxic emissions as waste. Substituting dangerous or damaging inputs will reduce control costs and risk within the plant and decrease the environmental impact of the product outside the plant.

Apart from input qualities, input quantities also dictate the level of resources which must be committed to storage (handling, transportation, space, lighting, heating, etc.). These resources may be reduced if the quantities and frequency of delivery are altered to coincide with demand. If it is necessary to maintain stocks of raw materials, stock rotation will minimise wastage. This is particularly true should the raw material be perishable or unstable.

If the nature of the output alters, for instance if the company undertakes batch production, ordering inputs only when they are definitely needed will reduce the level of waste. Adopting the principles of just-in-time management will help to minimise raw material wastage and may serve to encourage the use of local suppliers thereby minimising the financial and environmental implications of distribution.

Finally, inputs must be assessed in relation to any packaging wastes that they generate. As in many cases the supplier delivers the raw material input, it may be particularly attractive to return packaging waste to the supplier so that it can be reused. Again this will reduce the level of wastes to be disposed of and will also reduce the costs of supply.

Process design and management

Given that the raw materials have been selected and managed according to the criteria established above, attention must then focus on the process itself and any wastes that are generated. While many of the criteria will be process specific, there are, however, a number of general principles which can be applied in order to encourage the development of waste minimisation and these are outlined in Table 7.2.

It is vital that the manager knows the exact amount of raw materials entering the production process and that all wastes are monitored and recorded. Aside from aiding compliance with environmental and health and safety legislation, this will also allow measurements of conversion efficiency to be established. Over time conversion efficiencies will act as a measure of waste management performance. Also, by measuring the difference between the level of material inputs and outputs (both as products and as waste materials), an indication of the amount of waste that is not collected can be ascertained. The identification of emissions of this nature will ensure that all wastes generated can be accounted for and will hence protect the company from any liabilities that it may have been unaware of.

Unidentified releases may arise as a result of leakages or spillages which may appear to be very minor, however, over time they can lead to significant pollution problems (notably in the contamination of land and ground water) and a loss of valuable resources. Energy loss is a particularly important area as energy efficiency measures are easy to instal and can be extremely cost effective. All stages of the production process, including the building which houses the process, should be insulated against heat loss, and loss of energy through steam and air pressure leaks should be minimised. Energy efficiency should be closely monitored, and potential to recycle heat within the production process should be evaluated.

Table 7.2 Waste minimisation: process design and management objectives

- Establish the level of material and energy inputs into the process.
- Measure the material and energy outputs of the process.
- Generate process conversion efficiencies.
- Develop conversion efficiencies for individual components within the production process, including building energy management.
- Identify inefficient components and assess the potential for alternative technologies or techniques to fulfil the same objectives while producing lower or less hazardous levels of waste.
- Identify unrecovered waste emissions in relation to solids, liquids, gases, heat, light, noise, air pressure, steam, etc.
- Assess the potential to contain unrecovered wastes.
- Establish the value of the components of the waste stream.
- Evaluate the potential to segregate the flows of valuable wastes in order to minimise contamination and maximise the potential for reuse and recycling.
- Identify the scope to recover value from non-reusable and non-recyclable waste.
- Analyse potential for reductions in hazardous wastes and the overall volume of waste through on-site waste treatment.
- Ensure safe disposal of any remaining wastes.

By dividing the process into a number of components, a clearer picture of the areas of inefficiency can be established. This will then allow inefficient stages of production to be addressed. At each stage it is necessary to assess whether the minimum quantity or quality of resources are being used in order to provide the desired services. The over-specification of machinery and materials is also a major source of inefficiency. It is therefore necessary to specify the characteristics demanded of both materials and machinery in relation to the demands that must be placed upon them and then ensure that each component is operating to the levels of its specification.

Once the process itself is operating to its full efficiency, the waste stream should then be analysed. This analysis should identify the wastes collected and whether or not they are in a condition to provide a reusable resource within the plant. The potential for the segregation of waste streams to avoid mixing and contamination must also be studied. Waste treatment and recovery procedures must also be assessed, along with their potential to provide reusable or resaleable materials or wastes which are either less harmful or are cheaper to dispose of.

Where all options for reduction and reuse of materials and energy within the plant are economically exhausted, the waste management review should evaluate the disposal routes in operation for the remaining wastes. This must be carried out in relation to solid, gaseous and liquid wastes, and in all areas relevant consents and compliance with legislation must be ensured. Waste disposal practices should also apply the principles of Integrated Pollution Control and select the 'best practicable environmental option' for disposal. Under EPA and health and safety legislation, waste disposal practices should also include an assessment of appropriate handling, storage and record-keeping obligations.

Finally, it should again be emphasised that it is not only actual failure that should be highlighted by the waste audit, but also the risks of potential failure. Should the waste audit focus solely on the normal working practices of the plant to the exclusion of the abnormal practices, a major element of industrial crisis, health and safety violation and environmental degradation will not be addressed. The waste audit must therefore include some element of risk assessment and suggested measures for risk management and reduction through an assessment of day-to-day operational management and emergency procedures.

The results of the waste management review must then be extrapolated to offer a financial review of the waste management practices of the firm in order to establish the true costs of current waste management performance. The waste management review will thus present a baseline (both physical and financial) against which to compare future performance. The results of the review must then be integrated with the wider environmental and business strategies of the organisation.

The waste management review should highlight a number of areas where action is necessary. Issues of non-compliance can be prioritised so that risks to the environment, the company, its employees and the surrounding communities are reduced before seeking to improve performance more generally.

The most efficient process design will facilitate the management of waste at all stages within the process. This will allow the optimal input mix and the integration of more efficient alternative technologies. It will also allow the segregation of wastes at source, thus avoiding the mixing of wastes and their subsequent contamination and will aid the collection and treatment of all non-reusable and recyclable wastes. This necessitates a move away from the conventional output-oriented (end of pipe) production process and toward the preventative input-oriented (along the pipe) production process which seeks to combine production goals with the minimisation of inputs into the process through the waste minimisation strategy. The two approaches are depicted within Figure 7.3.

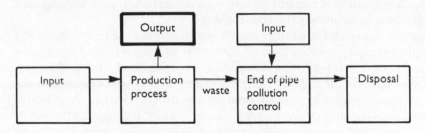

Figure 7.3(a) Output-oriented production process

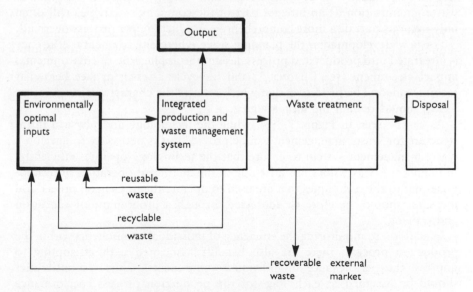

Figure 7.3(b) Input-oriented production process

Under the output-oriented approach, inputs are ordered without assessment of environmental impact before, during or after the material has passed through the production process. The production process then manufactures an output and generates waste. This waste is then captured by add on pollution control technologies and disposed of in accordance with environmental legislation.

Under the input-oriented approach, the production and waste generation processes are approached in a more integrated way. Inputs are assessed in relation to the criteria presented in Table 7.1 and are introduced to a production process that complies with the points set out in Table 7.2. Thus, reusable and recyclable wastes are segregated and re-introduced into the production process. The remainder of the waste is treated, any recoverable value, for instance through waste-to-energy incineration, is either re-introduced into the production process or passed on to external markets. It should be noted that even if waste is given away, waste disposal costs are avoided. Any waste that remains must then be rendered harmless and disposed of in the most environmentally efficient way.

The waste management strategy should aim to develop the technologies and techniques necessary to move from an output- to an input-oriented production facility. However, for existing companies, an integrated 'along the pipe' solution as displayed in Figure 7.3(b) is a longer-term goal constrained in the short- to medium-term by existing product and process designs. As a result, improved product and process design (from a waste management point of view) are normally carried out as a matter of course upon the productive or legislative obsolescence of existing equipment or, in marketing terms, at the end of the product's life cycle. For economic reasons, therefore, designing-in waste minimisation as an integral part of the company's activities will often only occur as part of a more comprehensive product and/or process overhaul.

For new developments, the planning stage where environmental efficiency is integrated into product and process design, the application of environmental impact assessment (see Chapter 3) and life-cycle assessment (see below) is recommended. The process design which reflects the characteristics of Figure 7.3(b) should remain the ultimate goal.

As can be seen in Figure 7.3(b), while the technology and physical infra-structure for waste management can be provided, it is necessary to develop a waste management system to ensure that the technology operates efficiently. In many cases waste does not arise due to the inefficient operation of techno-logies but to the techniques that are used to operate them. General procedural measures should therefore be addressed through a programme of education and training.

In addition to monitoring the efficiency of individual components within the production process, there are also benefits associated with attempting to improve the performance of individual components. Thus responsibilities should be assigned at each stage of the production process, performance measures should be published and recognition offered for improved efficiency.

The use of incentive and suggestion schemes will help to involve all staff in the improvement of environmental performance. Team-building exercises for each component will help to motivate staff to improve operational as well as environmental performance. It is once the process is operating to its maximum efficiency that the more fundamental measures relating to waste management can be addressed.

The collection of quantitative performance statistics through the waste management review will offer a baseline for future comparison and aid the target-setting process. Conversion efficiencies can be adjusted to reveal increases in reuse, recycling and recovery, and decreases in final waste disposal. It is important that performance measures are easily understandable, and that staff are aware of the ways in which they can improve their performance. Management systems must be developed to monitor progress and to work towards targets.

Therefore, by highlighting problems and potential, the waste management review acts as the catalyst for change in waste management procedures. Once the results of the review have been assessed, objectives set and management structures developed, it is necessary to undertake regular waste management audits in order to monitor progress. The waste management audit will follow a similar pattern to the more general environmental audit as discussed in Chapter 6.

While the waste management review and the following waste management strategy provide essential services for a company, focusing on the plant alone provides a constrained image of waste performance. It neglects any analysis of the wider implications of the firm's activities, for instance those up and down the supply chain external to the plant. Such an obligation to minimise the damage caused at all stages of a product's life (i.e. product stewardship) is beginning to be more widely applied than in certain specialist areas such as the manufacture and treatment of chemicals. The process of establishing comprehensively what the impact of a product may be and therefore how it may best be addressed is the role of life-cycle assessment.

ASSESSING THE TOTAL WASTE IMPACT

This is an era where prices will more realistically reflect the value of a natural resource and where the principles of 'polluter pays' and product stewardship are set to become more widely adopted. Effective environmental management cannot therefore start when the raw material is delivered and end when the final product is dispatched through the factory gate. The process of life-cycle assessment (LCA) aims to collate and analyse the information with which the environmental management system expands its outlook in response to these wider demands.

In attempts to ensure the environmental integrity of raw or semi-finished materials as they enter into production, certain companies have tried to assess the environmental impact of their demand for material inputs. The information that such an assessment provides will help to alter company purchasing policies to minimise the total environmental impact of the company. Such an assessment has included analysis of the source of the raw material, the sustainability or otherwise of its extraction, processing, packaging and transportation. It therefore seeks to identify the total environmental impact of the company's demand for raw materials. Such an assessment has normally been carried out through the use of a questionnaire issued to all companies who must offer this information if they are to be accepted as a potential supplier.

The use of supplier questionnaires is becoming more common, and is mainly applied by larger environmentally proactive companies who, alongside the more traditional product quality and price characteristics, demand good environmental performance from their suppliers. In recent years, the diffusion of improved environmental performance has been significantly stimulated through the heightened environmental demands placed on suppliers by a number of large companies. This is a trend which is set to continue as environmental pressures and awareness mount.

As with the spread of quality management and its assessment through standards such as BS5750 or ISO 9000, it is the larger companies and authorities who are most able to afford such measures and who will consequently be the first-movers in the field of environmental management. Through the environmental demands that they place on their suppliers, the technologies and techniques of good environmental management will subsequently trickle down to smaller companies over a number of years. The diffusion of environmental management techniques via the supply chain is therefore a very important factor influencing the improvement of industrial environmental performance.

However, the use of supplier questionnaires relies on the ability, integrity and willingness of suppliers to offer such information. Even if such information is made available, and the chance of a significant contract usually ensures that it is, variations in approach in different firms will indicate that the information supplied may not have been gathered or assessed in a consistent manner. The need therefore exists for an objective, systematic and standardised approach to collecting environmental information from a company's suppliers. Furthermore, while supplier questionnaires can be used to gather the necessary environmental information up the supply chain (i.e towards the raw material source), the comprehensive assessment of a product's environmental impact necessitates a still wider assessment, namely an assessment of the environmental impacts of production, distribution, use and disposal.

A combination of legislation, environmental standards such as the eco-management and audit scheme or BS7750 and industry programmes such as the Responsible Care programme of the UK Chemical Industries Association may offer some affirmation that relatively high environmental standards are being maintained in production. However, other standards are necessary to ensure that at all stages of the product's life, efforts are made to minimise environmental impact and to communicate these efforts in a rigorous and credible way.

Life-cycle assessment (LCA) aims to assess, and therefore help producers to minimise, the environmental impact of a product at all stages in its life. As an internal management tool for the company, the application of LCA is a way of clearly establishing the impact of a product throughout its life and hence a way of identifying key areas for attention. Within the firm, whether this is carried out in an exact, objective or quantitative way is not of fundamental importance. The benefits of LCA accrue through the focusing of managerial minds on all aspects of the product's environmental profile. The undertaking of this process will automatically aid future decision-making to better incorporate the environmental dimension and therefore to lessen impact.

The EC eco-labelling scheme (also discussed in Chapter 8) is based on the application of LCA. It aims to assess and recognise best practice in minimising overall product impact and to communicate these achievements to potential customers. It is therefore necessary to compare and rank the environmental impact of a number of different products and to award the label to the best environmental performers. As such, once the label becomes widely adopted it could provide the necessary information on product environmental impact to all those who are interested and negate the need for supplier question-naires. To do this effectively, the process of LCA must be developed to provide an objective and widely accepted framework though which the environmental impact of similar products can be measured and compared. However, the process of LCA is as yet far from being an exact and objective science.

THE PROCESS OF LIFE-CYCLE ASSESSMENT

As is discussed within Chapter 3 on Environmental Impact Assessment, the potential for waste avoidance from a particular production facility is at its greatest when it is designed into new or significantly altered plant. Environmental impact assessment provides the information through which this can be achieved. Similarly, the potential for minimising the environmental impact of a product is at its greatest when the product is being designed. Unlike the production facility, however, the design of the product once established is more open to redefinition and fine-tuning in order to reduce its environmental impact.

Life-cycle assessment seeks to highlight those areas in the environmental profile of a product where producers should focus their attention in order to minimise their environmental impact through redesign. Should the major area of environmental impact be that of production, then efforts to reduce the impact of the good should centre on the production facility. Alternatively, if the major area of environmental impact occurs as a result of the source of the raw materials used, then alternative sources should be sought. If the major area of product environmental impact is the production process, then the tech-niques of environmental management outlined throughout this book should be utilised. In all cases, those aspects of the product and its production which generate significant environmental impact should be revised.

In essence, the aims of LCA and EIA are very similar. Both are information gathering exercises aiding the minimisation of environmental impact through design and redesign. Indeed, a comprehensive EIA could subsume the process of LCA in establishing exactly what the potential impact of a proposed development and its outputs may be, although a very proactive and comprehensive EIA would be needed. Traditionally however, EIA, as with environmental auditing, focuses on the direct environmental effects of the plant itself rather than the wider and less direct impacts of the company's activities through its demand for raw materials and the impact of its product. As a result LCA carries great potential as a stand-alone, product-specific technique for providing the information with which a product's environmental impact may be reduced.

Life-cycle assessment, also known as 'cradle to grave' assessment, attempts to provide information on all facets of a product's environmental performance. The results of both the waste audit and of the LCA must then be incorporated into the overall environmental management strategy of the firm to provide an integrated and comprehensive waste management profile for a particular product. As process and product design are inextricably linked, the importance of an integrated approach which aims to minimise the overall environmental impact of a company cannot be over emphasised.

Undertaking LCA necessitates a number of stages with clear parallels to EIA or environmental auditing. Briefly, the stages are:

● to quantify energy and material inputs and emissions;
● to identify the areas of environmental impact in order to enable further study;
● to assess the environmental impact of inputs and emissions at all stages; and
● to establish the options for improving any stage of the life cycle of the product.

The chosen options should then be incorporated into the wider objectives that are worked towards through the environmental management system.

While many of the outputs of the LCA may appear to be obvious, the systematic and objective collation of quantitative data will firmly establish the extent of the impact and the scope for improvement. Merely undertaking the LCA will focus issues which are normally taken as read, will confirm or challenge pre-conceptions and will facilitate a greater understanding of the issues involved. Measuring and documenting the findings of the LCA will enable many of the lessons learned to be transferred throughout the company to change the attitudes and behaviour of those concerned with producing the goods. As an internal management tool aiming to achieve results such as these, the benefits of LCA are clear and unequivocal.

The controversy relating to LCA arises when it attempts to quantify and rank a range of different environmental impacts. To offer a practical example,

LCAs undertaken for washing machines establish that the major environmental impacts for all washing machines are in their consumption of energy and water during use (Hemming, 1992). Should one particular washing machine use less water and energy than a competitor, it is clear that its environmental impact is the lower of the two. However, should one be more energy efficient and thus make a lower contribution to global warming while a second uses less water and detergent and thus has a lower impact on water consumption and pollution, then objectively establishing which has the lower impact becomes impossible. With the extraordinary range of material inputs used in modern production and the infinite range of interactions when emissions are released into the environment, quantitatively assessing and ranking the environmental impact of many products with many different impacts with any accuracy becomes virtually impossible. It is then vital that some consensus is reached where the data upon which decisions are taken is transparent and the subjective views of all those concerned can be reconciled. As the methodology of LCA evolves and becomes more rigorous then the necessary subjectivity associated with ranking environmental impact can be reduced. The external application of LCA under the EC eco-labelling scheme is discussed in greater depth in Chapter 8.

Before beginning the process of LCA, it is important to decide upon the scope and objectives of the exercise. Should a company wish to select the best environmental option in each link in its supply chain, then in theory at least, all of the options available in the supply chain should be assessed. Clearly it is necessary to set the boundaries of the LCA within manageable limits. Current applications of LCA select those facets of the process which are likely to provide the most relevant information, for instance in highlighting any inputs which are especially damaging or any stages of packaging, distribution, use or disposal which can be readily improved. In practical terms, LCA provides a systematic framework through which the constituents of the product and their environmental impacts which are selected for study can be analysed and the potential for impact reduction assessed. For internal use, the scope of LCA may be very selective, however, for external use where comparative measures of total environmental impact are needed, the LCA must be much more comprehensive.

Focusing on the use of LCA as an internal management tool, there are a number of generally accepted stages in its methodology. These are as set out in Figure 7.4.

1. **Inventory analysis**

   Inventory analysis gathers information relating to the material and energy inputs into a product and its production and any emissions associated with it. This should relate to all stages of the life cycle from extraction and cultivation, processing, transportation, manufacture, packaging, distribution, use and disposal. Resources used and emissions generated should be measured per unit of output produced. Although this stage may demand

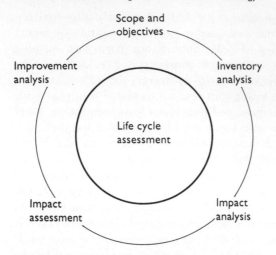

Figure 7.4 Life-cycle assessment
(*Source*: Charlton, C. and Howell, B., 'Life Cycle Assessment: A Tool for Solving Environmental Problems?',
European Environment, Volume 2, Part 3, April 1992.)

extensive research, particularly for companies which use a large number
of inputs or who operate within long supply chains, it is relatively
straightforward.

2. **Impact Analysis**
   Impact analysis is much less straightforward than inventory analysis. It
   involves establishing the environmental impact of each of the areas
   documented under the inventory analysis. This may be extremely complicated as in many cases the impact of an emission depends upon the nature
   of the emission, the environment into which it is emitted and the interaction of a significant number of characteristics of source emission and
   receptor environment. The boundaries of this stage of LCA will therefore
   be defined by the depth of analysis which is deemed both necessary and
   possible.

3. **Impact assessment**
   Once the scope and level of environmental impact has been established,
   some assessment or measurement of this impact is necessary. Impacts can
   be established both quantitatively and qualitatively. Quantitative impact
   assessment develops a list of the amounts of emissions and some measurement of their impact. In many cases, this is as much factual assessment as
   is possible in the absence of an element of subjectivity. To this point an
   LCA can provide an internal benchmark against which to compare future
   performance and is therefore of considerable use.

4. **Improvement analysis**
   The final stage of LCA is that of improvement analysis where the environmental profile of the product is altered through redesign of the product and

the methods of its manufacture. As with the waste management system, a formal and systematic appraisal of the product's environmental impact will often reveal areas where relatively simple fine tuning will reduce environmental impact. Improvement analysis will therefore assess the technically and economically feasible options available at all stages of the products life which can be utilised to improve the environmental impact of the good. Obviously, the attention of managers should focus on those areas of their operations where the environmental impact and the potential for its reduction is highest.

For greater analytical use and external ranking between products, qualitative assessment is needed so that some nominative measure of total environmental impact is gained. This may be achieved where each environmental impact is assigned a nominal value, for instance high, medium or low impact, so that some aggregated measure of total environmental impact becomes possible. This provides a quantitative measurement for use either as an internal baseline for future comparison or for external comparison.

As is mentioned above, however, the scope of the study may not necessitate such a comprehensive LCA. The process of LCA can be simplified in a number of ways. Different components of the study can be collated in relation to separate impacts, for instance all those areas where solid waste is generated, energy is consumed and so on. This will reduce the number of variants and simplify the process considerably. Also, for some commonly used inputs such as energy, databases of environmental impact are being established in order to provide common LCA solutions. These databases will offer standardised impact assessments for a range of energy and material inputs. However, for non-fund emissions where the environmental impact depends on the nature of the environment into which they are emitted, the development of such a common database is not possible and measures of environmental impact must be developed on a case-by-case basis. Furthermore, developing a selective list of criteria to be assessed may also simplify the process while still enabling internal baseline comparison and external ranking, should the same criteria be consistently applied. The selection of these criteria will in itself be a subjective decision, and once these criteria have been published, products may be designed to minimise environmental impact according to these criteria while ignoring all other areas.

However, as the experience of LCA progresses the present levels of subjectivity in impact assessment will be reduced. The application of LCA under the eco-labelling scheme will scrutinise the data and methodology used and will offer external verification and peer review of the claims made relating to aggregate environmental impact. Furthermore, as LCA becomes more widely applied the availability of widely accepted data will increase and hence the process will be simplified. The external application of LCA, although considerably more complex, is therefore set to increase as competing claims relating to product environmental impact are formally assessed through the criteria set out by the eco-labelling scheme.

The main application of LCA should be as an internal management tool to assist in the minimisation of product environmental impact. Life-cycle assessment provides an analytical framework through which this can be achieved. As such it should be incorporated into all environmental strategies and the management systems which seek to improve environmental performance.

CONCLUSION

The links between waste, environmental damage and business success are clear. As disposal routes decline, resource prices rise, legislation tightens, and public scrutiny increases, the motives for effective waste management strengthen. However, waste management is about more than the reduction of the costs of waste disposal. It is about the development of new technologies and techniques for waste minimisation. Effective waste management must therefore reconsider the traditional design of production processes and the ways in which they are managed.

Waste management must also look at the wider implications of a firm's activities. Life-cycle assessment offers an advancing framework through which the overall environmental impact of the product can be minimised. The motivations for LCA recognise the critical role that industry plays in environmental protection, not only through its processes but also through its products.

Effective waste management therefore demands that companies redesign their processes and products in order to minimise their total environmental impact. However, the objectives of the waste management strategy and the LCA must be integrated into the wider environmental objectives and management systems of the company if their full potential is to be realised.

References

Charlton, C. and Howell, B. (1992) 'Life Cycle Analysis: A Tool for Solving Environmental Problems?', *European Environment*, Volume 2, Part 3, April, pp. 2–5.

European Community Policy Document (1989) 'A Community Strategy for Waste', (SEC (89) 934), 18 September.

Hemming, C. (1992) 'Eco-labelling of Washing Machines: A UK Pilot Study', *Integrated Environmental Management*, No. 2, September, pp. 17–19.

CHAPTER 8

Communicating the difference: green marketing, packaging and eco-labelling

Strategies for marketing, in its widest sense and including packaging and eco-labelling must be at the heart of any company's forward planning. This is where environmental differences will be communicated and where a company's commitment will often be judged. It is also where companies are likely to be judged by consumers and the wider public and it is important that the integrated approach developed in the environmental management system must continue. It is often suggested that there are two options on the environment: either to control your own destiny, or to have it controlled for you. Legislation is requiring companies to address its environmental impact and what is voluntary now may be regulatory in the future. From a marketing perspective there is a need to recognise the potential gains which can be achieved by being proactive and therefore controlling your own destiny. This has been the experience of companies like The Body Shop, Sainsbury's and Tesco who have successfully integrated environmental considerations into all their activities. It has also been suggested that consumers do not expect their favourite brands and favoured companies merely to jump on the green bandwagon, they expect them to be at the forefront and so successful companies will need to push forward on environmental themes if they are to retain their market shares.

GREEN MARKETING

One of the key marketing challenges of the 1990s is to re-examine product portfolios as consumers switch to buying more environmentally friendly goods. This will involve the company in new areas of market research and new marketing strategies to inform consumers about the environmental attributes of their products and to persuade consumers to buy these products rather than others. This whole process will bring with it a range of new opportunities and threats. However, green marketing, which has too often been treated as a gimmick in the past and ridiculed for its cynicism, is more than about changing the characteristics and advertising of a product. It must be part of an overall philosophy for business which is consistent with whole-company approach. This is perhaps best demonstrated by firms such as The Body Shop where deeply held personal values are translated into sound business activities. The founder of The Body Shop, Anita Roddick, has a clear message:

> Our products reflect our philosophy. They are formulated with care and respect. Respect for other cultures, the past, the natural world, our customers. It's a partnership of profits with principles. (Body Shop Promotional Literature, 1990)

Marketing has to be seen as a key part of a corporate philosophy concerned with the identification, development and promotion of products and markets. Marketing strategies aim to satisfy the consumer and should therefore be seen from the customer's point of view. It is in effect the management process for identifying, anticipating and satisfying customer's requirements at a profit. The key task of the organisation must therefore be to determine the needs and wants of the target markets and to adapt the organisation to delivering desired satisfactions more effectively and efficiently than its competitors. Green marketing requires that this is done in a way which improves the environmental performance of products and of the business and therefore enhances the consumers' and society's well-being.

A key problem or contradiction often exists in this strategy, however, because consumers' wants do not always coincide with the long-term interests of the environment and a key element in any green marketing strategy needs therefore to be education and the provision of accurate information. As we shall see below, simply claiming that a product is green is unlikely to make a real difference to sales in the long run; but explaining to consumers the real environmental benefits of one product over another is likely to have more far reaching effects.

Changing consumer demands

The 1991 *British Social Attitudes Report* (Jowel, 1991) indicates that for the UK, like many other countries, changing consumer preferences are resulting in a cultural shift with environmental considerations permeating society more widely. More than simply buying environmentally friendly products when faced with a number of alternatives, increasing numbers of consumers are now actively seeking out products which are less damaging to the environment. Quite simply therefore, firms which are able to provide environmentally friendly products will see their sales rise. Moreover, consumer awareness in relation to the environmental impact of their consumption is increasingly global in its dimension with greater concern about the destruction of rainforests, acidification of water sources, global warming and ozone depletion. Younger adults and children, in particular, are better informed about the environment and more willing to adjust their own consumption patterns to reflect their perceptions of the environment. In the 1991 report, 50 per cent of those interviewed thought that damage to the environment was the biggest single concern facing Europe in the 1990s.

In 1992 the advertising agency McCann Erickson and the Harris Research Centre undertook research into the consumer care about the environment. It found that in Germany, France and the UK many consumers were more concerned about the environment than the economy, jobs and crime. More importantly perhaps, the survey began to look at the often cited trade-offs between environmentally friendly goods and other key aspects such as quality. It has often been the perception of consumers that environmentally friendly goods are less effective. The survey found, however, that only 31 per cent of consumers had been disappointed with green product performance, and 51 per cent were prepared to sacrifice some loss of quality for an improvement in the environmental performance of the product. More than half the consumers were willing to pay more for a product which had environmental benefits.

Consumers are now better and more accurately informed and the criteria for buying products is increasingly being based on social and environmental criteria as well as traditional characteristics such as price, delivery and quality. This is being accelerated by a plethora of publications aimed at both informing the consumer and promoting and campaigning for more environmentally friendly consumption. Companies, and particularly retailers, who recognise this are also putting pressure on their own suppliers to provide them with environmentally friendly alternatives and the whole supply chain is therefore under pressure to adapt to the demands of the end user.

The whole concept of brand management also needs to be reviewed within a green marketing strategy. In the past product brands have been developed which bring with them consumer loyalty and enable firms to raise prices over time. In the future however, consumers are less likely to buy a brand *per se*, but will increasingly be attracted by whole company philosophies and policies. Branding will increasingly have to be done at the organisational level and will therefore go hand-in-hand with eco-labelling and wider public relations exercises. This requires a deeper strategic response than the type of green marketing demonstrated by so many opportunistic firms of the 1980s. Of most importance will be the need for a wider, more holistic approach which satisfies demands made not only by consumers but also the whole range of stakeholders. Corporate, production, human resource management, marketing and environmental strategies have therefore to be consistent and integrated.

Nor is it enough for the end-product alone to reduce its negative impact on the environment. A whole life-cycle assessment from 'cradle to grave' has to be adopted to assess the total environmental impact of a product or service. This must include all stages of the pre-production and production process and the use and disposal of the product. In addition, a precursor to any attempt at green marketing must be the establishment and implementation of an environmental policy, the adoption of regular environmental audits of existing facilities, processes and systems, integrated environmental management systems and environmental impact assessments on the development of new facilities.

F

The overriding approach to satisfying consumers' needs must therefore be consideration of strategies which ensure sustainable development. The practical implications of this concept need to be considered by all green marketers who must respond to an ever increasing number of consumers for whom the purchase of environmentally friendly products is becoming more a habit than a decision associated with impulse buying.

The credibility gap

As the environmental issue found its way on to the consumer agenda in the 1970s and 1980s so the growth of green marketing began. This first phase of environmental strategies saw little more than short-term corporate responses with relatively minor adaptation being made to existing products. These were too often associated with spurious and inaccurate claims about the environmental friendliness of products and led pressure groups such as Friends of the Earth to expose these inaccurate claims and to introduce its 'Green Con Award'. This often did firms more harm than good in the longer term. To some, the claims might have seemed like cynical attempts to increase market share, and while there is undoubtedly some truth in that, the real root of the problem was a fundamental lack of accurate information on the part of both producers and consumers. As a result of this, many environmental claims have lacked credibility.

The increasing use of environmental labels by manufacturers and retailers has often left consumers confused and many consumers have believed that such labels were officially sanctioned. Undoubtedly considerable confusion still exists and will remain until the EC's official eco-label is well established. The 1990 report of the Consumers' Association *Which?* into green labelling and environmentally friendly claims found considerable misunderstanding on the part of consumers. In particular, it identified four general areas where inaccurate claims were being made.

1. **Excessive claims**: no manufactured products can possibly claim to have no negative impact on the environment. For example, although aerosol manufacturers might replace CFCs with other agents, these too may damage the environment.
2. **Multiple claims**: different forms of words were often used to try to describe the same environmental attributes. For example, research has indicated that aerosols labelled as 'ozone safe' were perceived to be superior to those labelled as 'ozone friendly'.
3. **Meaningless claims**: labels claiming that a product contains 'no phosphates', is 'recyclable' or is 'biodegradable' are meaningless if all such competing products do indeed have these attributes, which many did.
4. **Claims which are not explained**: due to a lack of consumer information many claims such as 'phosphate free' were not clearly understood and therefore often accepted as evidence of an environmentally friendly product when that was not the case.

The outcome of this sort of approach has been that pressure groups and consumers are increasingly demanding that firms supply more information about their environmental claims on a right to know basis. This means that firms must be both open and honest in their communications with the public.

The importance of environmental issues has also left many firms confused and it may not be surprising that inaccurate claims have often been made. However, there is increasingly a wider understanding that green marketing is more than simply attaching a label to a product and many more firms are working hard at a more integrated environmental strategy. Modern green marketing strategies recognise that simple short-term solutions are insufficient to make a lasting difference to a product portfolio and that there is a need to take a more strategic approach to marketing. It is to this that we now turn our attention.

THE GREEN MARKETING STRATEGY

A good starting point for analysing any corporate strategy is to examine the demands being made of that strategy. The stakeholder concept emphasises the need to satisfy a whole range of often disparate demands. This will include demands from customers for environmentally friendly products at reasonable prices with high quality attributes, demands from shareholders for high profitability and growth, and demands from employees for reasonable wages and job security. Although difficult, firms must try to satisfy these demands and reduce the tensions which exist between competing objectives. Local communities demanding less localised pollution may be in conflict with shareholders demanding higher output levels and sales in order to increase profitability for example. Directors of the company trying to cut costs may be in conflict from regulators insisting that new pollution control technology is installed. Nevertheless, a useful starting point must be to make stakeholders aware of each other's demands in an open and honest way. This approach, which has been alien to so many organisations in the past, must be part of an organisation's corporate culture if the company is to claim honestly that it is seeking to improve the whole of its environmental performance. For example, local communities need to be informed about the activities and potential dangers of a site. This is not only paramount in the case of an accident but also necessary to maintain good relations with those living near to a site. At the very least, some sort of report following the implementation of environmental audits needs to be disseminated to the local community. For example, the environmental audit reports of the Norwegian company Norsk Hydro are published and distributed to every household and organisation in the vicinity of one of their sites.

Thus, the most important lesson to be learned from the stakeholder concept is that cooperation is as important as competition. Trust relations have to be developed with stakeholders and this is best built up by honesty and openness.

Companies who are serious about improving their environmental performance should have nothing to hide and therefore the disclosure of as much information as possible, without giving away competitive advantages, is an obvious strategy.

Although environmental considerations are increasingly important to the consumer, environmental attributes alone will be insufficient to sell a product. The product must still be fit for the purpose for which it was intended, deliver the same attributes, have the desired quality and be price competitive. Failure to meet these basic requirements will result in the failure of the product. Therefore green marketing has to be integrated marketing. Indeed, green marketing is no different from traditional marketing insofar as its aim must be to satisfy the end consumer and provide an acceptable profit margin. Many marketers would claim that green marketing is not even a separate concept from marketing and if this involves a holistic approach to the product and organisation then we must agree with that.

Green marketing cannot therefore be looked at in isolation. The effects of launching a new product or re-orienting an existing one to have superior environmental attributes will have ramifications for procurement, finance, human resources, production processes and delivery. The fundamental key to a green marketing strategy is to approach the problem systematically and to undertake appropriate research and planning. The general approach may be little different to a conventional marketing strategy but if 'greening' is to be a consideration at the outset, a number of questions will have to be addressed:

- Has the marketing plan identified the key environmental considerations involved in the market for the product?
- Has sufficient scientific and technological research been undertaken to ensure that the product will have superior environmental performance to that produced in the past?
- What effect will new environmental attributes have on costs, revenue and profitability?
- Has the company planned on changes in the overall size of the market which may result in changing consumer attitudes?
- How much new investment will be required in the modification or development of the product in question?
- Has the whole environmental impact of the product from 'cradle to grave' been assessed?
- Has the product undergone sufficient testing to establish its environmental credentials?
- Have environmental pressure groups been consulted and is the company prepared for any adverse criticism of its product?
- Do the communication strategies relating to the product emphasise environmental aspects and benefits?

Consideration of different time scales for different activities is also important. While we have recognised the importance of longer-term strategic planning, the day-to-day operation and success of the company cannot be neglected either. The logistics by which a company improves its environmental performance will depend in part on its functional organisation, its geographical spread and its markets. Ultimately though, the organisation must make the environment a priority. Within the marketing mix there are a number of areas which can be addressed:

1. **Product policy.** Design products which minimise the use of non-renewable resources and are capable of being recycled. Use accredited eco-labels to mark products clearly but do not overstate or be dishonest about the environmental aspects of the product. Ensure that the customer uses the product as it is intended by providing aftersales and advisory services.
2. **Packaging.** Design packaging which, while fit for its purpose, uses the minimum amount of materials. Use materials which do less damage to the environment and arrange for packaging to be recycled or taken back and where possible reused. Avoid excess packaging used as promotional material.
3. **Promotion policy.** Ensure that all stakeholders have an input into the communications of the organisation. Enhance the environmental reputation of the firm by public relations and advertising exercises but make sure that all claims are honest and true. Be involved in broadly based campaigns to improve the environment and be evangelical with other firms and organisations. Be open and hide nothing which has an environmental impact.
4. **Pricing policy.** If environmental measures cost extra money then pass this on to the consumer making it clear that the price differential is a result of environmental improvements. If costs are reduced through environmental measures then be equally honest and consider offering discounts to those who can match your own environmental performance.
5. **Transportation and distribution.** Give preference to transportation systems which have reduced environmental costs in terms of energy consumption and pollution. Set up distribution channels with distributors, wholesalers and retailers which minimise transportation and packaging needs. Establish systems to ensure that used products and packaging can be recycled.
6. **Quality and effectiveness.** Try to ensure that environmental attributes do not detract from quality or the effectiveness of the product. If this is not possible then explain that to the consumer. They might be quite happy to accept it.
7. **People policy.** Ensure that the whole workforce is sensitive to environmental issues and committed to environmental improvement. Enhance awareness and skill by training and education and reward ideas and schemes which improve the environmental performance of the organisation. Provide incentives for surpassing environmental targets such as reward schemes.
8. **Systems.** Ensure that an integrated environmental management system is in place and is followed and that marketing is consistent with this. Ensure

that there is an adequate environmental monitoring system which is capable of identifying potential and real problems. Ensure that suppliers are clear of your requirements and are part of your overall environmental policy. Make the organisation responsive to stakeholders and participative.

Although this does simplify the issue somewhat, it can provide a starting point and a checklist for an organisation embarking on a new green marketing strategy. There are some key areas which deserve rather more attention, however, and it is to these we turn now.

GREENER PRICING

Traditional economic theory tells us that prices are established when property rights are exchanged and, within the market mechanism, this can be very efficient so long as property rights exist and are well defined. The problem with much of the environment is that there are no clear property rights and traditionally much of the environment has been treated as a free good and therefore overused. Nevertheless, general environmental awareness and, more specifically, the 'polluter pays' principle enshrined in environmental legislation have meant that there has been a steady growth in attempts to incorporate environmental considerations into the pricing process.

It is important to recognise that pricing policies themselves can also improve the environment. A good example of this is the government intervention on duty charged on leaded and unleaded petrol which has brought about improved consumer behaviour and benefits to the environment. For the individual firm the pricing decision will be much more complex but any environmentally friendly organisation will at least seek to reflect its environmental performance in its pricing policy.

The most basic question which any firm will have to address is whether a new environmentally friendly product will be sold at a lower price, the same price or at a higher price than its predecessor or non-green alternatives on the market.

1. A lower price, perhaps reflecting cost savings, will encourage consumers to buy the environmentally improved product and improve environmental performance. Where demand for the product is generally price sensitive, a lower price will be a successful strategy both for the firm and certainly for the environment.
2. Where price is left the same then the environmental attributes of the product will have to be used as a form of non-price competition. This will involve stressing the differentiation process and requiring the firm to look closely at its promotional policy.
3. In the case of the price of the product being higher, not only will a differentiated, green product have to be promoted but there must exist consumers who will be willing to pay a premium for the product. The extent of the price differential may be crucial here.

In most cases prices will bear a direct relationship with costs and therefore any pricing policy will have to reflect the lower or higher costs associated with the greening of the product and the business in general.

EXPLAINING THE DIFFERENCE

A key element in the marketing process must be communicating messages about products and wider environmental aspects, such as processes, to all stakeholders and particularly customers. There is, of course, no magic green method or style of promotion. Essentially, explaining the attributes of an environmentally friendly product should be approached in just the same way as any other communication message. The basic techniques are the same and the same key questions need to be asked.

1. Is there something substantial that can be said about the environmental performance of the product or company?
2. Who should the organisation be talking to and how do they currently feel and behave?
3. What are the aspects of a business which can be used to encourage them to buy a particular product?
4. Will the style of communication adopted be visible, be understood, be relevant, and be honest?
5. Is the company prepared to prove what has been said and be open to further questions about its overall environmental profile?

Companies which are promoting an environmentally friendly image will have to be very precise about what they say and truly practise what they preach. Drawing attention to the environmental aspects of a business will increasingly draw attention from a more sceptical public and better-informed media. To be successful a company must be able to demonstrate that it has responded to the key issues presented earlier in this book: that there exists an environmental policy and that it demonstrates commitment from the highest level, and is sincere; that products and processes are examined for their environmental attributes; and that there exists a proper management system to ensure consistently improving environmental performance.

If there is something about a product or organisation worth communicating then the key question must be to whom do you communicate? Undoubtedly the first group to concentrate on are the consumers of the product. That does not mean that a company has to communicate directly with them but that they must be the target audience ultimately. We know that there is a market for greener products and we know from questionnaires that consumers seem to want to buy those products. However, in practice it has been shown that a majority of consumers who are 'green' when they are answering the research questionnaire, are more conservative at the checkout. For instance, although research suggested that 50 per cent of their customers would be willing to pay extra for greener products, an analysis of checkout behaviour at Tesco suggested that only 10 per cent actually did.

The green message may therefore be rather more difficult to communicate than surveys might suggest. There is clearly only a limited trade-off that consumers are prepared to make in the real world. Although theoretically willing to buy alternative products, we know that most consumers are not, in practice, happy about giving up the brands they know and the price, quality and performance standards they have come to expect, especially for alternative, more uncertain purchases which might actually be at a higher price. One of the problems is that past marketing campaigns with respect to greener products have made situations worse by being deceitful. Many consumers have become confused, cynical and disillusioned with many greener products. Companies cannot therefore jump to conclusions about consumers' understanding of, and likelihood to respond to greener communications. There is a need to look very closely at markets and consumer behaviour before effective communications can be developed. In the main, the onus will be on the marketers to educate consumers, simplify environmental issues and then offer product solutions.

The consumer will also be affected indirectly through the behaviour of competitors and through the media, politicians and environmental pressure groups. There are therefore many other key targets for any greener communications. Increasingly, business-to-business communication is becoming more and more important for manufacturers and suppliers. If a company (and particularly a retailer) is developing an environmental stance, it is going to be more demanding of the environmental practices of its suppliers. The major retailers are good examples of this. Gateway issued a report on packaging in 1990, which introduced a tough and proactive policy on supplier packaging and they promised to phase out materials that did not conform to their green standards. The policy was not immediately popular, but is a good example of retailer actions forcing supplier compliance.

As discussed above, the first consideration concerning green communication is often not what to say about your company or product, but whether there is anything to say at all. There are two concerns here. Firstly, communicating a less-than-thorough or dubious environmental initiative runs the risk of alienating consumers and opinion formers if there are gaps in the message, inaccuracies in the claims or secrets in the organisation. In over-stating environmental claims, negative regulatory, pressure group and media responses could endanger the product, service or corporate integrity. Bad publicity could negate everything which the company was trying to achieve and would certainly act against any positive corporate image which a company was trying to foster. Secondly, there is an issue concerning whether a green message is appropriate to consumers at all. The impact of the message will depend on how aware, committed and educated the consumers of a product are and on the particular market characteristics in which the product is sold. In the first instance, a company needs to establish whether environmental considerations are or could be significant in their markets, and whether appropriate messages could confer a competitive advantage.

There are a number of communications techniques which can be used to get the message across. However, in order to be effective it is important that, whichever methods are chosen, they are used within an integrated and coordinated environmental strategy, consistent with other aspects of the company's environmental strategy. Even now, consumers are still swamped with the clichéd, generic imagery of greening in environmental messages: rainbows, trees, plants, green fields, dolphins, and smiley planets. These images have been used over and over again and as a result, consumers have tended to remember generic product categories, such environmentally-friendly detergents, rather than particular brands. At the other end of the scale, far too many messages have assumed detailed consumer knowledge across the range of environmental issues. There is a need to explain each issue where appropriate and then stress the reason why the consumer should prefer one particular product over its competitors' products.

In terms of executing communication, companies should not over-assume people's knowledge or altruism when it comes to any green issues. Neither should they under-assume how much consumers like their current brands. The majority of consumers will not be impressed with complicated explanations of why one product is more environmentally friendly than another. Those communicating the difference need to find simple and honest messages about why one product should be preferred.

There are a range of tools which can be used across the communication and promotional spectrums. Each has its advantages and disadvantages depending on the time and place it is used and there will be a range of specific points which any organisation will need to ask itself with regard to particular elements and practical procedures.

1. **Advertising**. If advertising is to be used as a communication medium, a firm must decide whether an advertising campaign is to be product-specific or company-generic. As the new green culture becomes more firmly embedded within the eyes of a consumer and as a growing number of products gain green credentials, so the emphasis may shift away from advertising specific products to communicating the wider environmental characteristics of an organisation which makes it unique.

2. **Corporate and public relations**. Many organisations have sold themselves as much as their product. When one thinks about companies such as The Body Shop it is difficult not to think of their stance on environmental issues and animal testing. Many firms who are environmentally proactive will also have things to be proud of. These might include the results of an environmental audit for example. Part of the PR exercise must also include the ability to communicate with the public when they ask questions and

therefore organisations need to know exactly what they would say in answer to enquiries about their 'green credentials'. As we have stressed before, such answers need to be fundamentally honest.

3. **Direct marketing**. Direct marketing is used with success in fund-raising by some organisations, but it is still much associated with 'junk mail' in many consumers' eyes. Nevertheless, there is considerable efficiency to be derived from direct marketing. But like everything which the environmentally aware company does, there are many issues to consider. Firstly, can the mailings be justified in terms of bulk and weight? Secondly, is the mailing itself environmentally friendly, using appropriate paper and packaging? Thirdly, will consumers object to this particular marketing technique as being fundamentally environmentally damaging through waste creation? If the target audience is well-defined and the quality of mailing lists good then these problems can be mitigated, but otherwise the technique may be quite damaging.

4. **Sponsorship**. Sponsorship has the twin benefits of raising the profile of your organisation and allowing the organisation to spend money on a worthwhile activity. Increasing numbers of firms have been willing to sponsor a range of events and activities which are associated with the environment. Sponsorship also allows companies to target support directly and there will be obvious spin-off benefits for both the organisation and the environmental project being supported.

5. **Personal selling**. In many situations it is the 'personal touch' which can add quality and success to a firm's marketing campaign. If the environmental message is to be pushed then the sales force needs to be well-trained and committed to their role. They need also to be fully aware of the broader issues surrounding the environmental initiatives of the company. Direct selling works best when the sales force is developing a relationship with clients rather than selling one-off products. And again, the process of selling needs to be looked at carefully. For example, does the car fleet use unleaded petrol and are new cars fitted with catalytic converters?

MARKET RESEARCH AND ENVIRONMENTAL INFORMATION

Successful marketing has to involve a proactive and creative search aiming to find and exploit new opportunities for product and market development. Greener marketing aims to do this in an environmentally responsible manner. Opportunities will arise in a number of areas and strategies will differ accordingly. However, there are ten key questions which will need to be addressed in all circumstances.

1. Does the product or service fulfil a real demand?
2. Does the new opportunity justify the research and development which will be required?

3. Does any new development really take into account its impact on the environment and what specific issues need to be addressed to ensure that the product is more environmentally friendly?
4. What price, quality or delivery trade-offs will consumers be willing to accept in place of positive environmental attributes?
5. Is the product or service likely to be acceptable over the long term?
6. Are there changing legislative requirements or consumer attitudes which will need to be taken into account?
7. Has thorough primary research been undertaken and completed?
8. Are the environmental issues and impacts fully understood?
9. Are marketing strategies and management information systems in place?
10. Are management and employees aware of the environmental issues and do they understand their role within the new opportunity?

Along with potential new opportunities there are likely to be new threats facing any organisation. Firms will have to monitor these proactively as markets change to respond to new environmental issues and developments. Potential markets and existing markets need therefore to be researched on an ongoing basis. Central will be the identification of new issues, market imperatives and the state of scientific knowledge, and accurate information is needed in all these aspects.

Marketing requires information to be effective and therefore greener marketing is nothing without accurate information on the environmental impact of both the company and its competitors. A continuous flow of information and data is needed on both processes and products and central to this will be life-cycle assessment, environmental audits and environmental impact assessment. At least the first two of these should be ongoing activities. On top of this there is a need for information relating to the overall performance and environmental conduct of the whole organisation. All these requirements point to the need for some sort of environmental information system. The aim of such a system must be to enable managers to make more effective decisions and to act as a database for answering queries from stakeholders.

Table 8.1 demonstrates how an environmental information system might be structured and identifies the type of information needed and the use to which it can be put over different time scales. It is important to realise that the system has to be integrated and no information collection exercise can really be viewed as discrete. It is also important, however, to distinguish between ongoing monitoring needs, information relating to the performance of the company and wider, often external, information needed for longer-term strategic planning. Companies have to consider information requirements at all these levels and introduce appropriate monitoring and measurement procedures. Decision-makers need to have access to a database of environmental information and this sort of system provides that.

Table 8.1 An environmental information system

	Immediate monitoring needs	Company performance indicators	Strategic planning needs
Timescale	Continuous, daily, weekly, monthly.	6 months–3 years.	2 years onwards.
Information coverage	Specific measures of environmental performance needed by division, site or function. Adherence to corporate policy and legislation needed.	Adherence to company policies and overall measures of company environmental performance. Needs to identify new priorities for action.	Transcends divisional structure and should concentrate on market trends, consumer behaviour and forthcoming environmental legislation.
Monitoring horizon	Covers short time periods and should be regularly repeated.	Assesses performance at regular intervals, assessing improvements over time and impediments to improvement.	Needs to look forward over long time scales and focus on strategy development.
Orientation	Demonstration of adherence to pollution standards and legislation and identify areas for further improvement and cost savings.	Needs to demonstrate a continuous cycle of environmental improve-ment, an assessment of company policies and the environmental management system. Assessment needs to be repeated periodically and measured against a baseline.	Provision of information for forward planning, forecasting and diversification activities. Assessment of competitor practices and environ-mental initiatives within the industry. Planning for uncertainty.
Instruments	Monitoring and control equipment, testing and sampling.	Environmental auditing. Life-cycle assessment, general performance indices.	Modelling, consumer and market research, corporate change assessment.
Examples	Discharge and emission control.	Planning for and assessment of environ-mental management systems.	Long-term profiling of consumer markets, identification of new market opportunities. Risk assessment.
Impact/ benefits	Adherence to legislation, less likelihood of fines and litigation.	Data on which to base environmental claims and information for adherence to standards. Lower insurance premiums.	Competitive advantage enables proper strategic planning and marketing campaigns.

PACKAGING

Packaging is increasingly on the environmental agenda. Many surveys into consumers' attitudes towards the environment have consistently found that a company's reputation on environmental issues had a strong effect on attitudes towards its products. There is considerable support for the use of bio-degradable or recyclable packaging, with around three-quarters of all consumers suggesting that they are more happy to purchase a product packaged in this way. Many consumers have demonstrated that they would be willing to pay more for such a packaged product and stating that there should be legislation requiring manufacturers to use recyclable or bio-degradable packaging.

Packaging is often seen as environmentally damaging because when it is discarded after use it becomes waste. Companies which are therefore committed to improving their environmental performance need to look carefully at their packaging strategies and requirements. The use of packaging has often been seen as a marketing tool, whereby promotional packaging can help to sell a product. Now the situation is almost reversed. A growing consumer awareness in relation to packaging will make the use of excess packaging a reason for not buying a product. Firms therefore have to balance their packaging usage carefully, considering:

- its utility value in protecting products and consumers;
- its positive marketing value for display and communication purposes; and
- its negative marketing value if it is seen as being excessive.

These three competing objectives mean that the design of packaging becomes crucial. Well-designed and appropriate packaging will enable a product to be differentiated from its competitors and as such it is an important aspect of marketing mix.

In the case of products designed for retail outlets, packaging will be influenced by the need to market the product successfully to the consumer. Packaging of products traditionally considered as gifts is one example where marketing of the product can result in excess packaging. However, the purchasing of these products tends to occur on a one-off basis and it might be argued only contributes marginally to a waste problem. There are many other reasons why retailers may be less willing to reduce packaging. For example, the introduction of blister packs has been attacked by advocates of green issues. This form of packaging does indeed cause increased waste, but its introduction was largely a result of pressure to respond to shoplifting. For this reason it seems likely that manufacturers and retailers will remain reluctant to reduce the use of such packaging until cost-effective alternatives for dealing with the shoplifting problem can be found.

One needs to be careful about exactly what entails excessive packaging and a definition which simply looks at the size of packaging in relation to the size of the product is too simplistic. This can be demonstrated by an examination of the use of modified atmospheric packaging (MAP) which are commonly plastic, sealed containers used for fresh food products. MAP has been introduced in response to a change in lifestyles. Consumers are increasingly demanding fresh food but have less time for shopping. Modified atmospheric packaging uses a mixture of plastic film and laminates to keep the right gases in the package and the wrong gases out. This enables meat, fruit and vegetables to be kept fresher for longer without freezing and reduces food wastage. When viewed in isolation, however, because the packaging surrounding the product is larger and seemingly more elaborate than that used previously, this is often cited as excessive.

It should always be borne in mind that since packaging costs money it is always in the best interests of the manufacturer to minimise its use within the constraints posed by storage, safety and marketing requirements. This does not necessarily result in the most environmentally friendly packaging since the cheapest may be less environmentally benign or result in greater or more toxic waste earlier in its production chain. With this in mind industry has made progress in recent years in producing both lighter and thinner materials for packaging. Examples where improvements in packaging have been made include the packaging of milk and juices in rectangular cartons and the packaging of biscuits in a thinner single plastic film. The former approach enables both storage space and distribution to be simplified and reduced in cost, while the latter represents a considerable saving in resources over the old approach of packing biscuits in corrugated paper. Improvements in product technology also have their implications for packaging. An example of this is the introduction of concentrated washing powders and refill packs for conditioners which have resulted in a dramatic reduction in the requirement for packaging.

The chief purpose of a pack is the containment and protection of its contents from the time of manufacture through storage, distribution and sale, and for a period of time thereafter. Secondary functions include the provision of information and guarantees about quality and purity and there will be marketing and promotional aspects of packaging. There is a great balancing act between the 'conventional' benefits of packaging and the environmental demands of consumers and governments. The extent to which source reduction of packaging can be carried out without prejudicing product protection and consumer convenience is an important issue.

The environmental issues surrounding packaging do not, however, make it easy to categorise materials into acceptable or unacceptable groups. One of the main problems has been the over-simplification of the issues by the media and sometimes by environmental groups. This does pose problems for the retailer or manufacturer who tries to choose a greener pack, and for the design, PR and advertising company which tries to design or advise on greener packaging. There are, however, some general criteria which can be applied to the choice of a greener pack.

Choosing and designing a greener pack

When one considers the complex set of roles which packaging may have and then lay on top of this environmental considerations, it is not really possible to claim superiority for one particular type of packaging. Furthermore, by solving one problem, care must be taken not to cause another. There are also a large number of key players who must work together in order to achieve packaging waste reduction. There are, however, ten very useful questions which can help in choosing and designing more environmentally friendly packaging.

1. Does the packaging material come from a scarce or seriously declining source?
2. Is production of the packaging material energy-intensive?
3. Has the design of the packaging ensured that materials can be easily reused or recycled?
4. Does any combination of packaging materials create difficulty for recycling?
5. Is the packaging associated with the use of chemicals which may cause environmental damage (e.g. aerosols and CFCs)?
6. Do current or anticipated environmental protection laws in any proposed market either constrain the use of chosen materials or increase their production or disposal costs?
7. Can concentrated products that fit into smaller packages be developed?
8. Can reclaimed (secondary) materials, which will also encourage the development of the recycling industry, be used?
9. Has proper consideration been given to pollution that may be caused during the manufacture of packaging?
10. Does the packaging, the information on it and its overall appearance encourage the efficient use, reuse and disposal of the contents and the pack itself?

Like most environmental issues, control at source is the first and best solution. One way of achieving packaging with better environmental performance is by source reduction. This means simply reducing the amount of materials used. In turn, this will reduce the extraction and processing of raw materials, reduce the need for disposal and will even reduce the energy and pollution caused by processing and recycling. Lightweight materials and energy-saving techniques can reduce the production costs of packaging products and will have additional environmental benefits. After reducing environmental impacts by using as few resources as possible, the next priority must be to design the pack which is recyclable. However, these two aims may be contradictory. Combining different materials in one pack may use less material overall, but may make the pack less easy to recycle. Another important consideration is that less packaging to transport through the distribution chain may provide significant savings in fuel and storage costs.

The useful life of a pack can be extended by refilling or returning it. Refilling results in significant energy savings and helps to keep empty bottles, cans and cartons out of landfills and incinerators. Repeated studies have shown that cleaning and reusing a bottle, for example, takes less energy than melting the same bottle and making a new one, or making a new bottle from scratch. However, more energy is usually needed in order to manufacture a refillable bottle than a non-refillable one in the first place, because it needs to be stronger to last over multiple uses. On top of this must be added the energy and water required for the bottle cleaning process. The initial investment in energy and resources required to manufacture the refillable bottle can be gradually recouped as the bottle is reused, but if the bottle is lost or broken before the break-even point has been reached, the overall environmental impact will be negative.

In the USA and the UK, unlike some other developed countries, the market share for refillables has sunk dramatically over the last twenty years. The decline can be attributed to reduced competition in the beverage industry where national brands with centralised packaging procedures have replaced local or regional products. The trend towards fewer bottlers with increased distribution networks increases the distance from consumers back to the plant, reducing the cost advantage of refillables over throw-aways.

Packaging legislation across Europe

Worries across many countries about waste emanating from packaging have led to some governments taking swift and forthright action. For example, in 1991 the German government introduced packaging legislation resulting from the realisation that industrial waste levels for the new unified Germany were as high as 40 million tonnes per year. Moreover, packaging materials accounted for more than 50 per cent of the volume of domestic waste in Germany. By introducing its packaging ordinance, the German government transferred the costs of waste disposal to the manufacturers, suppliers and distributors of packaged goods. By implicitly incorporating the 'polluter pays' principle, the legislation provides a strong incentive to reduce levels of packaging while ensuring that the packaging that is used is more environmentally friendly.

Germany is by far the most active of the Member States of the European Community in the area of packaging and has become the baseline model for EC developments. The German government, through its controversial Waste Packaging Ordinance, has made producers and retailers accept greater responsibility for its products. Retailers, who are also obliged to offer a refill service and provide more facilities for recycling, must accept all used packaging material returned by the customer. The most important provisions of the Waste Packaging Ordinance require that:

● producers and retailers must accept for recycling and disposal all returned transport packaging;

- the consumer can leave all packaging material at the point of sale;
- retailers must accept all used packaging material returned by the consumer and in order to encourage the consumer to do so, a deposit must be levied on all drinks, detergents and paint containers.

In fact, the Waste Packaging Ordinance operates by imposing a duty all along the supply chain to accept back used packaging from customers and to arrange for its recycle or reuse. The logistics behind this and the costs of so doing are both very high. However, the unique use of this route is not really the purpose of the legislation. Article 11 of the Ordinance enables organisations to employ a third party to undertake their recycling responsibilities and thereby waive their obligations to undertake the recycling themselves. The intention of the Ordinance is therefore to encourage organisations, wherever they are in the supply chain, to establish a network for the collection and reuse or recycling of used packaging that is independent of the public waste disposal system.

A key part of any company's marketing mix is the use of sales packaging. In article 3 of the German Waste Packaging Ordinance, sales packaging is defined as that packaging which is used by the consumer to transport the goods or until such time as the goods are consumed. In order to conform to the principles of the Ordinance, manufacturers, distributors and retailers have joined forces to create the 'dual system' organisation (DSD). The DSD, a limited company, is responsible for organising an independent recycling system and provides a regular collection facility either from the consumer or from the vicinity of the consumer. The Ordinance stipulates minimum quotas which have to be achieved which includes the attainment of an overall collection rate of 50 per cent of total waste sales packaging by June 1995.

Suppliers who are able to demonstrate that their packaging is recyclable are provided with a licence by the DSD enabling them to display a green dot on their sales packaging. The green dot guarantees the recyclable nature of the packaging and thus enables the waste material to enter the dual system. Financing of the dual system is achieved by charging a fee calculated on the basis of the number of packs sold and on the volume of packaging. Thus the green dot provides companies with an environmental label which can be displayed on their packaging. Many large customers, such as supermarkets, have a policy of only buying products packaged in 'green dot' materials. Moreover, by buying only 'green dot' products retailers can avoid direct responsibility for the recycling of packaging and this requirement passes backwards along the supply chain resulting in pressure throughout the system to use only the minimum amount of packaging required with the maximum amount of recyclability.

The German Waste Packaging Ordinance also covers transport and secondary packaging. Transport packaging is defined as that which serves to protect goods from damage during transportation. Secondary packaging is packaging which is intended as additional packaging around the sales packaging to:

● allow goods to be sold on a self-service basis;
● prevent the possibility of theft; or
● serve advertising purposes.

Manufacturers and distributors of transport packaging are obliged to accept the return of used packaging and to reuse or recycle it independently of the public waste disposal system. Distributors providing goods in secondary packaging are required to remove the secondary packaging on handing it over or delivering the goods to the final customer. Alternatively, the final consumer must be given the opportunity to remove the secondary packaging at the point of sale.

The German Waste Packaging Ordinance also defines mandatory deposits which have to be levied on some packaging and repaid when the packaging is returned. In the case of non-refillable drinks packaging with a net volume of between 0.2 and 1.5 litres, for example, the deposit has to be 0.5DM. Above that, the deposit rises to 1DM. However, this instrument can be suspended if the final target of the policy is met. The final target is for:

● a comprehensive recycling system for the packaging to be established;
● the percentage of refillable packaging not to fall below the level registered for the particular region; and
● the percentage of refillable packaging for the whole of Germany not to fall below 72 per cent.

Although the Packaging Ordinance only applies to Germany there are implications for any company wishing to supply and market products within that country. Since the obligation to recycle packaging is passed back along the supply chain, the importer will be responsible for all packaging up to the point of import. This has meant that German distributors have exerted tremendous pressure on foreign companies to supply goods in packaging which conforms to the Ordinance.

Some firms in Germany have found the packaging legislation costly to implement in the short run and non-German firms have also had to adjust their packaging specifications. However, many companies are now finding that the new packaging rules are actually helping their marketing and sales strategies. In particular, retailers in Germany tend to have a greater confidence in German suppliers meeting the specified packaging standards and are often showing a preference towards them in their purchasing policy. The Waste Packaging Ordinance has therefore precipitated a powerful response within Europe. Many countries, including France and the UK, have complained that the Ordinance breaks the EC regulations on free trade. The German government has defended its right to impose the legislation since countries are allowed to adopt measures to protect the environment even though these may result in barriers to trade.

However, Germany is not alone in introducing strict packaging legislation. In the Netherlands firms operating in the packaging chain have signed a voluntary agreement or covenant covering packaging waste. The key elements of this covenant are:

- By the year 2000 the disposal of packaging waste through landfill or incineration without energy recovery will cease.
- By the year 2000 the weight of packaging placed on the market will be below the levels of 1986 and where possible reduced by a further 10 per cent.
- Over-packaging will be avoided, multi-packs will be reduced and where packaging materials cannot be recycled, these will be replaced. Polymers used in packaging are to be reduced and inks, lacquers and dyes containing heavy metals and solvents are to be phased out.
- Refillable packs should be used where such a change will result in reduced environmental impacts.

Belgium has established a variety of voluntary agreements between the authorities and firms in the area of packaging and waste management. The agreements, coordinated by the Belgian Institute for Packaging, aim to:

- develop and apply more environmentally friendly production processes;
- develop and promote the use of lightweight packaging;
- remove from packaging anything which causes pollution in the waste stream;
- incorporate recyclability in the design, production and application of packaging; and
- promote packaging which is refillable, recyclable and/or compostable.

In 1992 a French packaging decree was introduced which forces producers, importers and distributors to either provide for or contribute to the reuse, recycling or elimination of waste packaging. A recycling organisation, Eco-emballage, was established by the packaging industry to attain these objectives and any firms not subscribing to the scheme are forced to introduce a deposit scheme for their goods or to introduce their own government-approved collection schemes. Membership of Eco-emballage confers the right for participating companies to use an identifying mark similar to the German green dot.

In Italy regulations have been introduced which have resulted in the establishment of consortia for each packaging material. These consortia work with local authorities and all packaging manufacturers and importers are required by law to join the relevant consortia. The operating costs of the consortia are divided among the members according to the market share of their products. The government has also incorporated targets into the legislation which stipulate that at least 40 per cent of plastics and 50 per cent of glass and metal containers have to be recycled and these targets will be increased over time. In 1991 a law was passed which required consumer products or packaging to be labelled in such a way as to inform the consumer of the materials used and declaring the presence of any materials or substances which might be harmful to people, goods or the environment.

With the introduction of the Environmental Protection Act in the UK, the government made clear its wish to see industry improve its environmental performance. Traditionally the UK has disposed of 90 per cent of its waste through landfill sites. But with such sites decreasing in number and more stringent regulations being imposed in relation to them there has been an urgent need to look at alternatives and to reduce the amount of waste being generated. The UK packaging industry, therefore, has had to make resources available for its own environmental improvement. However, the UK has lagged behind its competitors and by 1993 it had not introduced any regulations similar to the German scheme even though many firms which export goods have had to adhere to best practice in Europe. The UK government has essentially left industry itself with the responsibility of reducing packaging.

The packaging waste policies of individual Member States have run in many different directions and the Commission has recognised the need to tackle packaging waste on an EC-wide basis. The European Commission has already set up systems in some Member States to quantify and monitor packaging waste, while a complete 'cradle to grave' life-cycle assessment of all packaging types is undertaken. The Commission's proposals are broad enough to include packaging waste created by materials used for the distribution of goods, industrial packaging, agricultural products, retail and office waste, and consumer product packaging. These sectors account for an estimated fifty million tonnes of packaging waste each year in the EC as a whole. The Commission has insisted on:

- at least 60 per cent of all packaging waste being recycled within five years of the Directive ratification (compared with only 19 per cent in 1992);
- no more than 30 per cent of the waste is to be incinerated within the same time period; and
- no more than 10 per cent of packaging waste being placed in landfills.

In time we can expect that each packaging unit should feature markings indicating what it is made of, if it is returnable, and if it can be recycled. Ultimately, much greater priority will be placed on the reduction of packaging waste, the refill and reuse of containers, recycling, and energy conversion.

ECO-LABELLING

Over time eco-labelling schemes have been devised in a number of countries in an attempt to promote the use of production methods which are less harmful to the environment. The first such scheme was introduced in the Federal Republic of Germany in 1978. Canada, Japan and Norway established their own schemes in 1989. The schemes were also introduced to prevent the often spurious environmental claims already discussed at the beginning of this chapter. In countries such as the UK, where eco-labelling developments have been part of the EC development, environmental claims have been covered by advertising standards. For example, the UK Advertising Standards Authority (ASA) has criticised companies for failing to substantiate claims of environmental benefits and the ASA has issued the British Code of Practice on the Use of Environmental Claims which includes five basic principles.

1. Full documentary evidence must be held for all claims made.
2. Claims should not be absolute unless there is convincing evidence that a product will have no adverse effect on the environment.
3. The basis of any claim should, if possible, be clearly explained.
4. The cloaking of claims in extravagant language should be avoided as this will only cause consumer confusion.
5. Spurious claims should not be made.

The German Blue Angel scheme

Germany's Blue Angel eco-labelling scheme is probably the world's best established programme. Launched in 1978 by the German government, it now has almost 4,000 products carrying the label. The organisers of the scheme claim that 80 per cent of German households are aware of the scheme and it receives widespread support from manufacturers. Like the EC scheme, the label is not restricted to domestic made goods. The Japanese multinational Konica was the first company to win a Blue Angel label for use on a photocopier, for example. Many firms are aware that they cannot be without the Blue Angel award because the public sector and many large German companies will make every attempt to buy only products which carry the label.

The EC eco-labelling Regulation

The objectives of the EC's eco-labelling Regulation, agreed at the end of 1991, are to promote products with a reduced environmental impact during their entire life cycles and to provide better information to consumers on the environmental impacts of products. These must not be achieved at the expense of compromising product or workers' safety or significantly affecting the properties which make the product fit for use. The EC scheme is designed to reduce confusion by providing an authoritative and independent label to identify those goods with the lowest environmental impact in a particular product group. That is not to suggest that those products are environmentally benign, but simply that their environmental performance is superior to other products in the same group which do not have a label. The scheme should also encourage the production and sale of more environmentally responsible products and so aid the impact of consumption on the environment.

The label should affect all businesses along a supply chain even if some suppliers cannot use the label themselves. This is because suppliers will have to provide detailed information about their own components and their manufacturing process in order that the suppliers of the end product can apply to use the eco-label on the basis of a life-cycle assessment. Thus, in time, the label may become a minimum standard, specified by an increasing number of buyers, who practise green procurement policies.

All products, excluding food, drink and pharmaceuticals are potentially eligible for an eco-label if they meet these objectives and are in conformity with the EC's health, safety and environmental requirements. Products comprising substances or preparations classified as 'dangerous' under EC legislation will also be barred from receiving an eco-label along with any product manufactured by a process likely to cause significant direct harm to humans or the environment.

The EC scheme, issued as a Regulation, applies directly to all Member States and is EC-wide. It is a voluntary scheme and self-financing. It assesses individual products and their manufacturing processes so that a multi-product firm will have to make multiple applications if they wish all of their products to have eco-labels. The criteria for the award of an eco-label is ever tightening. Indeed, upon application for the renewal of an eco-label producers cannot assume that just because their environmental performance has remained unchanged it will be awarded the label again.

Judgement of the products must be made on the basis of a 'cradle to grave' assessment or life-cycle assessment. The assessment matrix (Figure 8.1) must be used in setting criteria for the award of an eco-label. This will require account to be taken, where relevant, of a product group's soil, water, air and noise pollution impacts, waste generation, energy and resource consumption and effects on eco-systems. These impacts must be assessed in the pre-production, production, distribution, use and disposal stages. The criteria established for the award of an eco-label within a product group must be precise, clear and objective so that it can be applied consistently by the national bodies which award the eco-labels.

National competent bodies who are independent and neutral, actually award the eco-labels for products. They are made up of representatives from industry, government, environment pressure groups and consumer groups and the body has to reflect the full range of social interests. These bodies act as a kind of jury and assess the environmental performance of the product by reference to the agreed general principles and specific environmental criteria for each product group.

The first product groups to come under the EC's eco-label scheme were:

- Washing machines (UK)
- Dishwashers (UK)
- Light bulbs (UK)
- Soil improvers (UK)
- Hair sprays (UK)
- Solar heating systems (Germany)
- Laundry detergents and other cleaning agents (Germany)

	PRODUCT LIFE CYCLE				
ENVIRONMENTAL FIELDS	Pre-production	Production	Distribution	Utilisation	Disposal
Waste relevance					
Soil pollution and degradation					
Water contamination					
Air contamination					
Noise					
Consumption of energy					
Consumption of natural resources					
Effects on ecosystems					

Figure 8.1 The EC eco-labelling scheme: indicative assessment matrix

- Photocopier paper (Denmark)
- Kitchen rolls (Denmark)
- Toilet paper (Denmark)
- Writing paper (Denmark)
- Insulation materials (Denmark)
- Paints (France)
- Batteries (France)

Within each group there has been significant controversy with different interest groups lobbying for different criteria. Some of this lobbying was done by firms keen to keep out their competitors. For example, in the case of hair sprays, the UK firm Procter and Gamble which produces a pump-and-spray system argued that it is more environmentally friendly than any of its rival's conventional sprays. But others argued that the pump-and-spray system was less effective and therefore not fit for use when compared with sprays with hydrocarbon propellants, and that it should not therefore qualify for an eco-label under the EC rules.

The use of an eco-label is not necessarily open to any product. The first step is to get a particular product group accepted as suitable for the award of a label. It may be the case that a particularly polluting group of products will not be open to such an award. Requests for the establishment of new product groups may come from consumers or industry itself and are addressed to the competent body in the Member State. The competent body, if it so wishes, can ask the Commission to submit a proposal to its regulatory committee. In any event the Commission will consult with interest groups and take advice from a range of sources. If it is decided that a particular product group will be open to the award of an eco-label then this will be announced in the *Official Journal of the European Community*. This process is outlined in Figure 8.2.

Following applications from manufacturers or importers of a particular product for the award of an eco-label, the national competent body has to notify the Commission of its decision relating to the award of an eco-label, enclosing full and summary results of the assessment. The Commission will then notify other Member States and they have 30 days to make reasoned objections to the recommendations. If there are no objections the award proceeds and a contract to use the label for a specified time period is drawn up. Lists of products which are able to use the eco-label are published. In the case of any objections and disagreement the Commission, acting through its advisory or regulatory body of national experts, will make the final decision. This procedure is summarised in Figure 8.3. Companies applying for an eco-label have to pay a fee to cover administration costs and a fee is also charged for the use of the label if awarded. Companies which succeed with their applications can only use the eco-label in advertising the specific products for which it was awarded.

The whole process of life-cycle assessment (LCA) used in the assessment is also fiercely controversial. The key issue here is the depth to which companies are expected to subject their products. To undertake a complete LCA with accurate assessment of all the environmental impacts of a product would be very expensive and time consuming, and, like environmental impacts, cannot be guaranteed to be 100 per cent accurate because of a lack of scientific knowledge in many areas. On the other hand, anything short of this sort of

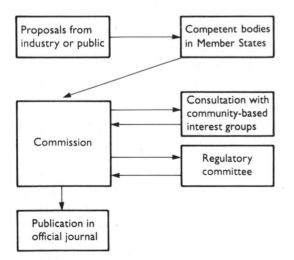

Figure 8.2 The EC eco-labelling scheme: selection of new product groups

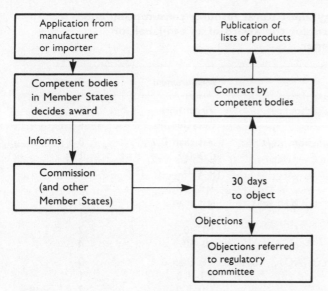

Figure 8.3 The EC eco-labelling scheme: award of eco-label to individual products

approach is open to criticism and might easily be destroyed by competitors or interest groups which were not involved in the process. In time the LCA will need a much more focused definition if it is to be successfully implemented and form the long-term criteria for the award of eco-labels.

It is clear from the EC eco-labelling Regulation that a full LCA is not actually needed. Products must be able to satisfy the criteria laid out for each product group and therefore any application for an eco-label needs only to address these key areas and show that there is no additional significant harm done by the manufacturing process. This has led many environmentalists to criticise the EC scheme on the basis that only a piecemeal LCA is needed. Indeed, many have gone as far to suggest that this is not true life-cycle assessment and that all the Regulation demands is that firms jump through some predetermined hoops.

This can be illustrated by reference to the draft guideline criteria for the award of an eco-label to paper products which were drawn up by the Danish eco-label working group in 1991. It demonstrates the approach which will be taken in judging whether products should be awarded an eco-label. The paper products criteria require that three main hurdles have to be cleared by any paper product before any more detailed analysis is undertaken. Firstly, wood used in the process would have to come from forests where replanting ensured that there was no net reduction in the volume of growing wood. Secondly, all manufacturing operations would have to comply with local regulations. Thirdly, the product should not contain substances in amounts exceeding any

Table 8.2 Energy and natural resource consumption and emissions: criteria for the award of an eco-label for photocopying paper

Area	Measurement	Points
Energy and natural resources	Virgin fibre	6
	Recycled fibre	4
Sulphur dioxide emission, kg/t	less than 0.2	0
	0.2–0.5	1
	0.5–1.5	2
	1.5–2.5	4
Organics to water (COD), kg/t	less than 1	0
	1–10	1
	10–40	2
	40–60	4
Chlorinated organics (AOX), kg/t	less than 0.1	0
	0.1–1.0	1
	1.0–2.0	2
	2.0–3.0	4
Releases to land	no releases	0
	controlled releases	1
	uncontrolled releases	4
Correction factor (fitness for use)		

national legal limits. On top of these three general requirements there are then specific criteria for energy and natural resource consumption and emissions and producers are awarded marks for their own performance against pre-determined 'score sheets' (see Table 8.2).

Using the criteria in Table 8.2, the best mills will have the lowest score of points. After the first batch of applications and submissions have been received a cut-off point for the attainment of an eco-label would then be selected. Eco-labelled products would also have to conform to EC specifications and standards where these exist and the assessment will include an arbitrary correction factor to compare fitness of use across products in the same category. The criteria say little, however, about the use of the product and disposal after use and therefore it can be argued that a full LCA will not be absolutely necessary. Nevertheless, the award does enable consumers to differentiate between products and if the award were to be made to around the best 10 per cent of products then this will act as a key competitive advantage for those firms as well.

CONCLUSION

Green marketing must be seen as part of an overall strategy for environmental management. It needs to be consistent and integrated with the environmental management system of the company and at all times be honest, truthful and open. It provides the main means by which companies can communicate their environmental achievements and the environmental issues which set them apart from their competitors. Key elements of the marketing strategy include the need to recognise and chart changing consumer trends, to have clear strategies aimed at differentiating the company's marketing mix and to have integrated and effective environmental information systems. It is not enough to promote products alone. Any organisation needs to examine its overall impact on and commitment to the environment.

Packaging will become a more important part of the marketing mix over time and traditional approaches to packaging will have to be reviewed by many firms. It is clear that in its attempts to reduce waste, the EC will introduce more stringent packaging legislation over time and companies will be expected to respond to this in a proactive way.

Companies which are keen to identify their more environmentally friendly products within their marketing strategy will also be aided by the EC's eco-labelling scheme which will be able to confer a recognised accreditation for a particular product. It will not be enough, therefore, to make minor changes to a product and call it environmentally friendly since environmental impacts need to be assessed from 'cradle to grave'. Increasingly, consumers' attentions will be based on corporate performance as well as individual product profiles and therefore any strategy will have to focus on the widest possible aspects of environmental impacts. Companies who take the environment seriously therefore need to adopt a proactive environmental marketing strategy which is much more holistic than the narrower marketing so often employed by more traditional firms.

References

Jowel, R. (1991) *British Social Attitudes Report* (8th Report), Gower Publishing Company, Aldershot.

Which? Consumers' Association (1990) 'Green Labelling', January.

CHAPTER 9

Small businesses and environmental management: a new model for development?

To improve the world in which we live everybody and all organisations need to be serious about environmental management. Small and medium-sized enterprises (SMEs) have an important role and although it might be argued that their individual contribution towards environmental degradation is small, taken together they have a very large impact. An obvious problem is that small business managers do not have access to information concerning environmental management and, in addition, many small firms do not have the capital nor the expertise to undertake the sort of strategies developed in this book, even though payback periods are often very short. Nevertheless, there are things that they can do at very little cost and if they can integrate environmental considerations into their everyday activities they are likely to save money, rather than spend it, in the longer term.

In looking forward to the ways in which environmental management can be integrated into the small organisation we need to consider wider aspects of small-firm development. Increasingly, small firms are being forced by the market to be more flexible and, at the same time, more specialised, producing high-quality goods. We know that quality standards are being forced along supply chains and that all firms are having to respond to the changes which the Single Market brings. Many of these issues and demands actually make the integration of environmental strategies easier. Indeed, there is a degree of synergy between these new demands and the demands of the environment. Moreover, a number of initiatives are encouraging SMEs to work together in a cooperative way at an industry level or a local level, sharing any costs of environmental management and, more importantly, sharing solutions and perhaps even environmental technology.

Throughout this book we have stressed the need for an integrated approach and in particular, we have identified important linkages between environmental improvement and quality, and between environmental management systems and the ethos of total quality management. These linkages are no different in the SME sector but are sometimes compounded by the developments which are occurring in the sector itself and the sorts of demands increasingly being made by the customers. SMEs have to respond to a market where they need to be more flexible in their operations and produce goods which clearly satisfy the particular needs of their consumers (who are often large firms with their own environmental agendas). The sort of approach which is increasingly being adopted by small firms is that of flexible specialisation: small firms have to respond to complex consumer demands in a flexible way and produce products which exactly fit customer requirements through introducing a degree of specialisation.

An ideal model for the sustainable development of small businesses is therefore one which integrates quality management, environmental management and flexible specialisation techniques. The sort of objectives which we might set for the potentially successful small business are that it is:

- profitable;
- environmentally friendly;
- competitive in the longer term; and
- produces a quality good or service.

Figure 9.1 provides the basis of the model discussed. Any company seeking to satisfy these objectives needs therefore to be right at the centre of the model integrating total quality management (TQM) systems, environmental management systems and flexible specialisation. The TQM system should be an important, integral part of an overall environmental management system and vice versa. While firms can follow the principal parts of an environmental management system and a TQM system without having flexible specialisation

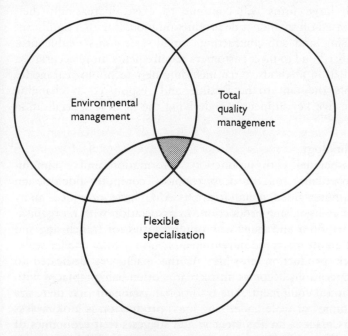

Figure 9.1 Quality, flexibility and environmental management: a model for the development of small businesses

characteristics, the particular type of company which best lends itself to achieving the objectives we have set out above is also likely to be the type of company able to take advantage of the principles of flexible specialisation. Thus the operational area which we need to concentrate on is the intersecting shaded area in Figure 9.1.

We also know that small firms will often be contractors, sub-contractors or suppliers themselves and will therefore find increasing pressure being applied to them as environmental management strategies are pushed along the supply chain. Such firms will have demands made of them and will have to adapt if they are not to lose markets to competitors who can offer better environmental performance characteristics. Small and medium-sized enterprises will therefore find themselves part of increasingly complex supply chains which will be driven by quality standards, environmental standards and a need to be flexible. We need therefore to consider each of these characteristics in turn and consider how the small firm can respond.

FLEXIBLE SPECIALISATION SYSTEMS

The environmental concerns about mass production and a trend away from production line (often termed Fordist production) techniques in the workplace tend to point in the direction of smaller, more flexible firms and divisions. Although large firms will continue to exist, increasingly their production will be based on smaller-scale production models with a significant increase in franchising and sub-contracting. Small-scale units enable production to be specialised and to meet customers requirements more accurately, while modern production methods, often including new technological modes of operation, enable the unit to be flexible and responsive to changing demands. There are five key influences underlying the flexible specialisation system.

1. **Appropriate technology**

    Technologies associated with production, information and communications and in particular, multi-process robotics, computer-aided design (CAD) and computer-aided manufacture (CAM) have provided many opportunities for reorganising production. In association with reorganisation on the factory floor and many new opportunities for franchising and sub-contracting, many of these developments have made smaller-scale, specialised, batch production possible. As the machinery dedicated to fixed-assembly operations becomes obsolete it is often being replaced with multi-purpose capital equipment. The traditional argument that there are benefits of economies of scale underlying mass production is looking less convincing. In its place is an argument which suggests that economies of scale are being replaced by economies of scope. In other words, economies which are associated with flexible, multi-product production. It should be noted, however, that the most advanced technology is not necessarily the most appropriate technology and investment in over-sophisticated technology can simply reduce profitability. There is a clear opportunity here to use clean technology and integrate waste reduction at source with the move away from production-line technology.

2. **Flexibility**

In the flexible specialisation system products will often be made to exact customer requirements. Therefore a degree of flexibility in terms of design, assembly, packaging and the associated marketing mix variables is vital. Flexibility in terms of production scheduling and working hours can often also add to environmental improvement. For example, by planning to run complementary processes together energy usage and costs can be reduced. Firms have to be prepared to supply goods meeting exact customer requirements at short notice and be flexible towards industrial customers expecting smaller suppliers to fit into just-in-time regimes.

3. **Contracts and sub-contracts**

At the limit, flexibility and the need to be responsive means that workers may be needed at one point in time but not at another. The implication of this is that increasingly, firms are only employing on a permanent basis those workers who can be fully employed for the full working week. Part-time working, casual employment and temporary contracts are therefore increasingly common along with franchising and sub-contracting. In many instances it will be cheaper and more efficient to use external firms, themselves specialised, to carry out particular tasks. Such firms are likely to be relatively small. Moreover, large firms are more often operating in this way, recognising that internalising all their tasks is not always the most cost-effective mode of operation. The use of small firms undertaking contract work enables the large firm itself to maintain a degree of flexibility and prevent over-employment. As environmental management techniques are pushed along the supply chain by these large firms, small firms will have to respond accordingly.

4. **Clearly defined products and markets**

In the past large mass-production techniques, which have been particular pollutants, have relied on mass demand for the product being produced. This meant that production was highly sensitive to changes in aggregate demand and to recession in particular. Now, smaller quantities of much more specialised products can be produced profitably because the technology is available to do it and because markets are growing internationally. Even the most specialised products are likely to have sufficiently stable markets in terms of demand. A Single European Market accelerates this sort of trend and small enterprises which may not be able to find a significant market in their own Member State may find a viable one in the wider European market. This also means that new smaller firms based on the twin characteristics of flexibility and specialisation are able to survive alongside their much larger conglomerate counterparts, relying on niche markets, meeting specialised demands and offering a more responsive and personal service.

5. **Workforce**

It can also be argued that workers have to become more versatile in the new flexible workplace. This often means that fewer, more skilled workers are employed and are expected to carry out a wider variety of tasks. Demarcation, therefore, has no place in the so-called post-Fordist production unit and is an issue which trade unions will have to address. The dominant ideology behind the post-Fordist scenario is that new flexible processes work most efficiently where workers themselves take on responsibility for the planning, programming and functioning of their work and begin to be responsible for the quality and environmental attributes of the processes for which they are responsible. With workers increasingly controlling their own work patterns, worker motivation can increase, and if care is enhanced, then quality and environmental performance will improve. Thus, the devolution of responsibility towards the factory floor can increasingly be seen as part of an environmental improvement package.

The SME has to think carefully about how to develop a flexible specialisation strategy in an environmentally friendly way. In purchasing new, clean technology, the cheapest may not be the most important consideration and the firm needs to think carefully about multi-process technology which can produce an increased number of variations to a basic product. In addition, it needs to look towards serving new and complementary markets and offering a high quality, personal service. The organisation and scheduling of production should enable a move away from batch processes wherever possible and working patterns need to be in line with levels of demand and not custom and practice. The workforce must become more flexible and specialised and there is a role for increased training and education. It may be that a core workforce is established with increased levels of part-time working. It must be noted, however, that the ethical firm will offer equivalent conditions of service to its part-time staff. Quality will also be an important factor in the small enterprise and it is to this subject which we now turn.

THE TOTAL QUALITY APPROACH IN THE SME

As we have seen in Chapter 5, it is a common misconception that quality costs extra money in terms of input costs. To recap: the theory behind a total quality management (TQM) system is that as quality improves costs actually fall through lower failure and appraisal costs and less waste. Total quality management is much more than assuring product or service quality; it is a system of dealing with quality at every stage of the production process, both internally and externally. It is a system requiring the commitment of senior managers, effective leadership and teamwork. This last facet is actually easier to achieve in the SME and in turn makes a TQM programme more easily implementable in a firm with flexible specialisation systems built into its operations. Total quality management is an approach which also aims to improve the effectiveness and flexibility of the business as a whole and attempts to eliminate wasted effort as well as physical waste by involving everyone in the process of improvement.

Central to the TQM approach is teamwork where people get together in process improvement teams and quality circles. Within the very small business a quality circle may actually involve everybody in the organisation. Clearly, as the organisation gets bigger, very large groups are difficult to manage and become unproductive. But one of the key functions of the quality circle is to make recommendations to management and, in turn, discuss suggestions made by others. This is actually very much easier in the smaller organisation where there are fewer management structures and shorter lines of communication.

Although quality circles have been traditionally linked with production-line technology, often their use has been associated with a move away from this towards a flexible specialisation system where several tasks in the production of a good are done by a group of people working closely together. The best example of this is the movement away from producing a car on a production line to a system where a group of people receive the shell of a car and assemble the whole product to an exact specification to meet the needs of the customer. Such a system was implemented by Volvo in Sweden and is now being adopted by other manufacturers in Europe.

The need to devolve decision-making and planning is clear in both a TQM approach and a flexible specialisation system and there are clear advantages associated with worker participation. Particularly in the SME, it is easy to make the workforce feel valued and involved, and participatory arrangements help to improve both productivity and commitment which are central to the needs of environmental management. In addition, it can be argued that the use of teamwork as an approach to problem-solving throughout the organisation has many advantages over allowing individuals to make decisions alone. When properly managed, teams improve the process of problem-solving, producing usable results quickly and economically. It builds up trust, improves communication and motivation, develops interdependence and helps workers to identify with the company.

THE ENVIRONMENTAL MANAGEMENT SYSTEM IN THE SMALL BUSINESS

The key to implementing an environmental management system (EMS) in an SME is no different from that in larger firms. Since communications and the whole organisation of the system are central and have to be transparent and clearly understood, the small size of the enterprise can make this process easier. Moreover, since we have identified several benefits of participatory arrangements and of teamwork, the SME needs to place these firmly within the design of the system.

The achievement of environmentally friendly production requires continual monitoring at all stages of the production and servicing process. While the working of this system may be a task for management, the system itself relies on the compliance and awareness of all members of the firm, whatever their status might be. Within the small organisation gaps which can occur because of a lack of commitment by only one person will be more serious in relative terms than in the large firm. Clear communication flows are therefore needed and workers need to recognise that it is better to highlight a mistake or error than to cover it up in case it gets them into trouble.

Environmental reviews and environmental audits are also clearly part of the environmental management system. The SME is less likely to have the expertise to undertake these in-house and is less likely to have sufficient money to bring in a team of consultants. Nevertheless, there are a number of sources of help and advice to which the SME can turn when some sort of environmental assessment is needed. Some local authorities may be willing to help in the process and in many areas organisations such as the Groundwork Trust will help SMEs carry out environmental reviews at very small, or sometimes no charge. Businesses in the same area can often get together, work cooperatively and spread costs, and it is always worth tying into local initiatives such as Business and Environment Forums and link up with sources of local expertise such as universities.

When it comes to energy audits and the assessment of possible new systems, many regional electricity companies offer a free (or at least very cheap) service which will assess the SME's needs and offer advice on possible actions. Local regulators are also likely to be helpful if approached for advice. Local authority departments responsible for registrations under the Environmental Protection Act, regional waste management regulators, local water companies and the regional offices of the National Rivers Authority will all be a source of help and advice although they will not undertake a full review for any business.

At the centre of an EMS has to be commitment on the part of all workers. This is worth repeating time and time again because gaps in an EMS system allow inefficiency to leak in and waste and pollution to leak out. The maintenance of that commitment cannot be taken for granted though, and it is through a reward system based on the environmental performance of the firm that the commitment can be held and enhanced. There are several options available to firms but the key must be to make the reward system transparent. The following are some systems which have been and can be used.

1. **Profit sharing**
   Since environmental management can impact positively on profits then profit-sharing schemes can be used as a reward. The problem with this system is that other factors also affect profits and the environmental

influence can sometimes cease to be apparent. Moreover, if there is a downturn in the firm's sales and profits fall, then the system can act as a disincentive.

2. **Sharing the waste dividend**

   The money earned from the recycling of waste can be put into a staff fund which can subsequently be redistributed or spent on social activities or collective goods. The problem with this system is that there is then an incentive to maximise waste for recycling whereas the primary aim must be to reduce all waste.

3. **Calculating an environmental dividend**

   A more complicated system is to make use of an environmental dividend. If the benefits of waste reduction, quality improvements, energy savings, lower input levels, inventory control and productivity increases can be measured, then a dividend based on this can be paid to staff. The problem here is that the reward system ceases to be transparent and there is a problem that staff might not believe management's calculations.

Whether an environmental management system is ultimately successful may depend in part on factors outside the control of the firm. But apart from the existence of a growing legislative framework aimed at directing firms, the most significant determinants of success will be a range of internal factors including commitment, the appropriateness of the organisation of the system and the success of the company in measuring and assessing its environmental performance. There also has to be a good reason for instituting the EMS and this needs to be thoroughly explained and discussed with everyone involved in the firm including workers, shareholders and customers. Over time the aim must be to develop a positive culture surrounding environmental management and its constituent parts. There is a very important role for managers here: they need to start thinking about more holistic management approaches and the EMS and TQM systems can easily constitute the core of that.

Reward and recognition provide the incentives to maintain the EMS culture – that is, reward directly related to performance for the workforce and recognition by customers, shareholders, pressure groups and regulatory authorities for the company as a whole. This can help workers to develop a sense of pride in their company which, in turn, feeds back into commitment.

COOPERATION AND NETWORKING

One key aim of the environmental challenge must be to help small and medium-sized enterprises develop and become resource-efficient, competitive, technically advanced and environmentally friendly. We have already noted that it is very difficult for the small enterprise alone to achieve all these requirements. The sort of technical expertise which large firms will have in-house to help with their environmental management will probably be lacking and few small businesses will have the money to buy-in consultants to do these important tasks. A clear way forward for the SME sector revolves around cooperation and networking. This entails creating links between small firms and between firms and institutions. For example, a useful and often unexploited link might be between businesses and local universities or between firms and economic development units of councils. Natural, geographical links often exist which can also be exploited, for example between firms situated in business parks.

Nevertheless, small businesses must begin to recognise the benefits which can be achieved from such a strategy. We have learned from the writings on worker participation that there are benefits in enlarging the boundaries of consultation and as a commonly cited phrase tells us, 'with every pair of hands you get a free brain'. By networking and cooperating beyond even the boundaries of the firm, managers can learn from other people's experiences and errors. What small businesses therefore need is a framework within which to achieve such advantages. These can be created by the establishment of industry-specific or multi-sectoral forums or simply within localities, but the common element which will determine the success of any of these initiatives is cooperation.

Lessons from the experience of business parks

Some business parks provide an excellent example of what might be achieved through cooperation and also reflect the model of small business development outlined earlier in this chapter. We have seen the establishment of many business parks (or sometimes called science parks or research parks reflecting their high-technology nature) and sometimes these are closely linked to one or more universities or other research institutions. Cooperation between those with expertise and knowledge in the university and those with capital and experience of products and markets feed into the system and can produce a powerful foundation on which to develop products in an environmentally responsible way.

Such business parks are often characterised by relatively small firms using sophisticated production arrangements. They are capable of producing products to order in a flexible way and of a high quality. Firms also have the ability to adopt an environmental management system across the business park, thus sharing costs but also providing an additional advantage of giving the whole park a green image with which firms can be associated. Local authorities will often be very keen to promote that image and there are a number of sources of finance to help promote such a development.

Commonly, business parks have also been attractively built and landscaped with environmental objectives in mind. The best parks are designed to encourage the formation and growth of knowledge-based businesses. Managers of business park companies are encouraged to innovate and be actively engaged in the transfer of technology and business skills to the other organisations on site. This sort of ethos encourages actions to improve environmental performance across all organisations.

Business parks do vary in their make-up but size does not seem to be an important factor. There is no evidence to suggest that there is a critical mass associated with a park, but rather, like the firms of which it is made up, a key characteristic seems to be flexibility, responsiveness and a degree of specialism. In some cases quite strict rules concerning what sort of firm may be accommodated on a park exist. Restrictions have included a need to be based in the area of research and design or on being high-technology associated companies, for example.

A major strength of small high-technology firms commonly found on business parks is the priority they have for identifying markets for their products and services. Business park companies therefore tend to be imaginative in their development. A common route forward in their development is to establish joint-venture activities with larger, more established companies. Small companies are capable of being more flexible and more specific than the large companies and are therefore often used for specific tasks which have to be done quickly.

Firms do not have to be situated alongside each other on business parks to adopt many of the principles outlined above. Opportunities exist for SMEs to network together within a geographical locality or to work together on an industrial sector basis. Many trade associations are providing information for their members on environmental issues and encouraging cooperation between companies. All that is really needed is a commitment to work together and some thought given to how competitive strategies can actually be born out of cooperative ones. This key idea is further developed in Chapter 10.

Innovation and technology transfer

There is little doubt that the process of 'greening' requires innovation at the firm level if society is to reap the benefits of more environmentally friendly products and processes. A great deal has been written about the innovativeness of SMEs in comparison with that of larger companies. On the one hand it has been argued that large-scale and high levels of monopoly profits are required for research, development and innovation, while on the other hand it has been argued that small firms are more efficient at performing innovative activities and are the major source of innovation. It is true, however, that very few SMEs engage in research and development expenditure. Nevertheless, small firms and independent inventors have played a disproportionately large part in producing major twentieth-century inventions, although at least half of these inventions owe their successful implementation to large companies.

The results of innovations aimed at environmental improvement will benefit the global environment only if they are shared. Such cooperation may at times conflict with competitive strategies and there is therefore a need to provide incentives to small firms not only to innovate but also to share the benefits of such a strategy. There needs to be a framework whereby both technology transfer and the transfer of information and knowledge can be achieved if small businesses are to achieve the same levels of success as their large counterparts. To this end the Department of Trade and Industry runs a number of initiatives for environmental research and demonstration.

Department of Trade and Industry (DTI) grants are available to firms which have identified an environmental project which will be of use to a wider audience, and collaboration in this work is encouraged to produce research materials and demonstration projects. Applicants can usually receive funding for up to 50 per cent of eligible costs. Additional funds are available if such projects involve firms and institutions in other Member States of the EC. The aim of such initiatives is to exemplify best technology in practice, to install innovative environmental technology, to show the practicability of a new example of environmental technology and to investigate environmental technology problems and solutions under a 'club' arrangement. This enables case histories to be developed and widely disseminated and events are held to demonstrate the best technology or practice in operation. This is seen as a highly effective way of promoting environmental improvement: suppliers can benefit from market exposure, users can attract attention as models of excellence and others can benefit from seeing feasible solutions that may have an application to their business.

To provide businesses with easy access to information on the environment the DTI also has an environmental helpline which can draw on the expertise of a range of research experts. The service is free of charge so long as the enquiry can be dealt with within four hours. Further work is undertaken on a fee-paying basis.

Other public support

If there is a role for the government and local government in helping small businesses be environmentally friendly, then this has to be evaluated carefully. In the past some government measures to support small businesses have been ineffective. We must remember that small businesses are often run by entrepreneurs and these people are more likely to be capable of gauging risk than public servants. Entrepreneurs also tend to be innovative, energetic and self-reliant and generally resent being coddled by so-called experts. However, it is the case that the skills and aptitudes of most proprietors of small firms are limited and with this in mind there is a clear role for the public sector to devise programmes to help small businesses introduce change aimed at environmental improvement.

The key strategy here has to be one of cooperation and not domination. We have seen how organisations such as the Groundwork Trust have succeeded in forging productive links between the private sector, voluntary initiatives and public agencies. We have also seen some links between the private sector and conservation groups. Urban regeneration, environmental education and community development have also brought with them benefits for the small business. But at the centre of all these successful strategies there has been an incentive for all involved to participate. Without proper incentives, which in most cases must go beyond mere altruism, we cannot expect small businesses to participate in environmental projects. However, many small businesses have not recognised for themselves the benefits of cooperative ventures and have concentrated too much on narrow cost minimisation strategies. With consumers there is a clear role for the environmental education of entrepreneurs and there is also a clear role here for public agencies.

CONCLUSION

The environmental revolution, which began in the 1960s and developed rapidly in the 1980s and into the 1990s, put much of the blame on large businesses and stressed the need for change in that sector. But increasingly attention is being turned to small enterprises and for them as well, environmental improvement will be an integral part of commercial normality in the future. Definitions of business success are likely to be wider in the future and every enterprise will have to demonstrate its contribution to the ultimate aim of zero negative impact on the environment. Even in the small business it will more often be the case that competitive advantage will be achieved not merely by keeping abreast of environmental developments, but also by initiating change within an organisation and responding with new environmentally friendly products and production processes.

Even though governments are seeking to make all polluters pay, the success of environmental improvement will be determined largely by the responsiveness of business. There is evidence that larger businesses are, at last, responding to environmental pressures but smaller enterprises are, in the main, followers rather than leaders and are lagging behind.

The environmental systems discussed in this chapter can be related to any business but it has been argued that the combination of an environmental management system, a total quality management system and a flexible specialisation system in a cooperative setting such as a business park, is a recipe for great success. In many ways the systems, the location and the interactive nature of the set-up feed off each other and develop new ideas, new products, new system designs and innovation.

The development of environmental networks among small businesses, voluntary organisations and the public sector will enable controlled and sustainable growth to occur. Ultimately what we do with our environment affects us all and future generations. If the environment is important then we should recognise that the systems and processes used in businesses are also important. It has been suggested here that collaborative arrangements, multi-sector networking and cooperative strategies and systems, associated with flexible specialisation, total quality management and environmental management meet the aims and objectives of a sustainable and developing economy to the extent that this provides us with a model for the promotion and development of industry. There is a need for small businesses to be given incentives to undertake environmental change. Some of these incentives are provided by the legislative framework and a need to survive in a more competitive and environmentally aware market-place. In addition, larger firms will push environmental improvement along the supply chain. But there is still a need to convince small businesses that environmental improvements will reduce costs in the long run and this can only be achieved by the demonstration of best practice. There is a clear role here for government and local authorities in supporting innovative developments and providing a forum where information can be exchanged.

CHAPTER 10

Regional development and environmental management: new opportunities for cooperation

In the previous chapter we saw that many environmental initiatives for small and medium-sized enterprises could be carried out at a local authority or regional level. This chapter develops that theme and looks at the sort of initiatives which are possible at a regional level and which, at the same time, will have an important part to play in the development of better environmental performance at the company level. The main thrust of this chapter is therefore to show how company-based environmental management systems and a regional environmental management system (REMS) can be compatible. It will show that there is a direct relationship between environmental quality and the industrial development and economic activities within the region, and that a key strategy for environmental management within businesses can be that of cooperation.

A region, for the sake of this chapter, is defined as any geographical area large enough for a project to be undertaken to improve the environmental performance of that area. It might be a local authority's area of jurisdiction (although this is almost certainly too wide), a particular city or town, or even part of a city which can be segregated. It might be an urban or rural area. However, it needs to be a manageable size so that the commitment of industry within the area can be channelled into action, and it needs to be sufficiently small to allow every participant industry to feel important enough to make an effort towards environmental improvement.

It is the method by which the environment of the region can be improved that can link possibly disparate regions. The underlying approach is to develop a conversion plan for the region leading to the development of a comparative advantage based on integrated environmental management, at both company and regional level. The REMS concept, in principle, is that commercial and industrial viability in the 1990s and beyond is synonymous with quality at every level, including environmental quality. Rather than regarding new environmental control and legislation as a negative factor and a cost, the thrust is to turn this apparent constraint into advantage. The REMS concept may also include a 'regional branding' of the area as one renowned for integrated environmental management, and economic benefits accrue from both regional- and company-level environmental management.

The development of the region must be based on high environmental and product quality at every stage of the production process and at every step in the production chain which will be integrated as far as possible within the region. At the product level, an emphasis on 'cradle to grave' responsibility and integrated supply chains leads to an increased control of the production cycle, from primary production right through to direct marketing and final sale. One specific aim might be to encourage different production steps to take place within the same region, including the disposal and treatment of waste. New opportunities for economic development may therefore arise in the region.

LINKAGES BETWEEN ECONOMIC DEVELOPMENT AND THE ENVIRONMENT

The original Treaty of Rome did not give the EC explicit powers to legislate on environmental matters but this was amended by the adoption of the Single European Act 1987, which now provides a firm legal basis for Community legislation on the environment. One of the provisions states that environmental protection requirements should be a component of all other policies based on the indisputable fact that measures in the sphere of other policies may have a significant positive or negative impact on the environment. This must be viewed as an important provision because it establishes a requirement that environmental protection must form an essential component of all Community policies, including economic development policies.

The EC's Fifth Environment Programme, which was introduced in 1993 and will run to the end of the century, has as a major theme the promotion of information and education of the Community's citizens towards the protection of the environment, and the direct involvement of the Community in achieving environmental protection through the use of voluntary agreements, codes of conduct, economic and fiscal measures. There will be a move away from dealing with environmental issues on an individual medium basis (i.e. air, water, noise, waste, etc.), to the handling of issues on a sectorial and regional basis involving local communities and local and national governments. This approach further emphasises the need for regional conversion plans which involve the integrated development of the economy and the environment involving all sectors of industry, the local community, and local authorities.

Integrated preventative action encourages actions to be taken to protect the environment at an early stage, requiring environmental management to go beyond the question of repairing damages, to stopping pollution from occurring in the first place. The 'polluter pays' principle is seen as an important instrument enabling the market to be adjusted to reflect the true costs of the production of goods and services, and is becoming adopted by both the EC and country governments. Pressures for regulatory compliance will be met, in the main, through the initiation of continuous and sophisticated monitoring systems, waste minimisation, more effective investments in process technology, and research and development. As these costs begin to impinge more heavily on an organisation's operating and capital costs, evidence of good practice will become a precondition for access to the wider investment community. These further pressures will obviously spill into most other stakeholder relationships.

Such trends confirm that industry will need to adopt a more strategic view of environmental problems. It needs to move away from predominantly short-term solutions to actual problem-solving, and towards the development of pre-emptive control strategies, striking a balance between regulation and the need to turn those regulations into competitive advantage abroad. The development of an REMS can help significantly here. Not only does it allow for a cooperative environmental effort on the part of firms in the region which can lead to synergy in research and development, waste management and energy efficiency, but a significant advantage can be derived from a common marketing approach. A regional conversion plan aims at focusing the marketing instrument not only on the company but also on the region in which the company is based. The region can develop a competitive advantage by way of an integrated, proactive, environmental policy and regional environmental management system. In other words, the product will be produced to the highest environmental standards in a geographical region where the quality of the environment is maintained through an efficient REMS.

THE REGIONAL ENVIRONMENTAL MANAGEMENT SYSTEM

There are inherent risks in treating economic forces and the environment as if they were separate and non-interacting elements. Economic policy which neglects to take into consideration environmental risks and damage is not sustainable. This is exemplified in so many semi-rural areas where economic development has resulted in the exploitation of the natural environment, leaving rivers biologically dead and parts of the landscape aesthetically degraded and sometimes contaminated.

One traditional starting point for dealing with this problem is that taken by environmental economists who argue that an economic value should be put on natural assets and that these costs should be internalised (see, for example, Pearce and Turner, 1990). Conceptually, there seems to be no quarrel with the fact that long-term economic benefits accrue from environmental management. When a landscape loses its productivity, standards of living are under negative pressure; when a landscape loses its aesthetic appeal, property values diminish. However, a significant tension between economies and environmental management often arises around short-term issues because of the difficulty of accurately valuing natural assets and the problems associated with the ownership of those assets. Even where prices can be identified it is often difficult to get these accepted by parties involved in a development (or perhaps more importantly their lawyers).

Where a region is already polluted or environmentally damaged the common approach to tackling problems is to deal with specific sources of pollution using regulatory controls. In addition, over time individual impact assessments can mitigate environmental damage, but they do not necessarily alter the larger picture. The effect of this *ad hoc* approach on the regional environment can often be seen as 'two steps forward, one step back'. Because of the non-integrated and non-coordinated approach, what is beneficial or, more often, 'not harmful' for one industry, may well be harmful to another.

The environment responds as a whole when stressed at a particular point but the traditional, piecemeal approach to environmental management does not provide any information about how the whole system reacts. There is therefore a need to develop a more integrated regional environmental management system (REMS) which is capable of exploring the synergistic effect of applying environmental management policies to all sectors of activity. This change from a piecemeal to a holistic approach can be seen as an important part of a 'sustainable development' approach. The concept of sustainable development recognises that there is an interdependence between the economy and the environment, not only because the way we manage the economy has an impact on the environment, but also because environmental quality has an impact on the performance of the economy.

Central to the development of a REMS is the cooperation and commitment of regional and local resources facilitated through partnerships between individuals, businesses, public sector institutions and other agencies. A regional strategy of regional environmental management is required which promotes and stimulates community-implemented development. It is particularly important, therefore, to involve the business sector and to make it clear that there are significant benefits to that sector of becoming involved. This process must begin through the provision of information, through education and training, and subsequently the provision of support, advice, and capital for local initiatives. Any environmental management system starts with, and depends strongly upon, the development of understanding and commitment from all people involved, and the REMS is no exception.

There is also a need to have a clear policy for the region which integrates both regional objectives and industrial aspirations. Such policies are already in place where local authorities have followed the advice of Friends of the Earth in introducing a declaration of commitment to environmental protection and policy development in the areas of recycling, energy, transport and planning, environmental protection and enhancement, health, and the monitoring and minimisation of pollution. Some authorities have also introduced regular environmental audits and invited public and industrial participation.

However, the REMS policy needs to go beyond this and fully integrate the needs of the region, industry and the public into a plan which binds them together with the objective of significantly improving all aspects of the region's environmental performance.

Regional environmental branding

The implementation of the REMS will help to give the particular region a comparative edge, and lead to more sustainable economic growth and development. The environmental quality-driven, market-led and proactive approach is increasingly used at company level, but is relatively new at a regional level. As a result of the implementation of the REMS, the area can be promoted as a 'green region' and a number of companies within the region may be able to take advantage of the 'environmental labelling' of the area. The message coming from the companies operating in the region must clearly communicate that the product comes from an area which is managed in an 'environmentally superior' way and where high threshold environmental criteria have been established.

Within the REMS, 'codes of conduct' relating to environmental performance and procedures can be established. These might include targets to reduce emissions, a protocol for handling waste in the region and a commitment on the part of all firms to introduce internal environmental management systems, for example. All institutions and companies in the region would be expected to adhere to these codes over time. Success will depend on commitment of all involved, but there will also have to be incentives provided by the local authority. Because the aim of the REMS would be to go beyond legislation, there will seldom be a 'stick' to go along with the 'carrot'. This is why businesses in an area will have to be convinced of the benefits of being involved in such a regional scheme.

Unlike existing labelling schemes, the focus of increased marketability of products produced within the REMS will not only be on the environmental impact of the product, but will also focus on the environmental performance of the company, which is rapidly becoming of more interest to the consumer, and on the environmental status of the region where the product is produced. As a result of the REMS, the range of products manufactured in a way which is least harmful for the environment will expand. 'Green products' will not only be defined in terms of price and performance, but products will convey real protection for the environment.

THE BENEFITS OF A REGIONAL ENVIRONMENTAL MANAGEMENT SYSTEM

Regional management centres around ecological improvement through environmental rehabilitation and prevention of further environmental degradation through the introduction of specific management and control systems. The REMS goes further than that because it not only introduces environmental management on a regional scale, but actively uses it as a tool to enhance the economic prospects of the region by integrating environmental, economic and social factors in the REMS. Regional management involving such an integrated approach, whereby all developments and all economic activities are seen as part of a larger structure, will have a number of general beneficial effects:

1. **Clear responsibilities for environmental improvement.** A conversion plan development team, with representatives from local communities and industries, and local government will set environmental targets and protocols at all levels. Targets will be continuously re-assessed and every person in the community will know that they have their own environmental responsibility.

2. **Cost reduction for companies through increased cooperation.** As a result of the integrated approach, different companies are more likely to cooperate in dealing with pollution and other environmental problems thereby potentially reducing costs. The Landskrona project in Sweden and the PRISMA project in the Netherlands are well-known examples which demonstrated that such a strategy can work, and that the environmental problems of companies, even if they operate in different industries, are often quite similar (Van Berkel *et al.*, 1991).

3. **Increased marketability.** Both the region as an entity, as well as the individual companies within that region may benefit from an increased marketability. Possibilities exist for marketing the region as a whole, bringing generic benefits to companies operating within it. It must be clear that the product comes from a region in which high threshold environmental criteria have been established. New investors may be attracted to the area, because of its more efficient management system.

4. **Landscape management and preservation.** The landscape and countryside will be better managed and preserved. Increased environmental planning in the REMS leads to innovative design and management and to an ecologically sound, socio-economic structure.

5. **Environmental rehabilitation.** A coordinated, cooperative and active approach to environmental rehabilitation will be undertaken, leading to a cleaner, healthier and safer environment.

6. **Quality of life.** A programme aimed at prevention of further environmental damage will integrate wider aspects of economic development and improve quality of life. The REMS is also likely to involve making the most of space, landscape, cultural and craft traditions, architectural and industrial heritage.

7. **Improved decision processes.** An integrated and structured approach to decision-making for new developments which involves wider representation in the region will reduce the chance of bad decisions.

Most of the synergistic effects of the regional environmental management system will only occur if all parties involved not only understand the conversion concept, but are also willing to cooperate and actively strive towards its success. The main strength of the REMS lies in the integrative approach towards environmental, economic and social factors.

CONVERSION PLAN DEVELOPMENT AND IMPLEMENTATION STRATEGIES

The goals for economic development inherent in the conversion plan for the REMS will be achieved through the development of regional, comparative advantage based on self-imposed, market-led codes of practice that ensure quality and integrated environmental management. An overview of the steps involved in the development of the REMS is given in Figure 10.1. Both the company-based environmental management system and the REMS build a strategic link between business objectives and environmental pressures. The two can no longer be seen as separate. The particular objectives of businesses and environmental improvement can no longer be seen as inconsistent, as has traditionally been the case. Moreover, the development of the REMS, as expounded here, is deliberately in line with company-based environmental management system standards such as BS7750.

The regional environmental management system requires a good source of up-to-date information about its starting point and its ongoing performance. There is a need, as far as possible, to undertake an initial review of the region which will act as a benchmark for future measurement. Using the same sort of approach adopted by businesses with environmental management systems, there is subsequently a need to regularly audit environmental performance and the REMS itself.

One possibility is to develop an interactive computerised database to create an environmental quality model (EQM) for the region. The model could be based on geographical information systems (GIS) modelling and it would also act as a database for environmental and socio-economic data. It would allow accurate criteria to be formulated and tested, and predict the effects of mediation work or of new development. Such a system would allow tradition-ally difficult factors such as land use and climate to be included in decision-making, and can be used to identify existing and potential sources of pollution. The model could be fully interactive, providing the holistic environmental quality control capability required by the regional environmental management system. However, the conversion plan needs to entail much more than 'just' an environmental management system. Environmental, economic, and social factors are included in the regional environmental management system and its conversion plan.

The key characteristics of the regional environmental management system are that:

● it is a management system for a specific region with well-defined, natural boundaries;

- it facilitates environmental rehabilitation and protection;
- it offers a management framework for coordinated development, with a clear sense of purpose;
- it integrates environmental, economic and social factors; and
- it emphasises local industry and local community interest.

The REMS should be regarded as a management tool, aimed at facilitating implementation of the regional conversion plan, and comparable to the function of the environmental management system at the company level. Instrumental to the development of the REMS will be a conversion plan development team. Specific tasks for this team would be the following.

- To further develop a detailed proposal for the installation of a regional environmental information system, including an environmental monitoring system.
- To conduct an extensive environmental and socio-economic study in the area, with emphasis on topics such as migration patterns, effects of infrastructural developments, employment, and the relative importance of the different economic sectors.
- To extend contacts and communication with local communities and industry.
- To develop internal strategies to promote information and education of all residents of the area towards environmental protection and the benefits and implications of the REMS, and to stimulate community involvement and environmental awareness.
- To design a template and model for processes and protocols within the area, resulting in improved communications and increased organisational control.
- To outline a regional environmental policy, with specific standards and targets, and to develop an environmental quality model (EQM).
- To conduct a detailed environmental quality survey and to identify and prioritise areas for environmental rehabilitation and development.
- To stimulate and coordinate further development and implementation of company environmental management systems.
- To identify and prioritise areas for economic investment and growth, and to identify new economic opportunities.
- To develop strategies to promote and market the area externally and to develop a scheme that gives recognition to 'green companies' within the region.

We know from previous discussion in this book that environmental development can best be established when there is a sense of cooperation and commitment from all parties involved. It is suggested, therefore, that for the development of a conversion plan, representatives of both local communities and industrial sectors are brought together in a development committee and not only help develop, but also ensure broad-based support for the final conversion plan.

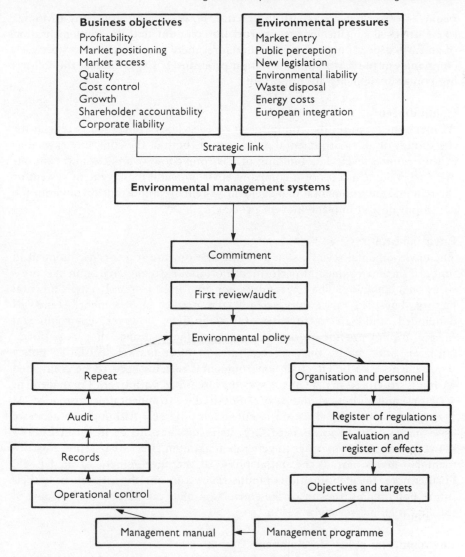

Figure 10.1 Development of the regional environmental management system

LINKS BETWEEN ENVIRONMENTAL MANAGEMENT AT THE COMPANY AND THE REGIONAL LEVEL

As stressed earlier there is a need to develop a strategic link between business objectives and growing environmental pressures. Figure 10.1 is taken as a basis for this comparison. The implementation steps shown in this figure closely follow the guidelines as set in the British Standard on environmental management systems, BS7750. In practice, however, each company EMS has to be designed specifically for a particular company and the implementation of an EMS depends on its format. Therefore, there may be differences between companies in the EMS implementation procedures. Nevertheless, the following common elements are important.

Commitment

As mentioned before, the commitment of everybody concerned is crucial for the success of all environmental management, both at the company as well as at the regional level. The building of environmental awareness and commitment to make a success of a company environmental management system or the regional environmental management system are important throughout the development and implementation process.

Environmental review

The environmental review is an accurate assessment, at a specific moment in time, of the environmental performance of, and extreme environmental pressures on a company. The review does not limit itself to purely environmental factors, but also takes into account the market environment, standards demanded, and barriers to entry. On their own, however, environmental reviews cannot provide an organisation with the assurance that its performance not only meets, but will continue to meet market legislative policy requirements. To be effective, environmental reviews need to be conducted within a structured management system; integrated with overall management activities; and address all indicators of desired environmental performance. At the regional level, the situation is not much different. Although an accurate assessment of the region is necessary, its results have to be integrated into a management system in order to generate maximum effect. A baseline environmental study is part of the initial phase of the development of an REMS. Furthermore, the identification of industrial sectors and the assessment of their future potential as a result of the conversion plan can be regarded as part of the first regional review.

Environmental policy development

Senior management must define and document the company environmental policy. This policy must take account of strategic objectives and be relevant for the company and its activities, products and services. At the regional level, a preliminary policy has to be written by the conversion plan development team.

Organisation and personnel

A management representative with defined authority for implementing and running the EMS is appointed in the company. The capacity of the current organisational structures to implement environmental management systems has to be examined at this stage and weaknesses should be identified. At the regional level, the management representatives' function can be compared with the function of the conversion plan development team and the environmental, economic, and social development committee.

Register of environmental legislation and effects
A list of current and anticipated relevant legislation and regulations has to be compiled. The environmental effects arising out of past, current and planned activities; normal and abnormal operations; incidents and possible emergency situations are identified. This applies for both company and regional level and is the responsibility of the company environmental manager and the conversion plan development team respectively.

Environmental objectives and targets
Objectives are set in the context of the environmental effects evaluation. Quantifiable, achievable and demanding targets are agreed. At the company level, this is done by senior management in conjunction with the manager responsible for environmental issues. At the regional level, this is done alongside the development of the regional environmental policy.

Management programme
At the company level, programmes to achieve environmental objectives are the key to achieving compliance with the environmental policy. Programmes may deal with past, present and future activities and the effects of new products and processes. Procedures for the verification and measurement of activities, proper documentation, and investigative and corrective action are set up. At the regional level, the development of management programmes is the task of the conversion plan development team. The conversion plan itself can, in fact, be regarded as the regional management programme.

Environmental manual and documentation
At the company level, a manual will be produced which states the environmental policy, objectives and targets, documents key roles and responsibilities of management and staff, and covers both normal and abnormal operating conditions. At the regional level, this again forms part of the tasks of the conversion plan development team.

Operational control
Objectives and targets are identified with regard to the processes and activities which affect, or potentially affect, the environment and which are relevant to the company policy. All activities are designed to be carried out in a controlled manner to minimise environmental impacts. At the regional level, operational control is the responsibility of the environmental, economic and social development committee, supported by their regional management and administrative team.

Records

A documented system of record-keeping is designed which, while keeping records to the minimum, will clearly demonstrate compliance with the environmental policy and the extent to which objectives are achieved. This is the task of the management and administrative support team at the regional level and will form an important part of the regional environmental information system.

Auditing

Following the implementation of a company EMS, periodic auditing is necessary to identify deficiencies and assess the effectiveness of previous corrective action. This auditing can be done in-house or by an independent third party. If a regional environmental management system is installed in a similar way as a company environmental management system (as proposed in this chapter) there are possibilities to have the REMS audited as well. If the audit is conducted by an independent third party, the region will be able to substantiate claims that the area is managed in an environmentally friendly way.

Repeat

Environmental management is an ongoing process. The company's management will periodically have to review the continuing relevance and effectiveness of the EMS in relation to the company's mission and objectives. In a comparable way, the targets and objectives set for the REMS will have to be reviewed. Then the whole cycle of environmental management, both at the regional and the company level, will be repeated.

COSTS AND BENEFITS OF THE REGIONAL CONVERSION PROCESS

The REMS cannot be introduced at no cost and therefore it is important to assess the benefits to be derived from the process which must weigh against the cost. However, the ultimate aim of improving the environment in a region is essentially priceless when considered as a long-term objective, and the benefits of introducing environmental improvements into smaller businesses, where they are traditionally more difficult to achieve, must also introduce a big plus. If public money is to be spent on the introduction of the system then the project clearly needs to be assessed very carefully. The following environmental, economic and social benefits need to be assessed.

Environmental benefits

- Even without the implementation of a REMS, instalment of company environmental management systems will lead to environmental improvements.

- The rehabilitation of derelict and polluted areas will restore the intrinsic value of the region.
- Implementation of a regional environmental management system will ensure that potential sources of pollution such as discharges, atmospheric emissions and solid wastes are controlled in order to maintain the quality of the environment.
- Integrated land management will enable commercial and industrial development to take place in harmony with the environment, leading to a diverse, appealing and well-managed landscape.
- The development of a 'green region' concept where economic growth and environmental quality go hand in hand.

Economic benefits

- The REMS will establish a set of standards for the area which will form the basis of planning requirements and will be used as an interactive environmental quality management system. Development planning procedures will be more coordinated and rapid, and chances for faulty decisions will decrease.
- Because of its integrated approach, the REMS will ensure that existing local, national and EC funds will be spent in a more coherent way.
- The company-based environmental management systems will ensure conformity with EC Directives and Regulations, guaranteeing maximum compliance and minimum barriers to trade.
- Enhancement of company management systems leads to increased product quality which may provide individual companies and industrial sectors with a competitive edge.
- A promotion scheme will identify the 'green region' concept and market the region, resulting in the development of a comparative advantage. The conversion plan will lead to economic growth and development, including new investments, in certain industrial sectors.
- The economic development of the area will result in improvements in transport facilities and increased mobility in the area, and will result in spin-off effects generating employment in all sectors.

Social benefits

- The rehabilitation of derelict and polluted areas will result in a cleaner and healthier environment.
- Both the establishment of a regional labelling scheme and the improvements in environmental quality and infrastructure will enhance opportunities for local initiatives and development.
- Implementation of the environmental management system will lead to regional integration and the emergence of a new community identity. Communication links between communities, industry, and government will

improve. Electing representatives will enhance democratic developments. Development of the tourist sector will result in improved leisure and amenity facilities, and in the establishment of community centres as focus points for tourism, local communities, and community-based initiatives.

Costing the conversion plan

The regional environmental management system ensures an efficient use of existing funds from local, national, and EC sources. Furthermore, it may often be the case that several new sources of funds may be applied for in order to develop parts of the conversion plan. The setting up of a company environmental management system is a relatively low-cost exercise. The benefits of a company EMS have been outlined in detail earlier in this book and research in the USA, with its high environmental standards and stringent laws, showed that costs of pollution control add up to a mere average of 0.54 per cent of a company's overall costs (Dodwell, 1992). Total environmental expenditures are on average 2.4 per cent of turnover (Winsemius and Guntram, 1992). Over a period of time, instalment of a company EMS will pay for itself several times over. Therefore, expenditure to install company environmental management systems should have a short payback period and can be self-financing.

As far as the costs of the plan itself are concerned, these will depend on the amount of expertise (i.e the use of consultants) which needs to be introduced into the region and the size of the project itself. Infrastructural investment is clearly required to address the issues of emissions and effluent management and rehabilitation, but expenditure of this kind is likely to take place anyway. An additional benefit of the REMS is that such expenditure is likely to be done in a more integrated and systematic way. There may also be a need to provide incentives to firms to undertake their own environmental improvements and this can be achieved if money can be found for the provision of small grants. The initial review of the region may be costly but it is invaluable in identifying priorities for action. In many cases, however, local authorities have already started on the process and there are growing sources of regional environmental information (e.g. Contaminated Land Registers).

Expenditure on the REMS needs to be seen as an investment good rather than a consumption good. It should be clear that any such investment will bring returns via improvements in the regional environment and new opportunities for businesses operating within that region. In turn, the increased wealth-generating potential in the region can mean that the project can ultimately pay for itself.

The conversion plan outlined here is involved with the competitiveness of the region. In this context, the conversion plan framework offers an opportunity to seek funding under EC research and development support programmes and other programmes, such as PRISMA, which are dedicated to levelling competitive disadvantages. The conversion plan addresses the issue of integrated development and, in this context, DGXXII of the European

Commission, as the coordinator of structural funds, may find research and experiment opportunities within the region.

CONCLUSION

It has been argued that there are benefits relating to the introduction of regional environmental management systems, which integrate environmental, economic and social factors. A REMS will only work if it is developed by people that have an interest in the region and central here is the participation, cooperation and commitment of businesses in the area. Coherent strategies and systems for environmental and developmental management, whether at the company level or at a regional level, have synergetic benefits to businesses within it and to the local community and the environment. Changes in regional management must be designed and developed by people from within the region, supported by professional staff. A central place in the management framework needs to be taken by representatives from local communities and industry. The role of local government is to provide linkage in the REMS.

Industry itself can benefit greatly by the additional help which will be provided by firms working together cooperatively with the support of a regional team. The REMS will complement the firm's own internal environmental management system and further add to the firm's competitive advantage if the region can attract a 'green label'. To a large extent the future of the environment and of the planet requires more cooperation and the concept of the REMS extends much of the best practice discussed in this book. A key concept of environmentalists has long been associated with 'local action, global impact'. At the centre of this concept is the need for increased cooperation and the regional environmental management system takes further what businesses alone can do towards achieving this important objective.

References

Dodwell, D. (1992) 'Environment better served by free trade carrot than protectionist stick', *Financial Times*, 13 May.

Pearce, D. W. and Turner, R. K. (1990) *Economics of Natural Resources and the Environment*, Harvester Wheatsheaf, Brighton.

Van Berkel, R. *et al* (1991) 'Business examples with waste prevention: ten case studies from the Dutch PRISMA project' in *Prepare for Tomorrow*, Ministry for Economic Affairs, The Netherlands.

Winsemius, P. and Guntram, U. (1992) 'Responding to the environmental challenge', *Business Horizons*, Volume 2, pp. 38–45.

INDEX